The German and Dutch Economies

Contributions to Economics

Gerhard Gehrig/Wladyslaw Welfe (Eds.)
Economies in Transition
1993. ISBN 3-7908-0721-4

Christoph M. Schneider
Research and Development Management: From the Soviet Union to Russia
1994. ISBN 3-7908-0757-5

Bernhard Böhm/Lionello F. Punzo (Eds.)
Economic Performance
1994. ISBN 3-7908-0811-3

Lars Olof Persson/Ulf Wiberg
Microregional Fragmentation
1995. ISBN 3-7908-0855-5

Ernesto Felli/Furio C. Rosati/Giovanni Tria (Eds.)
The Service Sector: Productivity and Growth
1995. ISBN 3-7908-0875-X

Giuseppe Munda
Multicriteria Evaluation in Fuzzy Environment
1995. ISBN 3-7908-0892-X

Boris Maurer
R & D, Innovation and Industrial Structure
1996. ISBN 3-7908-0900-4

Giovanni Galizzi/Luciano Venturini (Eds.)
Economics of Innovation: The Case of Food Industry
1996. ISBN 3-7908-0911-X

David T. Johnson
Poverty, Inequality and Social Welfare in Australia
1996. ISBN 3-7908-0942-X

Rongxing Guo
Border-Regional Economics
1996. ISBN 3-7908-0943-8

Oliver Fratzscher
The Political Economy of Trade Integration
1996. ISBN 3-7908-0945-4

Ulrich Landwehr
Industrial Mobility and Public Policy
1996. ISBN 3-7908-0949-7

Arnold Picot/Ekkehard Schlicht (Eds.)
Firms, Markets, and Contracts
1996. Corr. 2nd printing 1997.
ISBN 3-7908-0947-0

Karin Peschel (Ed.)
Regional Growth and Regional Policy Within the Framework of European Integration
1997. ISBN 3-7908-0957-8

Thorsten Wichmann
Agricultural Technical Progress and the Development of a Dual Economy
1997. ISBN 3-7908-0960-8

Ulrich Woitek
Business Cycles
1997. ISBN 3-7908-0997-7

Michael Carlberg
International Economic Growth
1997. ISBN 3-7908-0995-0

Massimo Filippini
Elements of the Swiss Market for Electricity
1997. ISBN 3-7908-0996-9

Giuseppe Gaburro (Ed.)
Ethics and Economics
1997. ISBN 3-7908-0986-1

Frank Hoster/Heinz Welsch/Christoph Böhringer
CO_2 Abatement and Economic Structural Change in the European Internal Market
1997. ISBN 3-7908-1020-7

Christian M. Hafner
Nonlinear Time Series Analysis with Applications to Foreign Exchange Rate Volatility
1997. ISBN 3-7908-1041-X

Sardar M.N. Islam
Mathematical Economics of Multi-Level Optimisation
1998. ISBN 3-7908-1050-9

Sven-Morten Mentzel
Real Exchange Rate Movements
1998. ISBN 3-7908-1081-9

Lei Delsen · Eelke de Jong (Eds.)

The German and Dutch Economies

Who Follows Whom?

With 15 Figures
and 37 Tables

Springer-Verlag Berlin Heidelberg GmbH

Series Editors
Werner A. Müller
Martina Bihn

Editors
Dr. Lei Delsen
Prof. Dr. Eelke de Jong
University of Nijmegen
Department of Applied Economics
P.O. Box 9108
NL-6500 HK Nijmegen, The Netherlands

ISBN 978-3-7908-1064-6

Cataloging-in-Publication Data applied for
Die Deutsche Bibliothek – CIP-Einheitsaufnahme
The German and Dutch economies: who follows whom?; with 37 tables / Lei Delsen; Eelke de Jong (eds.). – Heidelberg: Physica-Verl., 1998
(Contributions to economics)
ISBN 978-3-7908-1064-6 ISBN 978-3-642-59019-1 (eBook)
DOI 10.1007/978-3-642-59019-1

Softcover Design: Erich Kirchner, Heidelberg

SPIN 10648054 88/2202-5 4 3 2 1 0 – Printed on acid-free paper

Preface and Acknowledgements

In the fall of 1996 the Centre for German Studies of the University of Nijmegen celebrated its fifth anniversary. Main part of the lustral events was a conference on Friday October 25th which had as its theme: "Germany and the Netherlands: Who follows whom?". The conference was prepared and organised by the Centre for German Studies, the Department of Applied Economics, Nijmegen Institute for Academic Studies (NIVAS) and the Transferbureau of the University of Nijmegen. The conference's lingua franca was neither German nor Dutch, but '*Neu Deutsch*' as the president of the German central bank, Hans Tietmeyer, dubbed the English language at the beginning of 1997. This book contains a selection of the contributions to the international conference. The included six papers are revised and extended for this publication and supplemented by an introductory chapter and a concluding chapter by the editors.

The theme was chosen in spring 1996. An important reason for the organising committee to select this theme was that at that time the German newspapers and television almost daily described the Netherlands as the example (model) which the Federal Republic of Germany should follow. A risk of selecting such a topical issue is that after some months the attention for it may fade away. Fortunately (at least for the organising committee) this certainly is not the case for the theme addressed here. In October 1996 the topicality of it was increased by Helmut Kohl, the German Chancellor, who just a few days before the conference was held devoted an important part of his opening-speech of the '*CDU Parteitage*' to the issue of Germany's competitiveness. He held up the Netherlands and Austria as examples of countries where the wages and other production costs are lower than in Germany. "Our competitors in Western Europe and North-America have understood the signs of the times already. Almost all industrial countries change their social systems; tax rates are worldwide an essential element for attracting foreign investments" (according to Kohl). Other German leaders also pointed at the Netherlands as an example. Klaus Escher, leader of the '*Junge Union*', drew the attention to the problems in the Federal Republic of Germany with regard to the financing of pensions. He prefers a switch towards the Dutch system in which an essential part of the pensions is financed by means of a funding system.

In our view at present (June 1997) the theme of this book still is very topical. At the summit of Amsterdam the leaders of the member states of the European Union devoted much time to the high level of unemployment in many European countries. They agreed on an employment chapter in the Treaty of Amsterdam and called for studies, which should compare the institutions in the member states with a view towards selecting the best practices for enhancing employment in Europe. In many respects this book perfectly fits into this strategy, for a comparison is made of the institutional structures and features of the German and Dutch welfare states. The focus is on labour market policy and performance, the effectiveness of the Dutch and German wage setting institutions, the monetary policy of the central banks and the competition policy. The United Kingdom and the United States of America are used as benchmark countries.

We would like to seize this opportunity to thank some persons and institutions for their part in the organisation of the conference and the preparation of the manuscript for this book. First of all we would like to thank the contributors to this book for their willingness to write and translate (if necessary) their contribution. We thank Harry Garretsen for his comments on an earlier version of Chapters 1 and 8 and Bas van Aarle for providing Figures 1.2 and 1.3. Tine Verhey-van der Linden and her assistants are thanked for the organisation of the conference day and An Barten for her secretarial assistance. We also want to express a special gratitude to Jan van Megen, Director of the Centre for German Studies, for his support. Finally, financial support by the Centre for German Studies and the Rabobank is gratefully acknowledged.

Lei Delsen and Eelke de Jong
University of Nijmegen
September 1997

Contents

List of Contributors

Lei Delsen is Assistant Professor at the Department of Applied Economics of the University of Nijmegen, the Netherlands. His current research deals with a number of topical European labour market problems and issues, including new forms of work, retirement from work and employment policy. He published several books and articles. He is author of *Atypical Employment: An International Perspective. Causes, Consequences and Policy* (Groningen: Wolters-Noordhoff, 1995) and co-editor with Geneviève Reday-Mulvey of *Gradual Retirement in the OECD Countries. Macro And Micro Issues and Policies* (Aldershot: Dartmouth, 1996).

Raymond Gradus is currently working at the Dutch Ministry of Economic Affairs, The Hague, and is Associate Professor at the Research Centre for Economic Policy of the Erasmus University Rotterdam, the Netherlands. During the writing of his contribution he was working at the Ministry of Finance, The Hague. His main areas of research are growth theory and applications of microeconomics to policy problems. He published three books and about 40 articles in (inter)national journals and books. Recent publications include 'Pollution, Abatement and Long-term Growth', *European Journal of Political Economy*, 1996 (together with S. Smulders), and 'The economic effects of extending shop opening hours', *Journal of Economics*, 1996.

Bob Hancké is Research Fellow in the Research Unit on Economic Change and Employment of the Wissenschaftszentrum Berlin für Sozialforschung (Social Science Research Centre, Berlin; WZB), Germany.

Maja Helmer was student of political science in Bonn, Berlin and Durham/N.C. She was Research Assistant in the Wissenschaftszentrum Berlin für Sozialforschung (Social Science Research Center, Berlin; WZB) in late 1996 and is currently finishing her masters degree in political science at the Free University of Berlin, Germany.

Lex Hoogduin is currently working as Advisor to the President of the European Monetary Institute, in Frankfurt, Germany and is a Professor of Money and Banking at the University of Groningen. Before 1 July 1997, he worked at the Dutch central bank in Amsterdam as head of the Monetary and Economic Policy Department, and, related to that, he was, among other things, an Alternate to the Dutch central bank member of the Monetary Committee of the European Union. Previously, he worked at the University of Groningen. His main area of research is monetary and financial economics. He published several books and articles, among which his thesis *Some Aspects of Uncertainty and the Theory of a Monetary Economy* (Groningen: University of Groningen, 1991).

Henk Huisman is at the Monetary and Economic Policy Department of the Dutch central bank, Amsterdam, the Netherlands. His main research interests concern the structure of (international) financial markets, also in relation to the introduction of the euro. Previously, he worked for the International Monetary Fund, in Washington D.C., United States, the Ministry of Finance, in The Hague, and the Amsterdam Stock Exchange, the Netherlands.

Reimut Jochimsen, Professor of Economics, is President of the Landeszentralbank in North Rhine-Westphalia, Düsseldorf, Germany, and Member of the Central Bank Council of the Deutsche Bundesbank. Main fields of research are monetary policy, the European Economic and Monetary Union, the financial market and regional science. He published since 1960 several books and articles in international publications. Recent publications include: 'Europäische Wirtschafts- und Währungsunion: Auf Biegen und Brechen?', *Aussenwirtschaft*, 1996; 'Regional Science in Germany – From the Beginning to the Present' in: K. Peschel (ed.), *Regional Growth and Regional Policy within the Framework of European Integration* (Heidelberg: Physica-Verlag, 1996); 'Revisionskonferenz 1996: Wirtschafts- und währungspolitische Anforderungen an ein Maastricht II' in: D. Grimm, J.J. Hesse, R. Jochimsen and F.W. Scharpf (eds.), *Zur Neuordnung der Europäische Union: Die Regierungskonferenz 1996/97* (Baden-Baden: Nomos-Verlag, 1996).

Eelke de Jong is Professor of International Economics at the Department of Applied Economics of the University of Nijmegen, the Netherlands. He is coordinator of the postdoctoral programme 'Doing business in Germany' of the Centre for German Studies of the University of Nijmegen. Previously he worked at the University of Groningen and the University of Amsterdam. In 1994 he was a Visiting Professor at CERGE, Charles University, Prague, Czech Republic. He published two books and several articles in international journals on international financial issues. Among them are: *Exchange Rate Determination and Optimal Economic Policy under Alternative Exchange Rate Regimes* (Berlin: Springer Verlag, 1991) and 'Expectations of Selling-Prices in the EMS' in: P. de Grauwe, S. Micossi and G. Tullio (eds.), *Inflation and Wage Behaviour in the European Monetary System* (Oxford: Oxford University Press, 1997).

Arthur van de Meerendonk is a Senior Economist at the Economic Policy Directorate General in the Dutch Ministry of Social Affairs and Employment, The Hague, the Netherlands. He has contributed to the report *The Dutch Welfare State From an International and Economic Perspective* (The Hague: Ministry of Social Affairs and Employment, 1996). Previously he has worked for the Dutch Ministry of Health Care, The Hague.

Günther Schmid is Director of the Research Unit on Labour Market Policy and Employment of the Wissenschaftszentrum Berlin für Sozialforschung (Social Science Research Centre, Berlin; WZB), Germany. He is also Professor of Political Economics at the Free University of Berlin. His main research is on equity and efficiency in labour market policy. He is the main editor of *International Handbook of Labour Market Policy and Evaluation* (Cheltenham: Edward Elgar, 1996) and *Labour Market Institutions in Europe* (Armonk: M.E. Sharpe, 1994).

David Soskice is Director of the Research Unit on Economic Change and Employment of the Wissenschaftszentrum Berlin für Sozialforschung (Social Science Research Centre, Berlin; WZB), Germany. His main research is on the impact of education and training systems, financial systems and industrial relations systems on company human resource policies and product market innovation and competitiveness. He is Emeritus Fellow in Economics at University College, Oxford University, United Kingdom, where he taught from 1968 to 1990, and has been a Visiting Professor in the economics department at the University of California at Berkeley, in political science at Duke University, and in industrial relations at Cornell University, United States.

Gunnar Trumbull is a doctoral candidate at the Massachusetts Institute of Technology (MIT), Cambridge, United States and a Visiting Researcher at the Wissenschaftszentrum Berlin für Sozialforschung (Social Science Research Centre, Berlin; WZB), Germany.

Anne Wren is a doctoral candidate at the Harvard University, Cambridge, United States and a Visiting Researcher at the Wissenschaftszentrum Berlin für Sozialforschung (Social Science Research Centre, Berlin; WZB), Germany.

Part I

Introduction

1 Good Neighbours: Germany and the Netherlands

Lei Delsen and Eelke de Jong
University of Nijmegen, the Netherlands

1.1 Introduction

All OECD Member States are confronted with a number of important structural changes. These *common changes* include: the internationalisation of the economies, the advances in information and communication technology, and the ageing of the population and the labour force. There are many definitions of internationalisation in use. A broad definition is: "the intensification of economic, political, social and cultural relations across borders" (Holm and Soerensen 1995, p. 1). Partly internationalisation is the result of a purposeful policy to lift barriers on international trade and capital flows. The new information and communication technologies also intensify and facilitate the internationalisation process. The third common change, the ageing of populations creates considerable pressure on the financing of social programmes. While expenditure on social programmes is rising due to the ageing of populations, the number of working age people will be growing only slowly or declining. A consequential fiscal crisis has to be prevented.

In order to deal in an appropriate way with these changes, each OECD country has to consider the question whether its institutional arrangements facilitate the *adaptability of its economy*. In this respect one often makes a distinction between the relative importance of the market and of the government in coordinating economic activities. The institutional differences between industrial countries can to a great extent be ascribed to a different mix of mechanisms that correct the results of the market process.

From the economic point of view, the *consensus economy* is a mixed economic order in which, besides the market and the government, a third mechanism of coordination is used, namely consultation. For example, through consultation between the employers' and employees' organisations and the government these three bodies jointly give direction to social-economic policy. In particular product markets, producers and consumers organisations and the government will consult each other on issues like quality standards and prices. Following Albert (1991) a distinction can be made between two different variants of capitalism: the Rhineland model and the Anglo-Saxon model.[1] The Federal Republic of Germany and the Netherlands, together with Switzerland, Belgium, Luxembourg, the Nordic countries and Japan, are variants of the *Rhineland model*. These countries are characterised by relatively much government involvement and tripartism as a coordinating device. Concertation is used instead of conflict, and these countries are aiming at long-term investments. The United States of America (USA) and the United Kingdom (UK) may be considered as variants of the *Anglo-Saxon model* characterised by little government involvement and coordination by the market, aiming at short-term results. In this book the focus is on the Federal Republic of Germany and the Netherlands. The UK and the USA are used as benchmark countries.

The structural changes put pressure on the social market economies and its institutions. The optimum relationship between coordination by the market and non-market coordination is a flexible one. There is disagreement as to which institutional arrangements best support the performance of the economy. One of the conclusions drawn at present by many researchers, policy makers and policy advisors (see for instance Den Broeder 1996; Fukuyama 1996; Streeck 1995) is that coordination by the market is better suited to deal with these trends. In making policy advice the *OECD Jobs Study* (1994a) is biased towards the market. The basic starting point of that analysis is that non-market institutions and (social) policy arrangements do have detrimental effects, i.e. in the long run the market always gives better results without than with policy interventions. In other words a rise of the Anglo-Saxon model is expected and the end of the Rhineland model is inevitable. Albert (1991) sees a battle between the Rhineland model and the Anglo-Saxon model. He concludes that the Rhineland model on which the Dutch and German welfare systems are based is loosing ground since the 1980s in favour of neoliberalism, despite the economic and social superiority of the Rhineland model. The market is considered good, non-market coordination is considered bad. Deregulation and privatisation became dominant policy issues. Albert sees a real danger that capitalism will derail. The concerted economy seems to have lost legitimacy because the presently so dominant neoliberal ideology is rather critical and distrustful of concertation and cooperative competition. The question is to what extent this critique and distrust is justified (Van Waarden 1997, p. 13): does concertation among competitors really reduce competition to such an extent that undeserved rents can be extracted from consumers and inefficiencies are being produced? Are the resultant contracts and regulations really the rigidities they are made out to be? Do they reduce competi-

[1] A third variant of capitalism is the Latin model, characterised by relatively strong government regulation and strong government policy impact on economic development. Activities by economic agents are directed towards the government in order to put weight to their demands. France, Spain and Italy are variants of the Latin model.

tion and increase costs to business, as many neoclassical economists maintain? Do such institutions increase equity in the market? Could they also enhance allocative and dynamic efficiency, the competitive position of sectors and national economies?

The Rhineland model with its extensive social safety net is deeply entrenched in continental Europe. This *social model* refers to a set of habits, assumptions and laws which though varying from country to country, is based on a view that society is better off if the representatives of labour, capital and the people at large, i.e. the government agree how best to run an economy (*The Economist* 5 April 1997, p. 13). The institutions of economic coordination that make national economies differ are the outcome of a *path dependent* long-term historical process, a process in which structures and cultural values that evolved at one point in time predetermined subsequent policy choices and institutional developments. Each nation has its own specific history. That is why the outcome of this long-term process differs so much. This implies also that economic institutions are for their effectiveness and legitimacy dependent on other institutions and cultural values present in these societies. They 'fit' in a pattern of institutions and values, which are often deeply rooted. Particular forms of corporatist self-regulation may have great legitimacy in the Netherlands, but may be met with great hostility in the USA. As a result, the costs of such institutions may be much higher in the USA. This implies that there is not necessarily a 'one best way' to organise the economy for all times and all places. And also that it is not without problems to transplant American market solutions or Japan community allocation mechanisms to other societies (Van Waarden 1997, p. 13).

The core theme of this book is how the Dutch and German economies, variants of the Rhineland model, are changing and have to be changed, in the light of the above mentioned structural changes. To be more specific, the central question is: to what extent does the German and Dutch experience in this respect set an example for other (European) economies? Specific questions that will be addressed are:

- what are the advantages and disadvantages of the Rhineland model relative to the Anglo-Saxon model for structuring the economy?
- are the changes in the Netherlands an example for the necessary changes in the Federal Republic of Germany and other Member States of the European Union?
- will the increased internationalisation and the strife for integration in Europe result in a uniform structuring of the European economies?

In this chapter we summarise the major issues at stake when discussing the alleged controversy between state coordination and coordination by the market. Our point of departure is that no market can function without an appropriate institutional setting and that market institutions and regulations or government interventions are not simply sources of inertia and resistance to adaptation; they may actually act as the very vehicles for innovation and change. Neoclassical economists are inclined to perceive only the costs of regulation; intervention disrupts the 'natural' order and impedes an optimal allocation.[2] However, regulations also have functions and benefits, which become particularly apparent in the history of regulation. Many regulations, institutions and conventions, as they still exist at present in the Dutch economy, have been 'created' in the first half of this century. Their aim was to correct or mitigate the coordination failures, monopolistic practices and inequalities in the distribution of income and wealth connected with the free functioning of markets (see Kuipers 1996). In this sense states and markets are complementary, not substitutes (Rodrik 1996; 1997).

A relevant question is which institutions, arrangements and structures are better suited to perform their task within the changing international scene and various other developments mentioned above. Before this question can be answered we need:

1. insight in the differences in economic performance between countries;
2. insight in the institutional differences between countries, and;
3. insight in the role institutions and conventions play in market economies, i.e. why institutions exist in the labour, goods and financial markets.

This chapter is organised as follows. In Section 1.2 the major common trends in the industrial economies are discussed to illustrate the relevance of a comparison of the German and Dutch economies. In Section 1.3 a number of stylised facts are presented. A comparison is made of the social-economic performance of Germany and the Netherlands. The Unites States and the United Kingdom, representatives of the Anglo-Saxon model, are used as benchmark countries. In the 1970s and 1980s the German variant of the Rhineland model, the socalled 'Soziale Marktwirtschaft' was seen as a role model. During the 1990s the Dutch version, the 'Delta model', increased considerably. This shift in appreciation from the 'Soziale Marktwirtschaft' to the 'Delta model' as an example for other EU Member States is reviewed in Section 1.4. Section 1.5 discusses the theory and practice of the relationship between institutions and conventions and the performance of labour markets, financial markets, and product markets. Section 1.6 concludes and gives a summary of the contents and structure of the book.

1.2 Common Trends and Problems

As a result of the decline in the birth rate and the increase in the number of older persons, the proportion of persons employed will decrease in relation to the proportion of persons out of the labour force. Given the assumptions about

---

[2] Note, however, that political scientists and lawyers often start from opposing assumptions: the 'natural' societal condition is one of chaos, destruction, insecurity, and an unlimited and all-destructive battle of all against all (Van Waarden 1997, p. 17).

fertility, life expectancies and immigration flows, the old-age dependency ratio[3] is expected to increase sharply between 1990 and 2040, although the pace of ageing differs across OECD countries (see Figure 1.1). From around 20% in 1990 for most industrial countries, the ratios will be more than doubled to almost 50% in the Netherlands and Germany, and be almost doubled by the year 2040 in the USA to almost 35%. A strong ageing is projected for the Netherlands; starting with one of the lowest ratios in 1990 and reaching one of the highest in 2040. The opposite holds for the UK: while it started in 1990 at a relative advanced level, population ageing is projected to be less pronounced. Beyond 2040 the elderly dependency ratios are projected to decrease in all countries. The demographic developments – the double ageing process – will have important social and economic consequences for all OECD countries. These developments will put great stress on the systems of social security, pensions systems and health care of the industrial countries. In particular, higher pensions and social security premiums (wedge) will profoundly affect labour markets. Moreover, the need to transfer an increasing amount of resources to the elderly will have major consequences for the intergenerational distribution of welfare. Furthermore, growing pension funds are likely to substantially impact financial markets. At the same time increased life expectancy offers opportunities to extend productive working life (see Delsen and Reday-Mulvey 1996; *European Economy*, nr. 3, 1996; OECD 1994a; World Bank 1994). All industrial countries have to cope with these challenges and opportunities posed by these demographic trends.

Figure 1.1 Old-age dependency ratios, 1990-2050

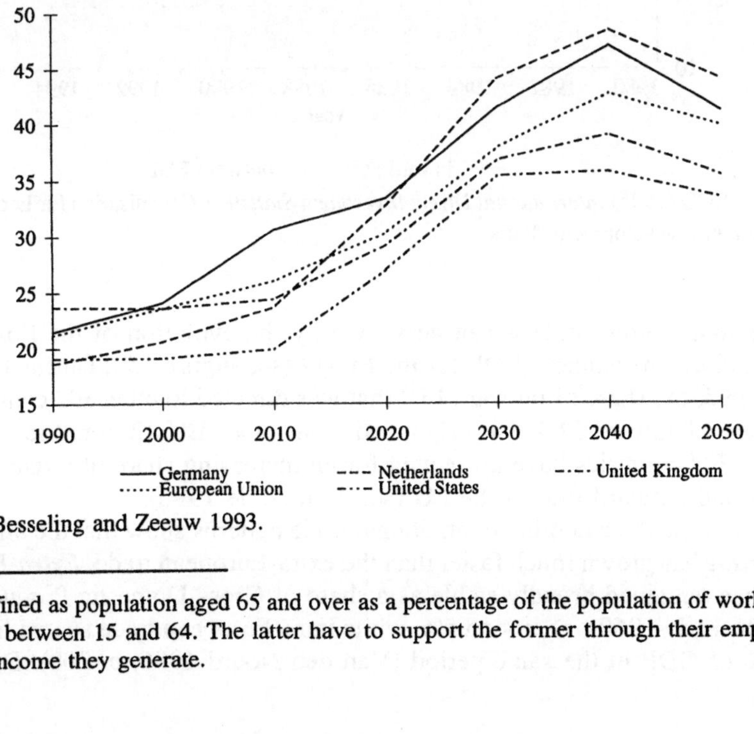

Source: Besseling and Zeeuw 1993.

---

[3] Defined as population aged 65 and over as a percentage of the population of working age, i.e. those between 15 and 64. The latter have to support the former through their employment and the income they generate.

The reduction in the transport and communications costs and the abolishment of legal barriers to international transactions (such as taxes) imply that to a large extent economic activities have become foot-loose. The cross-border flows of capital and the exchange of technology have increased markedly over the past decades. Also the international trade in goods and services shows an increasing trend. It is often referred to as 'globalisation' (Vernon 1996). However, the *internationalisation of the economies* is not global, in fact internationalisation is mainly regionalisation (see for instance Krugman 1991; Kleinknecht and Ter Wengel, 1996). As in social life also in economic life there seems to be much truth in the saying that "a near neighbour is better than a distant cousin". This is increasingly becoming relevant for European economies.

Figure 1.2 Intra EU Foreign Direct Investment, European Union 12, 1982-1993

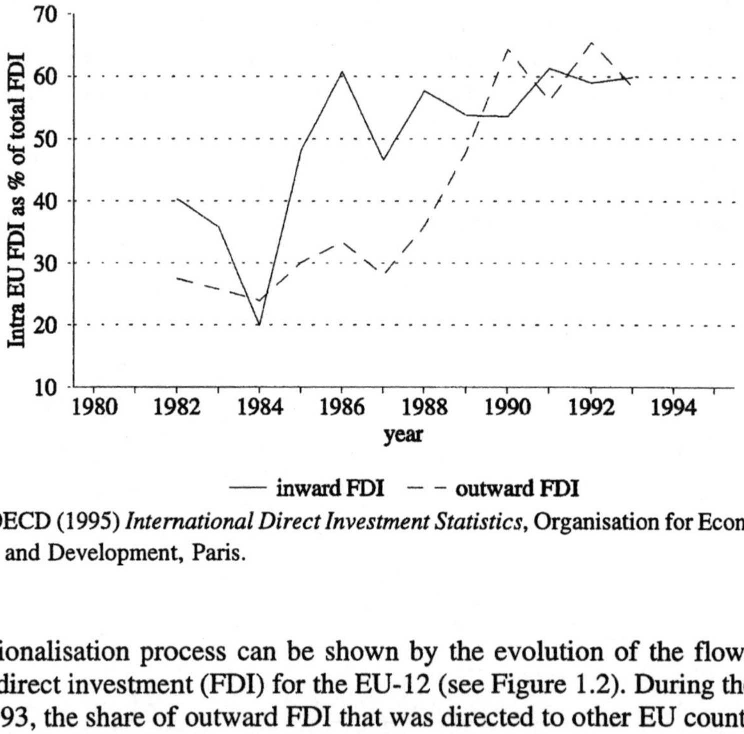

Source: OECD (1995) *International Direct Investment Statistics*, Organisation for Economic Co-operation and Development, Paris.

The regionalisation process can be shown by the evolution of the flows of the foreign direct investment (FDI) for the EU-12 (see Figure 1.2). During the period 1982-1993, the share of outward FDI that was directed to other EU countries and the share of inward FDI that originated from other EU-12 countries increased sharply. EU countries have accounted for an increasing share of a rising total of inward and outward FDI in the EU (see Van Aarle 1996).

For Europe the changing international trade patterns show that the *intra-European trade* has grown much faster than the extra-European trade. *Extra-European trade* has remained broadly stable as a share of Gross Domestic Product (GDP) since the early 1960s, at around 5%, while intra-European trade soared from 10% to 15% of GDP in the same period (Van den Noord 1996, p. 208). During the

1980-1995 period the import and export shares of the EU-12 economies remained relatively constant, fluctuating around a level of 21 to 26% of GDP. However, more importantly, the share of intra-EU exports and intra-EU imports rose from 50% to over 60% in this period (see Figure 1.3). With more or less constant import- and export-to-GDP ratios, the increasing shares of intra-EU trade imply trade diversion/substitution from extra-EU trade towards intra-EU trade (Van Aarle 1996, p. 129).

Figure 1.3 Intra EU import and export, European Union 12, 1980-1995

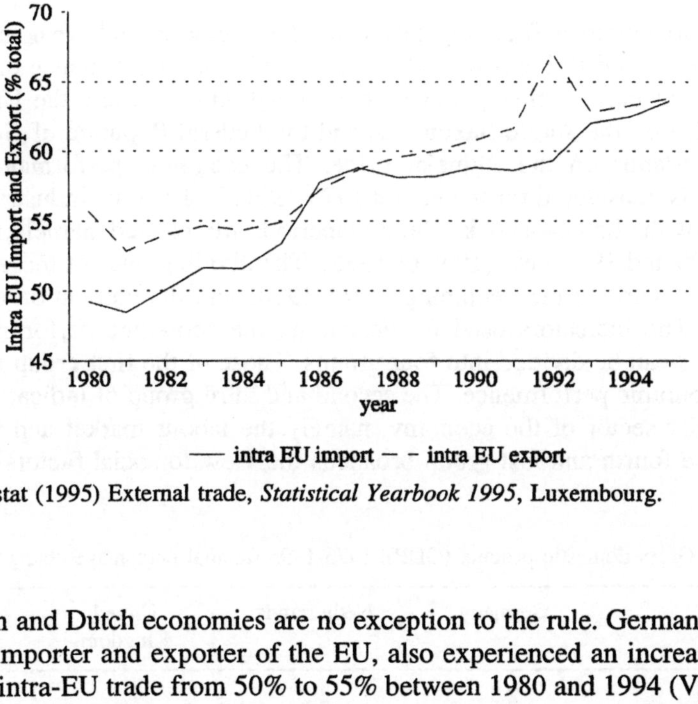

Source: Eurostat (1995) External trade, *Statistical Yearbook 1995*, Luxembourg.

The German and Dutch economies are no exception to the rule. Germany, by far the largest importer and exporter of the EU, also experienced an increase in the share of its intra-EU trade from 50% to 55% between 1980 and 1994 (Van Aarle 1996, p. 131). In 1995 almost 57% of German total exports was to EU countries and over 54% of all imports was from EU member countries, while both the import and export shares for other regions are below 10% (OECD 1996a, p. 9). For the Netherlands the data show a similar picture. However, the shares of intra-EU exports exceed intra-EU imports considerably. Between 1982 and 1994 the proportion of Dutch intra-EU exports in all Dutch exports increased from around 74% to around 78%. In the same period the share of intra-EU imports in all Dutch imports increased from around 56% to around 62% (see Van Aarle 1996, pp. 130-131; Jochemsen, Chapter 6 in this volume). Exports to and imports from Germany account for over one-third of Dutch intra-EU trade (OECD 1996b; CPB 1995, p. 95).

The data in this section not only show an increasing interdependency of regional (=European) economies and the common problems industrial countries face, they also show the economic importance of Germany and the Netherlands as good neighbours in the European Union and hence the relevancy of comparing the German and Dutch economies. In the next section some international comparative data on the German and Dutch social-economic performance are presented.

1.3 Some Stylised Facts on Economic Performance

In order to obtain a first impression of the strengths and weaknesses of the Anglo-Saxon and Rhineland models we describe the performance of two representatives of each of these models: the United Kingdom and the United States of America on the Anglo-Saxon side and the Federal Republic of Germany and the Netherlands on the Rhineland-side. The economic performance of these countries is considered for the period 1973-1996. In 1973 the industrial countries were hit by the first oil-shock. Three subperiods are selected, namely, 1973-1982, 1983-1990 and 1991-now (1995 or 1996). The dividing lines of these subperiods are the recession at the beginning of the 1980s and the unification of Germany in 1990. The indicators used for describing the economic performance of the economies can be divided into four groups. Those of the first group measure the macroeconomic performance. The second and third group of indicators focus on a particular sector of the economy, namely the labour market and the government. The fourth and last group broadens the view to social factors.

Table 1.1 Gross domestic product (GDP), 1976-1995 (annual percentage changes)

	Germany	Netherlands	United Kingdom	United States
1976-1996	2.5	2.3	2.1	2.7
1976-1982	2.3	1.6	1.4	2.3
1983-1990	3.0	3.0	3.3	3.3
1991-1995	2.2	2.1	1.3	2.2

Source: Central Planning Bureau (CPB), The Hague; own calculations.

An often used indicator of macroeconomic performance is the growth of *Gross Domestic Product* (GDP), which measures total production. During the last two decades the annual growth rate of GDP was the highest in the USA and the lowest in the UK (see Table 1.1). The differences between the four countries are small. More striking is that for the UK the differences between the periods are relatively large. In the second half of the 1980s the annual growth rate in the UK is one of the highest, in the other two subperiods it is clearly the lowest.

Table 1.2 Output per person, 1973-1996 (annual percentage changes)

	1973-1979	1979-1996
Germany	3.1	1.1
Netherlands	2.6	1.6
United Kingdom	1.5	1.9
United States	0.3	0.8

Source: *OECD Economic Outlook 61*, Organisation for Economic Cooperation and Development, Paris, 1997, p. A66.

A disadvantage of GDP as a performance indicator is that it does not relate the output to the input that is required for producing the output: a high growth rate of GDP might have required a lot of effort. Hence a measure of economic efficiency is needed. Only those increases in GDP unambiguously imply a better performance (in terms of increased efficiency) which follow from investment in more effective machinery, a more skilled labour force, better organisation of production or from increased opportunities for work for a previous excluded section of the population (Glyn and Miliband 1994, p. 10). Increase in efficiency could also be achieved in the form of shorter hours of work or less intensive working conditions, in which case GDP does not rise. In Table 1.2 output per person is used as a measure for *economic efficiency*. During the entire period the annual growth in output per person is in the two Rhineland-countries higher than in the two Anglo-Saxon countries. For the second period, however, the British figure is the highest. A reason for the low growth rate for the USA can be the high level of productivity in the USA (see Schmid and Helmer, Chapter 3 in this volume).

The number of people employed, the productivity per worker and trends in their real earnings will be key elements in coping with the increases in expenditure on social programmes due to demographic ageing. Moreover, a high number of inactive people leads to social costs in terms of social exclusion causing an increased probability of criminal actions. From an economic point of view inactive people loose their skills and thus inactivity leads to a loss of human capital. The *unemployment rate* gives a first impression of the level of inactivity. For the entire period the average unemployment rate is lower in the Rhineland countries than in the two Anglo-Saxon countries (see Table 1.3 row 1). Up to the beginning of the 1970s the German unemployment rate is the lowest, thereafter it increased so that during the last subperiod the Netherlands and the United States surpassed Germany. Except for the subperiod 1973-1982, the unemployment rate in the UK has been the highest of the countries concerned (see Table

Table 1.3 Unemployment rate, inflation rate and misery-index, 1973-1995

	Germany		Netherlands		United Kingdom		United States	
	mean	st. dev.	mean	st. dev.	mean	st. dev.	mean	st. dev.
A Unemployment rate								
1973-1995	5.1	2.1	7.3	2.7	8.1	2.9	6.7	1.3
1973-1982	3.3	1.4	5.8	2.6	6.0	2.7	6.9	1.4
1983-1990	6.4	0.9	9.9	1.6	9.9	2.1	6.7	1.4
1991-1995	6.7	2.0	6.4	0.6	9.5	0.8	6.5	0.8
B Inflation rate								
1973-1996	3.6	1.9	4.2	3.1	8.9	5.9	5.8	3.2
1973-1982	5.2	1.4	7.1	2.1	14.2	5.0	8.8	2.7
1983-1990	1.8	1.2	1.5	1.4	5.7	2.0	3.9	1.1
1991-1996	3.3	0.9	2.7	0.5	3.4	1.6	3.1	0.6
C Misery index								
1973-1995	8.7	1.7	11.5	2.7	17.0	4.4	12.6	3.4
1973-1982	8.5	1.5	12.8	2.7	20.2	4.7	15.6	2.8
1983-1990	8.2	1.6	11.4	2.5	15.6	1.4	10.5	1.3
1991-1995	9.9	1.8	9.1	0.7	12.9	1.3	9.7	1.2

Source: OECD, *Economic Outlook, December 1996*, Paris.

1.3, Part A). In the United States the unemployment rate has been remarkably stable at a level of about 6%. A striking difference between the USA and the other countries is that the unemployment rate in the USA was not effected by the first oil shock, whereas in the European countries this shock led to a significantly higher unemployment rate. In all countries the unemployment rate was at its highest level in 1983. From then the Dutch rate declined gradually and became lower than the German rate in 1992. Only in 1995 the British unemployment rate was lower than the German one.

Besides the level of macroeconomic activity its *stability* is important too. There are at least two reasons for considering stability. Firstly, risk-averse agents put value to stability as such. Secondly, it is generally believed that a stable economic environment will enhance economic growth. Stability increases the predictability of future developments and thus lengthens the time horizon of investors, so that they are more inclined to invest in projects for which the payback period is relatively long. In general these are projects which require much Research and Development, are relatively risky, and have a relatively large profit potential. A high *inflation rate* is the most important macroeconomic phenomenon that points at an unstable situation. The inflation rate of the Rhineland countries is almost always lower than that in the Anglo-Saxon countries (see Table 1.3, Part B). The German inflation rate is the lowest, except for the years 1991-1996. This temporary worsening of the German performance can be ascribed to the unification. The British inflation rate is the highest; also its variability is relatively large. In all four countries, the standard deviations show a decreasing trend, indicating a reduction in the variability of the yearly inflation rates and a more stable situation in each subperiod.

The *misery index* is the sum of the unemployment rate and the inflation rate. This index is inspired by the Phillips-curve trade-off between inflation and unemployment. Moreover, the misery index can be regarded as measuring both the level of economic activity and its stability. Once again Germany and the Netherlands appear to have performed better than the UK and the USA (Table 1.3, Part C). Both the mean and standard deviation of the misery index of the two continental European countries is lower than those of the two Anglo-Saxon nations. Until 1992 the misery index in Germany is the lowest, thereafter the index of the Netherlands and the USA (1994 and 1995) are lower. Overall the UK shows the worst performance. From the figures on economic growth, unemployment and inflation we conclude that in general the Rhineland countries have performed better than the two Anglo-Saxon countries. In many respects the macroeconomic performance of the British economy is the worst.

Table 1.4 Ratio of employed to total population and working age population in 1992

	Total population	Working age population
Germany	44.9	64.9
Netherlands	43.8	64.2
United Kingdom	44.0	67.8
United States	46.6	71.1

Source: Maddison 1995, p. 244.

The unemployment rate gives an incomplete picture of the level of inactivity in an economy. Other types of inactivity such as sickness, disability and early retirement are not included in the unemployment rate. In order to capture these forms of inactivity we relate the number of *employed people* to the total population and the potential working force (those between 15 and 64). According to both measures in 1992 the level of inactivity in the USA was lower than that in the other three countries (see Table 1.4). The difference between the USA and the other three countries is the greatest for the share of the number of employed persons as a percentage of the working force. This figure is relatively low in the Rhineland countries, whereas in the UK it is intermediate.

Table 1.5 Long-term unemployment, 1983, 1990 and 1995 (as a percentage of total unemployment)

	6 Months and over			12 Months and over		
	1983	1990	1995	1983	1990	1995
Germany	65.8	64.5	65.4	39.3	46.3	48.3
Netherlands	69.2	63.4	74.4	50.5	48.4	43.2
United Kingdom	65.7	52.2	60.7	47.0	36.0	43.5
United States	23.9	10.2	17.3	13.3	5.6	9.7

Source: OECD, *Employment Outlook*, various issues.

The functioning of the labour market appears to be of crucial importance for the performance of an economy. Therefore, in this book three chapters (Chapters 2-4) are devoted to the labour market. In this introduction we pay attention to some characteristics of the labour market. As stated above, a high level of inactivity will lead to a loss of skills and thus to a decline in human capital. In this respect it is not only the level of unemployment that is relevant but also (and maybe to a greater extent) the duration of the inactivity. There appears to be a great difference between the USA and the European countries. In the USA *long-term unemployment* is significantly lower than in Europe (see Table 1.5). During the last decades in Germany the proportion of long-term unemployment (12 months and over) in total unemployment has steadily increased, whereas in the Netherlands this proportion gradually decreased and was at the same level as in the UK in 1995. So with respect to long-term unemployment the same conclusion can be drawn as with respect to the unemployment rate; the main difference is not that between the two economic systems but between Europe and the United States.

Table 1.6 Unit labour costs, 1976-1996 (annual percentage changes)

	Germany	Netherlands	United Kingdom	United States
1976-1996	3.3	0.9	6.1	3.6
1976-1982	4.9	2.8	12.9	8.3
1983-1990	2.1	-0.6	3.4	1.2
1991-1996	3.2	0.6	2.0	1.3

Source: *Centraal Economisch Plan 1995*, The Hague.

Wage increases corrected for changes in labour productivity are important determinants of employment. During all subperiods the changes in the Dutch *unit labour costs* were the lowest (see Table 1.6), indicating an improvement of the competitive position of the Netherlands on world markets. In the second half of the 1980s the Dutch wage increases were even smaller than the improvements in labour productivity. With an annual rate of 6.1% the increases in the unit labour costs in the UK were the highest. Especial in the period before the Thatcher administration the wage increases were very high, but also in the years after 1982 the annual changes in British unit labour costs were higher than those in the other countries. During the last two decades the rise in unit labour costs in Germany and the USA was approximately the same. In the 1970s, the German rates were lower than those in the USA, whereas from 1983 onwards the reverse holds. Once again the differences between the countries does not correspond with the two models of economic systems. In part the differences may be related to differences in the phases of the business cycle.

Table 1.7 General government: outlays and financial balances, 1978-1995/1996 (as a percentage of GDP)

	Germany	Netherlands	United Kingdom	United States
Total outlays				
1978-1995	47.9	55.7	42.5	33.0
1978-1982	48.0	54.9	42.8	31.5
1983-1990	46.4	56.4	41.6	33.1
1991-1995	50.3	55.3	43.5	34.2
Financial deficit				
1973-1996	2.5	3.7	3.4	2.2
1973-1982	2.6	2.9	3.5	1.3
1983-1990	1.6	5.0	1.7	2.9
1991-1996	3.2	3.3	5.6	2.9

Source: Leibfritz et al. 1994, Table A6.

A striking difference between the Rhineland model and the Anglo-Saxon model concerns the role of the government. The market plays a dominant role in both models. However, in the Rhineland countries the institutional arrangements explicitly take into account the possibility of market failures. The government is supposed to create the circumstances under which the market process leads to outcomes that are just for all. In the Anglo-Saxon countries the results of the market process are accepted as such. Essentially, the government has almost no role in correcting these results. A consequence of this difference is that in general in the Rhineland countries *government expenditures* (as a percentage of GDP) are greater than in the Anglo-Saxon countries. The figures of total outlays of the government (central and local) affirm this statement (see Table 1.7). The ranking of the countries by the size of total outlays is: the Netherlands, Germany, the UK and the USA. Except that the total governmental expenditures in the Rhineland countries are higher than in the Anglo-Saxon countries, within each group the outlays of the more open economies are the greatest. This results corresponds with Rodrik (1996; 1997), who claims that countries that are more exposed to trade have a larger government sector because governments provide social insurance to counter the effects of exposure to external risk.

The *financial deficits* of the government are the highest in the Netherlands and the UK (see Table 1.7). A striking difference between these two countries is that during the 1990s the Dutch deficit declined, whereas the British increased. This increase can be ascribed to the recession in the UK during the first years of the 1990s. The German deficit was very low in the second half of the 1980s; it increased in the 1990s, due to the costs associated with the German re-unification. Mostly the deficits in the USA are lower than those in the other countries. From these figures no significant difference between the two models can be distinguished.

Figure 1.4 Gross public debt (as a percentage of nominal gross domestic product), 1978-1995

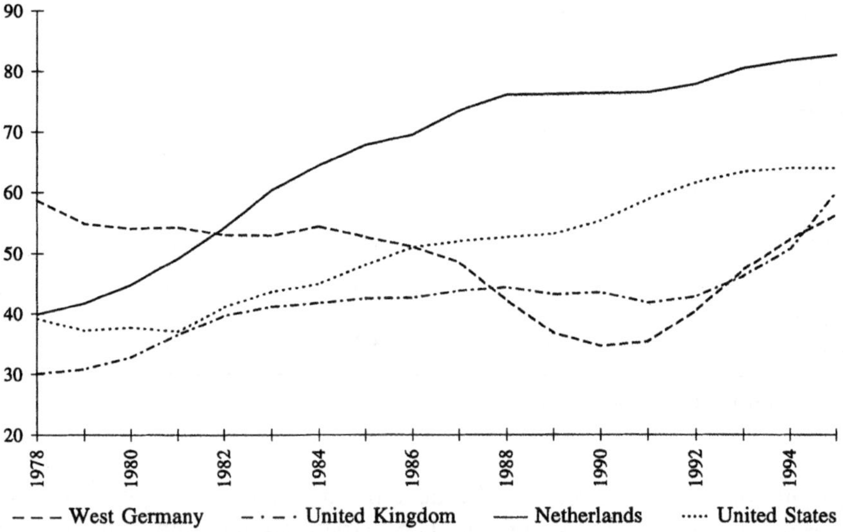

Source: Leibfritz et al. 1994, Table D8.

Also the data on the level of the debt show no significant difference between the Anglo-Saxon and Rhineland model (see Figure 1.4). From 1982 onwards the Dutch *gross public debt* (as a percentage of GDP) is the highest of the four countries. During that period one of the Anglo-Saxon countries occupies the second position. Until the beginning of the 1990s the German public debt was relatively low. From then onwards, it increased fastly; once again, due to the unification.

Table 1.8 Gross domestic product and human development index, 1987, 1989 and 1993

	Year	Real GDP per capita (PPP$)[1]	HDI	GDP rank minus HDI rank[2]
Germany	1987	14 730	0.97	-1
	1989	14 507	0.96	-2
	1993	18 840	0.98	-2
Netherlands	1987	12 661	0.98	10
	1989	13 351	0.97	8
	1993	17 340	0.94	18
United Kingdom	1987	12 270	0.97	8
	1989	13 732	0.96	11
	1993	17 230	0.92	7
United States	1987	17 615	0.96	-17
	1989	20 998	0.98	2
	1993	24 680	0.94	0

[1] PPP$ = Purchasing Power Parity, US dollar.
[2] A positive figure indicates that the HDI rank is higher than the GDP rank, a negative the opposite.
Source: United Nations, *Human Development Report* 1990, 1992 and 1996, Oxford University Press, Oxford.

Hitherto we have compared various economic indicators of the four countries. However, an assessment of the social-economic order based on economic factors only, misses the greater part of the social component. We therefore conclude this section with a comparison of the four countries with regard to the Human Development Index (HDI) and the income distribution. The HDI is developed by the United Nations in order to incorporate in one index economic growth as well as some other factors which are relevant for the development of countries. The HDI contains measures of the life expectancy at birth, the adult literacy rate and the real GDP per capita (see UN 1990, p. 109 for details). The differences between the HDI of the four countries concerned are small (see Table 1.8). In 1987 and 1993 this index was higher for the Rhineland countries, whereas in 1989 the Anglo-Saxon countries had a slightly higher index. The real GDP per capita is the highest in the USA (see Table 1.8). Except for 1987, the ranking of the USA according to the HDI roughly corresponds with the ranking resulting from the GDP per capita. For Germany the difference in ranking resulting from the use of the HDI or the GDP per capita are always small. The rank of the other two countries is always higher when the HDI is used than when use is made of the GDP measure. Once again the United Kingdom shows the worst performance.

Table 1.9 Income distribution. Percentage share of income

	Year	Lowest 20 percent	Second quintile	Third quintile	Fourth quintile	Highest 20 percent	Highest 10 percent
Germany	1974	6.9	11.0	15.4	21.9	44.8	28.8
	1978	7.9	12.5	17.0	23.1	39.5	24.0
	1988	7.0	11.8	17.1	23.9	40.3	24.4
Netherlands	1977	8.1	13.7	17.9	23.3	37.0	22.1
	1981	8.3	14.1	18.2	23.2	36.2	21.5
	1988	8.2	13.1	18.1	23.7	36.9	21.9
United Kingdom	1979	7.3	12.4	17.7	23.4	39.2	23.8
	1988	4.6	10.0	16.8	24.3	44.3	27.8
United States	1972	4.5	10.7	17.3	24.7	42.8	26.6
	1980	5.3	11.9	17.9	25.0	39.9	23.3
	1985	4.7	11.0	17.4	25.0	41.9	25.0

Source: World Bank, *World Development Report, 1983, 1985 and 1995*, Oxford University Press, New York, 1983, 1985 and 1995.

Figures on the income distribution are only available for the 1970s and the 1980s (see Table 1.9). According to these figures the share of the lowest 20% of households in the income is the highest in the Netherlands and the lowest in the USA. In Germany, the Netherlands and the USA the share of the lowest 20% is relatively constant. During the 1980s in the United Kingdom this share declined from 7.3% to 4.6%, whereas that of the highest 10% increased from 23.8% to 27.8%. Hence, the income distribution has become more uneven in the UK. In both Germany and the USA the share of the highest income groups in total income has declined during these years. The changes in the income distribution in the Netherlands are small. Overall the income distribution is more equal in the Rhineland countries than in the two Anglo-Saxon countries.

The facts presented in this section suggest that during the last decades the economic performance of the UK has been worse than that of the three other countries. The USA perform better than the two Rhineland countries with respect to the annual growth of GDP, the level of employment and long-term unemployment. Moreover, the size of government expenditures and government deficit in the USA are lower than in the other countries. One of the two Rhineland countries outperforms the other countries with respect to the other criteria used. In every period in these countries income is more evenly distributed than in the Anglo-Saxon countries. During the last ten years the differences between the Rhineland countries and the USA have diminished with respect to the annual growth of GDP, the unemployment rate and the inflation rate. This may reflect that the American economy is more flexible and thus better able to react to the challenges of the structural changes discussed in Section 1.2. Within the group of Rhineland countries it also seems that the more flexible economy, that of the Netherlands, recently performs better than the German. This implies that the

German and Dutch economies have changed their relative position. In the next section we describe in more detail this change in rank and shed some light on the factors that have played in this respect.

1.4 From 'Soziale Marktwirtschaft' to the 'Delta Model'

In the 1970s and 1980s Germany for several reasons was seen as a role model. Hampden-Turner and Trompenaars, for example state "... who can doubt that it is the 'German model' that appeals most to the new Europe, rather than the American or Japanese models?" (Hampden-Turner and Trompenaars 1994, p. 201). Institutional arrangements of the German Federal Republic were considered as examples for building the European Union. Like Europe, the German states first drew together through the customs union ('*Zollverein*') with political union coming later. Germany exemplifies the federal decentralised structures most EU members wish to see on a European scale. The politically independent European Central Bank (ECB) is modeled on the German central bank, the Deutsche Bundesbank. The German-style capitalism is also the most important model for most ex-Communist countries. It is not simply closer geographically to the ex-Communist world than the Anglo-Saxon variant, but it is also closer psychologically and ideologically (Hampden-Turner and Trompenaars 1994, p. 202). The German model was associated with favourable economic performance in the 1970s and 1980s. At that time, as was shown in the previous Section 1.3, the growth rate was one of the highest, the increase in labour productivity was tremendous, the unemployment rate was low, the budget was under control, and debt was only 42-43% of GDP. These achievements have been attributed to institutional factors: the German '*Wirtschaftswunder*' was thought to be the result of its '*soziale Marktwirtschaft*'.

During the 1980s the German system of industrial relations was characterised by stability and adaptation and it was able to combine macro rigidity and micro flexibility. The German labour market relies more heavily on working time and internal flexibility than is the case in other EU countries. Trade unions and employers' associations, works councils and management have been able to cope with economic, technological and political changes, resulting in German industrial relations being among the most stable in the Western world. The German industrial relations have been presented as an enviable 'model' for other economies. Its huge economic successes have been attributed to its institutions: sectoral collective bargaining, labour law court, the independent Deutsche Bundesbank, the non-intervention in wage formation ('*Tarifautonomie*'), nationwide unions and employers' associations, works councils, dense local business networks and comprehensive training programmes. The German economy gained a comparative advantages in the 1980s by having a broadly skilled workforce and a well-developed system of education (see Den Broeder 1996; Visser and Van Ruysseveldt 1996; Soskice et al., Chapter 2 in this volume).

Inspired by the increase in unemployment rates, in the early 1990s the debate has shifted from '*Modell Deutschland*' to '*Standort Deutschland*'. Now the emphasis is on the costs of regulation, bureaucratic red tape, high labour standards, short and inflexible working hours and high non-wage labour costs (Visser 1996, p. 40). In the 1990s, the German model of industrial relations came under increased pressure, due to the poor performance of industry, and the social, economic and political problems which emerged after the unification (Paqué 1993). Is Germany still attractive enough as a location for domestic capital and for foreign direct investment ('*Standort Deutschland*')? German employers and their associations complain that it is becoming increasingly difficult to compete against foreign companies because Germany has high wages, shorter working hours, long holidays, high tax rate and government red tape (*EIRR* February 1994; Visser and Van Ruysseveldt 1996, pp. 163-172).

In the 1970s and the first half of the 1980s the Netherlands were characterised by the so-called 'Dutch disease'. The increasing government resources (gas exploits) were used to stimulate the economy and employment through higher consumption and lower premiums. It resulted in wage and price hikes and an appreciating currency, which lead to a loss of competitiveness and jobs in the open sector. Moreover, the financial deficit increased sharply, from 1.4% in 1971 to 5.3% in 1979 and 9.4% in 1983. The governments consisting of a coalition of christian democrats, liberals and socialists were not able or willing to take significant measures. The radical change occurred in 1982. Then a coalition consisting of the christian democratic party and the liberal party won the elections. The resulting cabinet Lubbers-I introduced various austerity plans to reduce the budget deficit. Finally the succeeding cabinets under prime minister Lubbers succeeded in reducing the budget deficit and controlling the government debt. Meanwhile and maybe of even more important was that in the Autumn of 1982 the social partners (trade unions and employer organisations) concluded the 'Accord of Wassenaar'. This agreement forms the basis of a long period of moderate wage increases (see Table 1.6 in Section 1.3), which led to a sharp improvement of the Dutch competitiveness.

So at the start of the last decade of this century the Netherlands by and large had their public finances under control and were implementing measures to enhance the flexibility of the economy. Partly as a result of these measures, the Dutch economy outperformed that of Germany and many other EU Member States: the average growth rate of real GDP and employment growth were above average between 1989 and 1995. Early 1994 the standardised unemployment peaked and declined to 6.3% in 1996. It is one of the lowest among OECD countries and sharply below the EU average of 11% (OECD 1996b, p. 15). Also in monetary terms the Dutch economy performs well. The inflation rate is lower than those in partner countries and comparable with the traditionally low rate in Germany. Also employment growth has been considerable in the Netherlands, relative to other European countries, while in Germany employment dropped. For 1996 and 1997 employment growth is higher than in the USA. Moreover, labour productivity in the Netherlands is one of the highest in the OECD area (see

Schmid and Helmer, Chapter 3 in this volume). This good performance implies that for the Netherlands it is easy to fulfil the EMU convergence criteria, especially that of the budget deficit of less than 3% of GDP. Although the public debt level is still higher than 60% of GDP it is declining and therefore the Netherlands also meet this criterium (see Jochimsen, Chapter 6 in this volume).

The '*Dutch model*', including the constructive role of the trade unions and the extraordinary growth of part-time work is considered as an example by Belgian, French and German politicians and employers. Also central bankers consider the Dutch approach a success and the reforms of the institutional structure over the past few years are praised. Hans Tietmeyer, president of the Bundesbank, Jean-Claude Trichet, president of the Banque de France, William McDonough of the Federal Reserve Bank of New York and IMF-Director Michel Camdessus have recently praised the adaptability of the Dutch model. The Dutch model is labelled '*Delta model*' referring to the symbol of change and to the Rhine delta. The EU-partners envy the Dutch employment growth and the developments in government finance. The trade unions are very cooperative. Dutch moderate wage increases are presented as a cure for Europe's unemployment and as an alternative for the Anglo-Saxon model (*The Economist* 5 April 1997, p. 20). The Netherlands – the pink Kok administration – are considered a political synthesis of the Rhinelandic social market economy and the Anglo-Saxon market model. In the labour market the Dutch have tried to combine the flexibility of the United States of America with the security of Germany (Den Broeder 1996). The Dutch example *seems* to suggest that adjustment of the labour market and the social security system can have positive results for job growth without sharply increasing social inequality, as in the United Kingdom, and serious social unrest, as in France.[4] The Netherlands show that change is achievable without wrecking the European 'social model'. Hence the Dutch experience shows that welfare states are flexible enough to adapt to new circumstances (see also Van de Meerendonk, Chapter 4 in this volume). Moreover, the Netherlands, seem to prove that meeting the EMU convergence criteria can go along with social policy and dramatic job growth (see also Schmid and Helmer, Chapter 3 in this volume).

Of course the differences in economic performance of Germany and the Netherlands, and the change from the *soziale Marktwirtschaft* to the *Delta model* becoming the role model can be partly explained by the asymmetric shock of the German re-unification. There is no doubt that from 1990s onwards in Germany the problems increased sharply. Section 1.3 showed that the unemployment rate increased and the share of long-term unemployment rose. The share of public spending in the GDP, the budget deficit and the increase in public debt can all three be ascribed to the unification of Germany. Another and maybe even more

[4] See for instance: Netherlands. To good to be true?, *The Economist*, 12 October 1996, pp. 39-40 and 42; Le modele hollandais, *Le Monde*, 18 October 1996; EMU targets pose very few problems, *Financial Times*, 29 October 1996; Abschied von der Norm, *Die Zeit*, 13 September 1996; Overvloed en onbehagen in de Rijndelta, *NRC Handelsblad*, 21 December 1996; Europe isn't working, *The Economist*, 5 April 1997, p. 13.

important explanation can be that, the differences between the two countries could be related to differences in culture and institutions. In this book the contributors concentrate on the latter. Differences between countries in the structure of labour markets, capital markets, and product markets are closely interlinked; together they form a cluster of complementary institutions. In the next section a brief review of the possible influences of norms, cultures and institutions on these three markets is presented. To some extent it provides the framework of the rest of this book.

1.5 Norms, Culture and Institutions and Economic Performance

1.5.1 Transaction Cost Theory and Institutional Economics

Neoclassical economics rely on open or simple "self-interest-seeking with candid disclosure": the position of individuals is fully and candidly disclosed before trade takes place, there are no surprises (Williamson 1975, pp. 26-27; 1985, p. 49). In economic science, this neoclassical 'perfect' market is often used as a benchmark to relate actual market relations. A market is considered to be more flexible, and is considered more efficient, when it shows more resemblance with the ideal type of the free unregulated market. The neoclassical analysis focuses on *production costs*. According to the standard version of the neoclassical theory, in the long run, the market mechanism will result in an equilibrium between demand and supply on all markets. As far as in the short term no equilibrium is established, this is related to restrictions on the functioning of the market mechanism.

In institutional economics the focus is on the *transaction costs*, the costs of running the economic system. Old, new and neo institutional economics have in common the argument that information is not acquired costlessly or even immediately as assumed in the simple neoclassical competitive paradigm. These theories recognise that information is acquired through time, by experience, by the process of learning-by-doing and is less than perfect. This lack of information causes coordination problems. Transaction cost economics assume that human agents are subject to *bounded rationality* and are given to opportunism, which is a condition of "self-interest seeking with guile". Individuals are "intendedly rational, but only limited so": they are rational but up to the limit of their capacity to receive and process information. So it is not just merely a question of deficiencies of information that determine market outcomes but of deficiencies in the human capacity to process that information, this leads them either to develop norms of behaviour, rules of thumb, or to adhere to social conventions. Both represent ways of economising on the resources devoted to process any new information. The most critical dimension for describing transactions is the condition of *asset specificity*. Asset specificity refers to durable investments in transaction specific assets. Asset specificity arises in an intertemporal context. Implying that unlike neoclassical transactions exchanges are neither faceless nor instantaneous (Williamson 1975, pp. 20ff; Williamson 1985, pp. 52-56). Specialised assets cannot be redeployed without sacrifice of productive value. One consequence of this is that long-term relations emerge in which contracting parties enjoy particular information advantages. 'Voice' rather than 'exit' is exercised to clear the market.

Incomplete information forces agents to act on predictions in case information is lacking, and extra information that makes predictions better enhances efficiency. Agents have to take care of coordinating their actions, by acting on their expectations of other agents. As these other agents act on their expectations as well, decisions become interdependent. In this way *multiple equilibria* may result, depending on the level of mutual expectations. Conventions and institutions have emerged to deal with these coordination failures[5] (Van der Lecq 1996, p. 397). As prices are information carriers, institutions can be seen as complementary to prices: "Social and economic institutions are informational devices that supplement the informational content of economic systems when competitive prices do not carry sufficient information to totally decentralize and coordinate economic activities" (Schotter 1981, p. 109). In the case of information asymmetry parties may seek to exploit this information advantage and this may result in a lower level of efficiency. This has been described by Williamson (1975, p. 9; 1985, pp. 47-51) as "self-interest-seeking with guile" (opportunism resulting in behavioral *uncertainty*) and it is in order to obviate such behaviour, and to mitigate the associated inefficiencies, that in certain markets institutions, rules and norms of behaviour have emerged.

Depending on the type of problem, the norm takes the form of a convention or an institution. A convention is self-enforcing; an institution needs an enforcing authority such as a sanctioning mechanism to support it. It is noteworthy that the rules that are devised are often of a cooperative, rather than a competitive, form. The stable or self-enforcing systems of norms are a starting point for the explanation of institutional differences between countries. Rules and institutions by definition imply a certain amount of (price/wage)rigidity. However, these institutions and conventions may reduce the uncertainties associated with trade and promote economic growth. Hence, price and wage rigidities are not necessarily a symptom of insufficient operation of the market mechanism as supposed by neoclassical economics (Garretsen 1997). On the other hand too much reduction in risk and uncertainty may give rise to *moral hazard.* In situations of uncertainty, *beliefs* and *trust* become at least as important as knowledge. Institutions than can become carriers of these beliefs and are able to persist because they are *believed* to do so (Van Waarden 1997, p. 15 and p. 20).

How do the agents coordinate their actions in order to reach a particular outcome, i.e. what are the mechanisms behind the emergence, the selection and

[5] Coordination failures is said to be present if "mutual gains from an all-round change in strategies may not be realised because no individual player has an incentive to deviate from the initial equilibrium" (Cooper and John 1988, p. 442).

the persistence of rules, conventions and norms? In the emergence of norms the above mentioned interaction and reciprocal expectations play a crucial rule, because the pay-offs actions agents choose depend on the actions taken by other agents. Conventions as the solution to coordination problems both need a macro and a micro underpinning: the social context influences the individual decision and is influenced by it. Three focal points that contribute to orderly markets are: contextual features, rules of thumb and common habits (Van der Lecq 1996, pp. 408-410). Contextual features, imply that the focal points are endogenously determined by the problem configuration. Rules of thumb are determined outside the problem. Habits emerge if for several periods of time the past choices determine (partly) the actual ones. Repetition of a problem creates a tacit agreement on the choice of a particular solution. This *path dependence* implies that the existence of institutions not only depends on their efficiency or utility increasing effects, but on their existence in former times as well. A coordinating norm may change once the coordinating problem or its context has changed significantly. Learning can also be a source of change for institutions if agents learn of a substantial more efficient institution to perform a task. The same holds for a convention shift. Shared mental models form a culture or an ideology and this may contribute to the explanation of different institutional configurations in different countries (Van der Lecq 1996, pp. 420-421).

After this brief overview of theories on the role of institutions, in the next three subsections respectively the labour market, financial market and product market institutions in relation to economic performance will be discussed in some detail.

1.5.2 Labour Market Institutions and Performance

Neoclassical labour market theory not only presupposes a perfect market, which i.a. means that labour is homogeneous, i.e. that the productivity of each worker is equal. Hence discrimination on the labour market is non existent and unemployment is only a rationing problem depending on the level of the market wage: unemployment is randomly distributed over the suppliers of labour, and unemployment is essentially a disequilibrium phenomenon. According to this neoclassic view 'rigidity' in the price of labour, the quantity and quality of manpower and conditions of employment are the hindrance to the clearing of labour markets. However, in reality labour markets are not perfect, if only because labour is *heterogenous*. Hence the probabilities of becoming unemployed, and to remain unemployed, are unequally distributed. Apart from the rationing problem there also is a distributional problem (see De Neubourg 1995; Delsen 1997). Given the heterogeneity of the labour force, left to itself the market tends to produce and reinforce inequalities – between those in and out of work, between strong and disadvantaged groups in the labour market, between regions and countries. Particularly vulnerable are the unskilled, older workers, disabled persons and minorities, especially in depressed regions. Non-intervention is likely to result in slower adjustment at higher social costs. This may explain why in the labour market competition-restraining institutions and anti-competition practices are introduced to a greater extent than in other markets. This may result in above market clearing wages. However, collusion among workers may save on transaction costs by giving a 'voice' to the workforce; it may also foster more harmonious relations between workers and management in the pursuit of common goals and strengthen social consensus in the society at large (OECD 1994b, p. 52).

Apart from the reduction in transaction costs, recent labour market theories like search, contract, insider-outsider and efficiency wages theory give economic reasons why wages are inelastic and explain the existence of involuntary unemployment as an equilibrium phenomenon. According to these theories offering wages above the market clearing level may be advantageous for the employer. For instance, it offers the opportunity to select good external candidates and to reduce turnover costs. Higher real wages moreover offer more effort and commitment of the employees.

The most important labour market institutions are unions and collective wage bargaining, job security and unemployment benefits. Until recently, in line with neoclassical thinking, there was somewhat of a consensus among economists that labour market problems in Europe are caused by these institutions. '*Eurosclerosis*', as it was dubbed, resulted from social policies, legislation and collective agreements, centralised bargaining, resulting in high benefits, dismissal protection and restrained wage competition. Unemployment benefits lower the incentive for job search and increase wage pressure by insiders. Minimum wages price the least skilled out of the market. Job security provisions and firing costs disturb the market process, deter hiring, thus reducing labour demand, reduce job mobility and hamper the economies ability to deal with uncertainty and structural change. The disincentive effects of the welfare system was considered a main cause for the high level of structural unemployment in Europe. High marginal and average tax rates (wedges) result in higher wages and are harmful for employment, reduce work effort or searching for work, reduce labour supply and result is less investments in human capital (see for instance OECD 1994b).

Recently more neutral or opposite conclusions are drawn in the literature. Deregulation of the labour market and decentralised wage bargaining may be at the expense of trust and commitment, or in general the social climate, the latter being a major source of good economic performance. The social climate is often excluded from economic analyses and overlooked by policy makers in reshaping the welfare states. Decentralisation may also result in non-competitive wage premia (Den Broeder 1996; Nyfer 1996). Countries which moved towards decentralisation or less coordination over the passed decade have experienced larger declines in the employment rate than countries which did not experience such decentralisation/uncoordination (OECD 1997, p. 83). There is evidence that in countries with less favourable social security benefits, because of the pressure of serious social consequences in case of redundancies (poverty) the necessary restructuring of enterprises is postponed. This resistance to change is analysed by Englander and Gurney (1994). When structured properly, the social security system may promote the willingness of people to take risks, resulting in a positive relationship between equality and efficiency (see Van de Meerendonk, Chapter 4 in this volume). Other research shows that sectoral institutions of concertation provide for necessary collective goods such as a skilled labour force and collective research and development. They create a certain order and stability on markets and reduce risk and uncertainty, thus facilitating long-term investment. They reduce labour unrest, all resulting in high labour productivity and high product quality (see Van Waarden 1997, p. 24). In the *OECD Employment Outlook 1996* it is concluded that cutting benefits and reducing minimum wages may not be a solution to lower long-term unemployment, because of the high social costs.

Different institutional settings, like wage bargaining, legal minimum wage and unemployment benefits and other benefits, rates of unionisation, have an impact on the volume of low paid jobs. These institutional features may create wage floors and reduce earnings dispersion, particularly at the bottom of the income distribution. However there is no hard evidence that countries with relatively few low paid jobs have reached this at the expense of higher unemployment rates and lower employment for the weakest groups in the labour market (OECD 1996a, pp. 75-76). Based on endogenous growth models it may be argued that minimum wage legislation does not necessarily have negative consequences on economic performance. In fact, it can have positive effects on growth by inducing more human capital accumulation: a low demand for unskilled labour, induced by a minimum wage, may create an incentive for workers to accumulate human capital. Moreover, it is possible that a decrease in the minimum wage lowers the welfare of each agent in the economy (Cahuc and Michel 1996). See also Dolado et al. (1996) for similar arguments.

1.5.3 Financial Systems and Economic Performance

The financial sector is of great importance for economic activity and economic growth, for it links savers and investors and selects the projects that will be financed and carried out. As Stiglitz (1992, p. 161) puts it: "if capital is at the heart of capitalism, then well-functioning capital markets are at the heart of a well-functioning capitalist economy". In a neoclassical world of perfect competitive markets and perfect information, the institutional structure of financial markets plays no role, i.e. the world could do without bonds and shares. However, in reality the financial structure is determined by economic factors and probably to an even greater extent, by non-economic factors, including culture and social norms (see Hoogduin and Huisman, Chapter 5 in this volume). Of interest is whether these differences in financial structure have an impact on the economic performance.

Related to national capital market systems three models can be distinguished. The *bank-based model* is characterised by close ties between banks and industry, concentration of company share ownership among small groups of shareholders, a relatively high proportion of debt capital in company financing and participation of banks in the shareholders' equity of business (Gelauff and Den Broeder

1996, p. 48; Ministry of Economic Affairs 1995, pp. 84-86). For instance in Germany and Denmark stock market development has been limited and banks play the most prominent role as providers of capital. The *market-based model* or Anglo-Saxon system is characterised by a strong separation of ownership and management, many small shareholders, a limited role for banks in risk-bearing corporate finance, highly developed stock markets, many suppliers of venture capital and almost no anti-take over measures. In the bank-based model with concentrated shareholders, there is more incentive to intervene and to exercise 'voice' rather than 'exit'. In the *Latin model* of the financial sector, the stock market is also relatively underdeveloped: many businesses are family-owned, financial holding companies and cross-participation are common, as are state owned companies. This system operates in countries like Belgium, France, Spain and Italy. The Dutch financial system can be considered as an example of an intermediate form between the bank-based system and the market-based system (see Hoogduin and Huisman, Chapter 5 in this volume).

To evaluate the performance of capital markets several indicators are used: private sector investment ratio; internal financing of investment by business; capital market possibilities for external financing and costs of capital. From the available comparative research results no clear cut differences in performance between the bank-based and the market-based system can be established (see Ministry of Economic Affairs 1995; Mayer 1996). However, this does not mean that there are no (still unobserved) differences in performance between the bank-based and market-based model.

There is an important interrelationship between the structure of financial and product markets. The willingness of financial institutions to finance investment is crucial for healthy competition in the product market. Financing of investment will typically require very patient investors. Short horizons can obviously constrain investment (OECD 1994b, p. 25). In the bank-based model, ownership remains concentrated and long-term relationships and commitment develop. In the Anglo-Saxon market-based system characterised by dispersed, anonymous shareholders it is difficult to sustain trust and commitment. Mayer (1996, p. 25) concludes that competition in the product market is generally associated with allocative and productive efficiency. Competition encourages the supply of goods and services at lowest costs and at prices which reflect the underlying costs of provision. He argues that this does not necessary apply to financial markets. Competition in the financial markets may undermine the development of long-term relationships between firms and financial institutions: the provision of rescue funding by banks may be discouraged. On the other hand, limitation of competition in financial markets may result in monopoly exploitation of borrowers.

1.5.4 Product Market Regulation and Performance

Apart from financial markets also properly-functioning product markets are essential for the adaptive and innovative capacity of an economy. If markets do not function well, this leads to cost inefficiency, deterioration of quality, risk-avoidance and lack of innovative behaviour. It can also have negative effects on the role played by small and medium-sized enterprises in the creation of new jobs (Ministry of Economic Affairs 1995, p. 101). Although all OECD governments embrace the principle that product prices should be determined by market forces, public intervention often weakens the strength of competition in the product market. This may be at the expense of employment. In most OECD countries, including Germany and the Netherlands, general competition legislation prohibits competition restraining measures (prohibition system) or the abuse of market power (abuse system) (see OECD 1994b, p. 25; Gradus, Chapter 7 in this volume).

There is an interrelationship between the structure of product markets and the labour markets. *Imperfect competition* in the product market can lower employment when employers share rents with their workers and results in above market clearing wages. Establishing a competitive environment could improve job prospects by both eliminating wage premia and encouraging output expansion. Initially, increased competition may result in job losses due to the elimination of existing inefficiencies. Rents come about because competitors cannot enter and eliminate supernormal profits. It is not the actual entry that matters but the threat of entry, i.e. producers in contestable markets are unlikely to earn any rents (OECD 1994b, pp. 23-24).

Regulations are not only necessary to constitute markets. There are also specific ones needed to maintain markets and competition. Regulations have to correct for too little and too much competition, which both reduce the *effectiveness of competition.* In order to prevent competition from destroying itself, anti-trust legislation is needed (see Van Waarden 1997, pp. 18-19). Too strict anti-cartel legislation may have opposite effects. The rather tolerant Dutch cartel policy thus far allowed for moderate forms of horizontal cooperation between competitors. A ban on such cooperation may force them to replace *horizontal cooperation* by *vertical cooperation*, i.e. cartels by firm hierarchies. This is exactly what happened in the American history (Van Waarden 1997, p. 18). According to the OECD (1994b, p. 53) the most efficient way to reduce the distortionary effects of imperfect product market competition on labour market outcome is to remove the opportunity for producers to earn rents. This will require tough enforcement of general competition legislation; pervasive statutory entry barriers and public subsidies to producers will have to be critically reviewed. But the most effective anti-trust policy is to maintain and to encourage a multilateral trading system, and to expose domestic producers to the rigors of international competition.

Indeed, related to product markets it is of importance to distinguish the sheltered or domestic sector from the open sector. The competition in the sheltered branches of industry, notably services, and public utilities is low or even absent. Less importance is attached to controlling *costs*. It results in higher prices and reduces employment and growth in the economy as a whole. In the internationally exposed sectors of the economy, strong competition is ensured by open markets and effectively enforced competition policy. Deregulation and competition policy are supposed to promote competition, resulting in a dynamic product market and more efficiency and prosperity.

There is evidence of harmful effects of limited competition in the product market. Various studies indicate a positive relationship between *flexibilisation and economic growth* (see Van Bergeijk and Haffner 1996; Koedijk and Kremers, 1996; Gradus, Chapter 7 in this volume for an overview). These analysis by means of general equilibrium models or the construction of indices for market regulation have in common that they start from a model in which more price flexibility is assumed to be better and full competition is the norm. Hence price rigidities have no benefits, only costs (see Garretsen 1997).

The impact of competition on *productivity* is likely to be more indirect. By allowing inefficiencies to persist, weak competition may affect productivity growth. A lack of competition may also put insufficient pressure on management to improve productivity performance and incorporate new technology. Pilat (1996) found support for the view that exposure to international competition promotes productivity growth: competition on the international market can contribute to cost minimalisation, but exports may also allow specialisation and economies to scale. Also a *dynamic product market*, as measured by entry rates, provides a positive contribution to productivity growth. High entry and exit rates ensure that only the best (and most productive) firms survive (see Nickell 1996). These analyses mainly focus on costs. Deregulation of the sheltered sector and more competition in this sector, may be at the expense of the quality of services. When endogenous growth factors are taken into account, competition reduces prosperity in the long run. The cheaper and expanding sheltered sector will result in a reallocation of production factors in the economy and a *crowding out* of the open, more innovative sector. At the macro level this implies less investments in Research and Development and other innovative activities, resulting in a drop of productivity. So, it is perhaps not market and dynamics but market or dynamics (Van de Klundert and Smulders 1997). Finally, a dynamic product market may not always contribute to productivity growth as supposed by neoclassical economists. For instance, where market entry and exit is easy, because of little investment needed, there may be a permanent overcapacity in the market. The high turnover of firms and the low profit rates may imply that such firms lack the continuity needed for long-term investment and creative innovation. In that case, regulation may be needed to protect the product markets from too much competition (Cf. Van Waarden 1997, pp. 18-19).

1.5.5 Culture and Performance

From previous sections it is clear that countries with similar market institutions may perform differently, and countries with different institutions may perform similarly. To a large extent this may be related to differences in culture, for institutions for their effectiveness depend on cultural values in societies (Cf. Van Waarden 1997, p. 13). Until recently, economics has confined itself to a study of transactions – how people utilise money, not why they do this or what there motives might be and lost sight of the one component, almost unmeasurable, that makes all economic activities possible: human relations. Behind every economic transaction are people making choices, acting on their values, given one thing high priority, another one low. Each culture brings a unique set of values to bear upon the act of wealth creation. These values characterise both the organisation that practises them and the products and services the enterprise creates (see Hampden-Turner and Trompenaars 1994, pp. 5-6).

Although neglected for a long time, increasingly economists consider norms and values as an ingredient in explaining differences between countries in economic performance. Economic life cannot be divorced from cultural life. The degree to which people value work over leisure, their respect for education, attitudes towards family, and the degree of trust they show towards their fellows all have a direct impact on economic life and yet cannot be adequately explained in terms of economists' basic model of man. Societies can save substantially on *transaction costs* because economic agents trust one another in their interaction and therefore can be more efficient than low-trust societies, which require detailed contracts and enforcement mechanisms. This trust is not the consequence of rational calculation; it arises from sources like religion or ethic habit (Fukuyama 1996, pp. 351-352). Trust may not be truly exogenous; it may increase with good past performance of a society's institutions (see La Porta et al. 1997). Based on World Values Survey data, Nyfer (1996) concludes that there are differences in the character of trust between Anglo-Saxon countries and continental Europe. In the European capitalism trust is based on *personal relations* build up over the years. In the more liberal market economies of the Anglo-Saxon countries the market parties base their trust on *objective criteria* like annual reports. There is a significant positive relationship between trust and average annual real growth of GDP per capita (Nyfer 1996).

Whether people trust their government and institutions like an independent central bank or a strong currency largely depends on social-cultural factors. Persons who disregard these European cultural differences may draw the wrong conclusions related to the potential of economic and political integration (Fukuyama 1996, p. 355). He considers social capital critical to prosperity and to competitiveness. *Social capital* is the ability of people to work together for common purposes in groups and organisations. In addition to skills and knowledge, a distinct portion of human capital has to do with people's ability to associate with each other, that is critical not only to economic life but to virtually every other aspect of social existence as well (Coleman 1988). The ability to associate depends, in turn, on the degree to which communities share norms and values and are able to subordinate individual interests to those of larger groups. Out of such shared values comes trust, and trust, has a large and measurable economic value (Fukuyama 1996, p. 10). Trust or social capital determines the performance of a society's institutions. The effects of trust on economic performance are statistically significant and quantitatively large. Based on the same World Value Survey data La Porta et al. 1997 show that trusts improves government efficiency, social efficiency, including infrastructure quality and adequacy, infant mortality, and educational achievement. Trust is also associated with lower inflation and weakly with a higher per capita GNP growth. The internationalisation of economies implies that social capital and trust are becoming as important as physical capital to compete.

Institutions have both positive and negative effects on economic performance. The theoretical and empirical understanding of the roles played by institutions, norms and culture in the functioning of markets still is limited. It is the editors hope that this book contributes to a better understanding of the role played by institutions in economic life and to more balanced and better founded policy decisions related to the (re)structuring of our economies in response to the structural changes they are confronted with.

1.6 Contents and Structure of the Book

The book is divided into four parts. In the present chapter, Part One, an overview is given of the issues at stake when discussing the pretended controversy between state coordination and coordination by the market and a number of relevant issues in relation to comparing national economies, and it is shown why it is of interest to compare the German and Dutch economies in particular.

Part Two 'Institutional differences in the welfare states' consists of four chapters which focus on the differences in wage bargaining, labour market policies and labour market performance between the Netherlands and Germany and on the impact of the German and Dutch welfare states on economic performance. The UK and the USA are used as benchmark countries. Chapter 2 by David Soskice, Bob Hancké, Gunnar Trumbull and Anne Wren focuses on the German and Dutch wage bargain systems in relation to macroeconomic performance. They review the role of the different institutions of the German political economy and the problems in the German political economy and discuss the various solutions to these problems. The authors argue that a deregulation of the labour market according to the Anglo-Saxon example is not a viable long-term option for Germany. Next, the applicability Dutch model is discussed. They argue that despite the fact that Germany and the Netherlands show a number of relevant institutional similarities, the import of the Dutch political-economic model would destroy institutions that have long been the foundations of Germany's competitive advantages in the world market. Three additional solutions are discussed to increase corporate profitability without deregulating the German labour markets. These options include: a more expansionary macroeconomic policy, admitting wage dispersion and moderation of wages.

Chapter 3 by Günther Schmid and Maja Helmer deals with the Dutch employment miracle. In the 1980s, the Netherlands had one of the highest unemployment rates in the European Community; Germany one of the lowest. Today, the reverse is true. Is there a Dutch employment miracle? If so, how can it be explained? This chapter tries to answer these questions in seven steps. Beginning with the development of an analytical framework within which to compare employment systems, the authors measure the performance of the two labour markets and economies, paying particular attention to the role of labour market policy in the process of adapting to structural change. It is shown that the Netherlands have an interesting, new configuration in which the advantages of competitive and coordinated capitalism are combined with a modernised form of the welfare state. A key shortcoming of both employment systems remains the hitherto highly passive character of employment redistribution. Transitional labour in markets would be a more appropriate strategy of redistributing employment in order to link long-term social needs and economic efficiency. On the whole, however, developments in the Netherlands point much more clearly than those in Germany to a path along which the European model could move.

In Chapter 4 Arthur van de Meerendonk analyses and compares the German and Dutch welfare states. A central issue in the chapter is the impact of the welfare state on economic performance, i.e. are there differences in economic performance between welfare states and liberal market economies? Two questions are addressed: to what extent are economic performances determined by welfare state institutions and are there differences in German and Dutch institutions that explain the current diverging economic performances of both economies? To examine these questions, Germany and the Netherlands are compared with the United States, the United Kingdom and Sweden. The current crisis in Germany in the aftermath of the unification reflects both internal and external causes. It is concluded that the internationalisation since the 1980s is not sufficient to explain the erosion of the German corporatist framework. Also the capacity of the government to act is crucial. The Dutch experience shows that corporatism can be altered, and that welfare state institutions can be reformed so as to contribute to the adjustment potential of the economy.

Part Three 'Financial and competition policies' includes three chapters which deal with the markets for goods and services and the financial markets in Germany and the Netherlands. The differences and similarities in the financial structure, monetary policy and competition policy are addressed. In Chapter 5 Lex Hoogduin and Henk Huisman discuss the differences and similarities of the financial structure in Germany and the Netherlands. The German financial system is a typical example of the continental 'bank-based' system, which is characterised by: risk-avoiding, co-operation, and long-term relationships between those who demand and those who supply capital. Although basically, the Dutch financial system is also 'bank-based', it contains more than the German system elements of the Anglo-Saxon 'market-based' financial system. The latter is characterised by risk taking, competition and short-term relations between the provider and user of capital. In the Netherlands there has always been a fairly open and relatively large stock market. Another difference is that in Germany the house-bank relationship between banks and firms are close and there is a widespread bank representation on the supervisory boards of firms. The third and final difference mentioned by the authors is the different way in which savings find there way to the capital market: the Dutch save through pension funds and insurance companies, whereas the Germans save through banks. Despite these differences between the two countries, the similarities seem to be more important. Moreover both systems move towards a more Anglo-Saxon system. A major difference between the latter and the system in Germany and the Netherlands is that in the Anglo-Saxon countries changes in official interest rates have a comparatively greater impact on economic activity than in most continental European countries.

This brings us to monetary policy, the topic of Chapter 6 by Reimut Jochimsen. Since 1983 the guilder-Deutschmark rate is very stable. It is the only rate within the European Monetary System (EMS) which still has a narrow exchange rate band of 2.25%. The nominal interest rates in the two countries have converged. These developments reflect that the monetary authorities of the two countries aim at the same goal: a stable and low inflation rate. During the greater part of the last decades monetary policy is supported by healthy public finance and a wage policy which takes due account of the stability requirement. In the 1970s and the beginning of the 1980s, in the Netherlands both public finance and the wage policy were out of control. Since 1982 the scene changed significantly; Dutch wage increases are very modest and public deficit and debt are declining. Nowadays the German public finance is burdened by the costs of the unification and German wages are far higher than those in neighbouring countries. Moreover the Dutch have reformed the pension system and have taken deregulation measures. In Jochimsen's view in this respect the Germans can learn lessons from the Dutch. The tight relations between Germany and the Netherlands and the shared goal for stability can be regarded as a good example of the way the Economic and Monetary Union (EMU) might work. The great importance of Europe for both countries make that they once again are in the same boat: in the EMU the standard of stability should be guaranteed.

In Chapter 7, Raymond Gradus compares the Dutch and German competition policy. He states that Germany acts as the leader and the Netherlands as a follower with respect to all three fields of competition policy: competition law, privatisation and deregulation. Based on the prohibition principle, since 1958 the aim of the German competition policy is to safeguard competition. Since World War II Dutch competition policy on the other hand has been based on the abuse system. The onus of proof lies with the Minister of Economic Affairs and therefore, implementing competition policy is more difficult. However, the situation in the Netherlands has changed very dramatically in recent years. Recently the Dutch parliament has accepted a new law on competition policy, which is based on the prohibition system. The procedure in the new act has many similarities with the German practice. In fact, Dutch deregulation and privatisation policy has been based on current efforts in Germany. An interesting observation in this respect is that the Netherlands seems to put more effort into continuing its policy of deregulation than Germany. The chapter also discusses the macroeconomic consequences of this policy.

Part Four 'Concluding Remarks' contains one chapter, Chapter 8, in which the editors collect from the previous chapters the arguments for answering the questions listed in Section 1.1. The following issues are dealt with. The pros and cons of the Anglo-Saxon and Rhineland model. The question whether the Netherlands is an example for the German economy. Finally the results of this book are used for answering the question whether the institutional arrangements in the European economies will converge toward one model and if so whether this model will contain more Anglo-Saxon elements than the present European economies.

References

Aarle, B. van, (1996), The impact of the single market programme on trade and foreign direct investment in the European Union, *Journal of World Trade*, 30, (6), pp. 121-138.

Albert, M. (1991), *Capitalism contre Capitalism*, Édition du Seuil, Paris (in French).

Bergeijk, P.A.G. van and R.C.G. Haffner (1996), *Deregulation, Privatization and the Macro Economy*, Edward Elgar, Cheltenham.

Besseling, P.J. and R.F. Zeeuw (1993), The financing of pensions in Europe: challenges and opportunities, *Research Memorandum No. 111*, CPB Netherlands Bureau for Economic Policy Analysis, The Hague.

Broeder, C. den (1996), Institutions at work. Commitment and flexibility on the German and Dutch labour markets, *Research Memorandum No. 131*, CPB Netherlands Bureau for Economic Policy Analysis, The Hague.

Cahuc, P. and P. Michel (1996), Minimum wage unemployment and growth, *European Economic Review*, 40 (7), pp. 1463-1482.

Coleman, J. (1988), Social capital in the creation of human capital, *American Journal of Sociology*, 94, pp. 95-120.

Cooper, R. and A. John (1988), Coordinating failures in Keynesian models, *Quarterly Journal of Economics*, 103, pp. 441-463.

CPB (1995), *Centraal Economisch Plan 1995*, Centraal Plan Bureau, Sdu Uitgeverij, Den Haag (in Dutch).

Delsen, L. (1995), *Atypical Employment: An International Perspective. Causes, Consequences and Policy*, Wolters-Noordhoff, Groningen.

Delsen L. (1997), Flexibilisering van de arbeid in Europa, *Tijdschrift voor Arbeidsvraagstukken*, 13 (1), pp. 23-36 (in Dutch).

Delsen, L. and G. Reday-Mulvey (eds.) (1996), *Gradual Retirement in the OECD Countries. Macro and Micro Issues and Policies*, Dartmouth Publishing Company, Aldershot.

Delsen, L. and E. de Jong (1997), Het wankele mirakel, *Economisch Statistische Berichten*, 23 april, pp. 324-327 (in Dutch).

Dolado, J., F. Kramarz, S. Machin, M. Manning, D. Margolis and C. Teulings (1996), The economic impact of minimum wages in Europe, *Economic Policy*, October.

EIRR (1994) Germany: Labour costs and international competitiveness, *European Industrial Relations Review*, February, pp. 13-17.

Englander, A.S. and A. Gurney (1994), Medium-term determinants of OECD productivity, *OECD Economic Studies*, No. 22, Organisation for Economic Co-operation and Development.

European Economy, no. 3, 1996, Ageing and pension expenditure prospects in the Western world, Directorate-General for Economic an Financial Affairs, European Commission, Brussels.

Fukuyama, F. (1996), *Trust. The Social Virtues and the Creation of Prosperity*, Simon & Schuster, New York.

Garretsen, H. (1997), *Terug naar 1937?*, Oratie, University of Nijmegen, Nijmegen (in Dutch).

Gelauff, G.M.M. and C. den Broeder (1996), Governance of stakeholder relationships: The German and Dutch experience, *Research Memorandum No. 127*, CPB Netherlands Bureau for Economic Policy Analysis, The Hague.

Glyn, A. and D. Miliband (eds.) (1994), *Paying for Inequality. The Economic Cost of Social Injustice*, Rivers Oram Press, London.

Hampden-Turner, C. and F. Trompenaars (1994), *The Seven Cultures of Capitalism*, Piatkus, London.

Holm, H.-H. and G. Soerensen (1995), *Whose World Order?: Uneven Globalization and the End of the Cold War*, Westview Press. Boulder CO.

Kleinknecht, A. and J. ter Wengel (1996), Feiten over globalisering, *Economisch Statistische Berichten*, 9 October, pp. 831-833 (in Dutch).

Klundert, Th. van de and S. Smulders (1997), Marktwerking of dynamiek, *Economisch Statistische Berichten*, 14 May, pp. 384-387 (in Dutch).

Koedijk, K. and J. Kremers (1996), Market opening, regulation and growth in Europe, *Economic Policy*, October, pp. 445-467.

Krugman, P. (1991), *Pop Internationalism*, The MITT Press, Cambridge (Mass).

Kuipers, S.K. (1996), Coördinatie, concurrentie en doelmatigheid, in: Nentjes, A. (ed.) (1996) *Marktwerking versus coördinatie*, Preadviezen van de Koninklijke Vereninging voor de Staathuishoudkunde 1996, Uitgeverij Lemma BV, Utrecht, pp. 37-51 (in Dutch).

La Porta, R., F. Lopez-de-Silanes, A. Shleifer and R.W. Vishny (1997), Trust in large organizations, *The American Economic Review*, Vol. 87, No. 2, Papers and Proceedings, May, pp. 333-338.

Lecq, F. van der (1996), Conventions and institutions in coordination problems, *De Economist*, Vol 144, No 3, pp. 397-428.

Leibfritz, W., D. Roseveare and P. van den Noord (1994), Fiscal policy, government debt and economic performance, *Economics Department Working Papers no. 144*, Organisation for Economic Co-operation and Development, Paris.

Maddison, A. (1995), *Monitoring the World Economy 1820-1992*, Organisation for Economic Co-operation and Development, Paris.

Mayer, C. (1996), Corporate governance, competition and performance, *OECD Economic Studies*, No. 27, pp. 7-34.

Ministry of Economic Affairs (1995), *Benchmarking the Netherlands. Test of Dutch Competitiveness*, The Hague.

Neubourg, C. de (1995), Switching to the policy mode: incentives by the OECD jobs study to change our mind set, *De Economist*, No. 4, pp. 521-535.

Nickell, S.J. (1996), Competition and corporate performance, *Journal of Political Economy*, pp. 724-746.

Noord, P.J. van den (1996), Globalisation and the European disease, *De Economist*, 144, pp. 195-222.

Nyfer (1996), *Kwartaal Bericht 1996-3*, Nyfer Forum for Economic Research, Sdu Uitgevers, The Hague (in Dutch).

OECD (1994a), *The OECD Jobs Study. Facts, Analysis, Strategies*, Organisation for Economic Co-operation and Development, Paris.

OECD (1994b), *The OECD Jobs Study. Evidence and Explanations. Part I Labour Market Trends and Underlying Forces of Change*, Organisation for Economic Co-operation and Development, Paris.

OECD (1996a), *OECD Economic Surveys. Germany*, Organisation for Economic Cooperation and Development, Paris.

OECD (1996b), *OECD Economic Surveys. Netherlands*, Organisation for Economic Cooperation and Development, Paris.

OECD (1997), *Employment Outlook*, Organisation for Economic Cooperation and Development, Paris.

Paqué, K.H. (1993), Germany: Living with tight corporatism, in: J. Hartog and J. Theeuwes (eds.), *Labour Market Contracts and Institutions. A Cross-national Comparison*, North-Holland, Amsterdam, pp. 9-29.

Pilat, D. (1996), Competition, productivity and efficiency, *OECD Economic Studies*, No. 27, pp. 107-146).

Rodrik, D. (1996), Why do more open economies have bigger governments? *NBER Working Paper No. 5537*, National Bureau of Economic Research, Cambridge (Mass).

Rodrik, D. (1997), The 'paradoxes' of the successful state, *European Economic Review*, 41, pp. 411-442.

Schotter, A. (1981), *The Economic Theory of Social Institutions*, Cambridge University Press, New York.

Stiglitz, J.E. (1992), The design of financial systems for the newly emerging democracies in Eastern Europe, in: C. Clague and G. Rausser (eds.) *The Emergence of Market Economies in Eastern Europe*, Basil Blackwell, Oxford, pp. 161-184.

Streeck, W. (1995), German capitalism: Does it exist? Can it survive?, *Discussion Paper 95/5*, Max Planck Institut für Gesellschaftsforschung, Köln.

The Economist (1997), The politics of unemployment, 5 April, pp. 19-20 and 25.

UN (1990), *Human Development Report 1990*, United Nations, Oxford University Press, Oxford.

Vernon, R. (1996), Passing through regionalism: The transition to global markets, *The World Economy*, 19 (6), November, pp. 621-633.

Visser, J. (1996), Traditions and transitions in industrial relations: a European view, in: J. van Ruysseveldt and J. Visser (eds.), *Industrial Relations in Europe. Traditions and Transitions*, Sage, London, pp. 1-41.

Visser, J. and J. van Ruysseveldt (1996), Robust corporatism, still? Industrial relations in Germany, in: J. van Ruysseveldt and J. Visser (eds.), *Industrial Relations in Europe. Traditions and Transitions*, Sage, London, pp. 124-174.

Waarden, F. van (1997), *Institutions of Socio-Economic Coordination: A European Style?*, Ministry of Social Affairs and Employment, The Hague.

Williamson, O.E. (1975), *Markets and Hierarchies: Analysis and Antitrust Implications*, The Free Press, New York.

Williamson, O.E. (1985), *The Economic Institutions of Capitalism*, The Free Press, New York.

World Bank (1994), *Averting the Old Age Crisis. Policies to Protect the Old and Promote Growth*, Oxford University Press, Oxford.

Part II

Institutional Differences in the Welfare States

2 Wage Bargaining, Labour Markets and Macroeconomic Performance in Germany and the Netherlands

David Soskice, Bob Hancké, Gunnar Trumbull and Anne Wren
Wissenschaftszentrum Berlin für Sozialforschung, Germany

2.1 Introduction

Dutch economic performance in the 1990s has drawn envious attention from Germany: unemployment is low (6% in 1997 and falling), economic growth is strong, and its combination of low inflation and small budget deficit should allow it painlessly to meet Maastricht criteria for European Economic and Monetary Union. While similar economic results have also been achieved in the United States, the extent of deregulation implied by this approach has made it unpalatable to important actors in the Federal Republic of Germany including trade unions, Chancellor Helmut Kohl, and the management of many large firms. Hence, as Germany looks abroad for solutions to its own economic woes, the Dutch experience increasingly appears to offer a third way between business-as-usual and wholesale deregulation on the Anglo-Saxon model.

We argue, however, that the Dutch model is not readily applicable in the German case. Moreover, the costs of its transfer would be high indeed. First, Dutch employment growth has come primarily from the service sectors, whereas Germany's economic engine has long been its large, high-skilled manufacturing sectors. Second, the impressive profitability of Dutch firms appears to result in part from the weak position of unions in wage bargaining; Germany, by contrast, has relied on strong union negotiators as a key component in its high-wage, high-skill production strategy. Third, the move towards more flexible contracts that has generated work-force flexibility in the Netherlands would likely undermine the integrity of the Germany training system, another central component of German industrial strength. In sum, the benefits promised by the Dutch model could only be realised by destroying institutions that have been and are the foundation of Germany's competitive advantage in world markets.

The structure of this chapter is as follows. Sections 2.2 and 2.3 describe the institutional components of the German labour market and the stresses they have faced in the early 1990s. Section 2.4 describes the central role played by sectoral wage bargaining and works councils in solving management problems associated with Germany's strategy of high quality incremental innovation. Section 2.5 describes the Dutch reforms of the past ten years, and the way in which similar reforms applied in Germany would subvert its critical labour market institutions. The final Section 2.6 draws lessons from the Dutch experience to suggest a viable home-grown strategy for Germany.

2.2 The Structure of the German Wage Bargaining System

Two central associations represent employers in Germany: the *Bund Deutsche Arbeitgeber* (BDA) focuses on employment questions; the *Bundesverband der Deutschen Industrie* (BDI) handles business issues more generally. The central *Deutscher Gewerkschaftsbund* (DGB) represents all industrial unions. While these associations play an advisory role in wage setting, actual negotiations are undertaken at the *sectoral level* between industry employer associations and industry unions. The government is excluded from a direct role in the negotiations. Disagreements are resolved through labour courts. Wages in Germany are negotiated annually.

Although these sectoral wage agreements are not formally linked in Germany, by convention wage agreements adopted by the *engineering sector* (through a set of regional agreements) have been used as a pattern for wage agreements in other sectors.[1] Within engineering, wages are negotiated between IG Metall, the largest union in Germany, and Gesamtmetall, the largest association of employers within the BDA. While other sectors engage in similar wage negotiations, in normal years they look to the engineering sector's outcome ('*Tarifvertrag*') and conclude wage agreements at approximately the same level. The result has been a system of highly coordinated wage agreements that relies heavily on union and employer input.

Accounts in the German press on collective bargaining convey the impression that Marxist nineteenth-century class warfare lingers in Germany today. Employers accuse the unions of attacking the very foundations of German capitalism, while unions describe employers as monsters lacking any sense of social justice. On closer inspection, however, such histrionics often belie rather mundane disagreements – should wages this year increase by two percent, for example, or rather by three and a half? Given this gap between the rhetoric and the reality, one may be tempted to see the negotiation process as a performance of ritual dances enacted upon a stage of profound consensus. Neither of these views is completely accurate.

A more faithful interpretation of German wage negotiation lies between these two extremes. Unions and employer associations have extensive professional contact, know each other very well, and fully understand the ramifications of their wage settlements for both sides. The problem is that both unions and

[1] For good English-language introductions in the (West) German system of labour relations, see Berghahn and Karsten 1987 and Streeck 1984.

employer associations are *constrained by their members*. Unions, for their part, must be responsive to the demands of powerful works councils in large companies in their sector. They must take care to protect less skilled workers, whom the works councils, who typically represent more skilled workers, might be likely to ignore. Employer associations, too, feel pressure from their own members to show that they are countering union demands. This need to please their respective constituencies drives both unions and employer associations to undertake difficult technical negotiations behind a curtain of public vituperation.

There is a third, largely 'invisible' player in the German wage negotiation process: the central bank, the Deutsche Bundesbank. All parties to the wage negotiation process are aware that over-inflationary wage settlements will trigger *retaliatory interest rate increases* by the Bundesbank. German wage negotiations have been particularly sensitive to this threat because the leading sector, engineering, relies heavily on exports. As higher interest rates are mirrored by higher exchange rates, and hence higher prices on foreign markets, export sectors are particularly sensitive to Bundesbank retaliation.[2]

2.3 Recent Strains on the German Model

Three different factors combined in the early 1990s to upset the balance in this complex game played by German unions, employers organisations, and the Deutsche Bundesbank over wages. The resulting imbalance has caused a considerable drop in the performance of the German economy.[3]

First, the immediate *post-unification boom* in Germany generated high levels of employment growth and falling unemployment. Skilled workers in particular benefited from the boom. Whereas emerging industries in the newly integrated federal states sought out skilled workers for their factories, the majority of the work force remaining from the German Democratic Republic was competing for unskilled or semi-skilled positions. The result was a disproportionate demand for high-skilled labour that extended across Germany. Within firms, this new *demand for skilled workers* put a finger in the scale of power on the side of the works councils, which have always favoured the interests of skilled labour. Unions, facing greater pressure for higher wages from emboldened works councils, nonetheless continued to embrace the goal of wage compression across all skill levels.[4] The result was a greater pressure for wage increases, driven especially by the works councils in large companies.

---

[2] The seminal paper arguing this point is Hall 1994.

[3] This treatment of recent strains on the German political economy is taken from Carlin and Soskice 1997. The reader is referred to that article for a more detailed account of the issues discussed here.

[4] While the works councils do not play a formal role in wage negotiation, informally they hold a lot of control over the outcomes.

Second, the unification process created difficulties in the relationship between the Bundesbank and the Federal government. When the Kohl government decided 1990, in the face of strong Bundesbank opposition, to *link the Ost mark* with the Deutschmark at a one-to-one parity, the Bundesbank felt that its reputation as the keeper of the Deutschmark's value had been seriously undermined. To restore its credibility, the central bank clung doggedly to a *tight monetary policy* in the face both of inflationary wage pressure and of government deficit spending that it considered excessive.

Third, the move toward European integration aggravated the economic damage that resulted from this strict monetary regime. With the exchange rates of other European countries pegged to the Deutschmark under the European Monetary System (EMS), movements in interest rates in Germany tended to be mirrored elsewhere in order to maintain exchange rate parity. A monetarily induced deflation in the Federal Republic of Germany was therefore generalised across Europe with *interest rates rising* and *exchange rates appreciating* relative to the US dollar.[5] Furthermore, European governments were constrained in their ability to compensate fiscally because of requirements imposed by the Maastricht criteria for European Economic and Monetary Union (EMU). National budget deficits in 1997 were not to exceed 3%, and total accumulated debt was not to exceed 60% of Gross Domestic Product (GDP). The effects on the German economy of the Bundesbank retaliation were thus much more severe than past experience would have suggested. The exporting sector in particular was damaged, not just by the appreciation of its exchange rate vis-à-vis the US dollar, but also by a generalised decline in demand in the European economies which constitute its main export market. Under these circumstances the traditional German strategy of recovering from deflation via export-led expansion became increasingly difficult.

In the face of these conflicting pressures the institutions of the German political economy have failed in their traditional role of facilitating the economic compromises necessary to maintain profitability, cost competitiveness, and employment growth. Even though the costs associated with Bundesbank retaliation have been high, wage demands have remained high as well (see Figure 2.1). The Bundesbank has responded in an unrelenting fashion by raising interest rates and reducing them only gradually in the face of a sharp recession in 1995. The outcome has been a deterioration in company profitability and employment performance.

---

[5] Though in 1992, these pressures led Italy and the United Kingdom to depreciate against the Deutschmark and hence opt out of the European Exchange Rate Mechanism (ERM).

Figure 2.1 Unemployment rate and wage inflation in Germany, 1974-1994

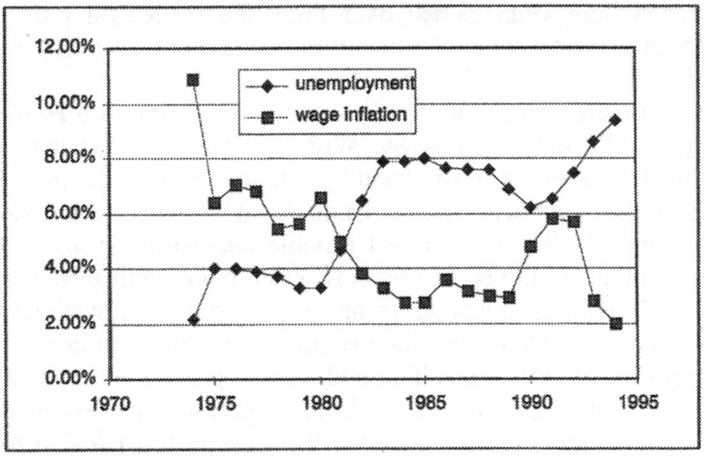

Source: OECD.

2.4 Is the Grass Greener? Deregulation in Perspective

This crisis in economic performance has led to much discussion of institutional reform in Germany. Among others Olaf Henkel, the head of the BDI, has called for dramatic labour market deregulation and large cuts in the welfare state. But, despite often vicious rhetorical rounds in the media accompanied by occasional deregulatory nudges from Chancellor Kohl, the German business community remains hesitant to implement wide-ranging *deregulation* that would push Germany toward the Anglo-Saxon model of labour relations. While this reticence in the business community undoubtedly reflects a genuine belief in the future of the social market economy, it also stems from the way German employers see their interests reflected in the current system. Employers are especially concerned about the deleterious effect that such deregulation would have on the German training system and on the co-operative work organisation of highly skilled employees, as these institutions have been critical to the competitiveness and innovative strength of German firms.

The competitiveness of the German engineering and chemical sectors is to a large extent grounded in a comparative institutional advantage in what has been called *high quality incremental innovation* (HQII).[6] HQII in Germany relies on two workforce characteristics. First, the strategy requires a workforce that combines extensive training in industry-specific skills with deep experience with company-specific product and process technologies. This kind of *specific knowledge* allows the work force to implement effective incremental changes in the

[6] For more details, see Carlin and Soskice 1997; Soskice 1997 and Matraves 1997.

face of changing technologies and shifting world markets. As company-specific experience can only been gained over time, the successful pursuit of HQII depends on an institutional environment that encourages enduring relationships between companies and employees.

The second requirement for successful implementation of a HQII strategy is a high degree of *worker autonomy*. With a highly experienced work force, decisions are best made at a low level by employees with the greatest specific knowledge of how changes should be undertaken. While such decentralised problem solving allows efficient and flexible adaptation, it also requires that companies combine a high degree of worker autonomy with sufficient coordination between decentralised worker groups to ensure that innovations in one area are matched with complementary innovations required in another.

These patterns of skill acquisition and work organisation create three potentially difficult managerial problems related to performance evaluation, worker management, and adequate skill provision. The first problem, that of *performance evaluation*, is that the strategy of decentralised problem solving that underpins HQII also makes it difficult for upper-level managers to evaluate how their employees are actually performing. Employees, recognising that they are not being closely monitored, face fewer obstacles to shirking.

The second problem posed by HQII is that managers, even when they do understand what workers are doing, may not easily be able to manage them. This phenomenon, which Oliver Williamson has dubbed '*collective hold-up*', occurs because workers with company-specific expertise have a strong bargaining position in their relationship with management. Not only do their company-specific skills make them difficult for the company to replace, but their deep technical knowledge also makes them extremely marketable in the industry as a whole. Furthermore, the emphasis in German companies on worker autonomy and strong coordination across decentralised groups allows for greater coordination among workers that intensifies the disadvantage of management in any negotiation process.

Finally, the high-level of industry and technology skills that underpins the HQII strategy would be a risky investment for any employer in a deregulated labour market. If German employers were free to offer individual discretionary wage contracts to workers, as in the United States and the United Kingdom, it would become more cost-effective for companies to *poach* skills by hiring employees from their competitors rather than to invest in training their own workers. This would be fine if individual workers could be expected to acquire necessary skills by themselves. But in an insecure labour market, individuals may be loath to take on the risk of investing in company-specific skills. The optimal level and mix of worker skills necessary to carry out a HQII manufacturing strategy therefore requires an institutional environment which diminishes the risks on both sides of the employment contract.

Manufacturers in Germany have been able to solve these three managerial problems thanks primarily to two institutions at the core of their industrial relations system: coordinated wage bargaining, and works councils. *Coordinated wage bargaining*, as described above, gives wage-negotiating power to actors at the sectoral level, namely unions and employer associations. On the one hand, this means that individual companies have no ability to poach workers from competitors simply because they are not able to offer substantially higher wages to lure away well-trained employees from competing firms. Without this threat of poaching, companies can confidently invest in broad skills for their employees without fear of losing their investment to competitors. Conversely, this also means that workers within a single company cannot hold management ransom because of their company-specific skills. Because wages are set at the sectoral level, firms can put a great deal of trust in their employees without falling prey to collective hold-up. In other words, by moving the wage-setting negotiation out of the individual firm, Germany's system of coordinated wage bargaining removes the risks of poaching and collective hold-up that would otherwise discourage firms from investing in deep skills.

The Works' Council Law of 1952 gave the *works councils* veto rights over management decisions on redundancies, work organisation, and training. This allows them to protect the employment of existing employees, securing their retraining when necessary. One consequence is that both companies and workers can confidently invest in firm-specific skills. Any individual company, aware that its competitors also have works councils that favour employee retraining, does not face a significant risk of poaching. Individual employees, in turn, recognising that works councils will work to retain their job, are therefore willing to make an investment in company-specific skills. Furthermore, works council participation in company decision making gives managers some confidence in the performance of their employees. This allows them to overcome the monitoring problems that otherwise would make Germany's HQII strategy untenable.

Were Germany to deregulate its labour market according to the Anglo-Saxon example, coordinated wage bargaining and works councils would be the most likely institutions to be eliminated. Yet they are absolutely central to the *training system*, which is, in turn, a crucial component of German industry's strategy of high quality incremental innovation. Hence, although a *deregulated labour market* might lower wage push in Germany, it could also be expected to decrease the level of company specific knowledge in the labour force while forcing management to adopt more hierarchical and less trusting relations with its employees. This in turn would upset the product market strategies of German companies that rely on cooperative relationships with their employees. In short, any advantages gained through lower wages would be overshadowed by a drop in Germany's long-term export success.

2.5 The Dutch Alternative

Having ruled out deregulation as a viable long-term option for Germany, politicians, journalists, and social scientists have recently begun looking for ideas closer to home. On first inspection, the Netherlands has been seen as an attractive third way. The Dutch political economy is institutionally similar to the German one in several key respects. As a member of the EMS and a close neighbour and trading partner of Germany, the Netherlands maintains a monetary policy that is linked to that of the Bundesbank (see Jochimsen, Chapter 6 in this volume). Important parallels also exist between the Dutch and German systems of industrial relations. Dutch wage negotiations, as in Germany, take place at a sectoral level within a framework of national accords. Dutch works councils have a structure and function that is similar to the German '*Betriebsräte*', including negotiations over decisions of hiring, firing, and work organisation (although they exert less influence in the wage negotiation process) (see Visser 1996). In addition, as in Germany, Dutch employers are strongly organised (see also Van de Meerendonk, Chapter 4 in this volume).

The Dutch economy has performed considerably better than that of Germany over the last ten years. Starting from a comparable base in the 1970s, Dutch rates of manufacturing profitability have increased significantly while German rates have stagnated and declined. Meanwhile, the Dutch have experienced a serious reduction in unemployment while German unemployment has risen slowly until 1989 and finally skyrocketed after 1991. Thus, despite their *similar institutions*, economic performance by the 1990s was very different in the two countries. This *divergence in performance* is what has attracted the attention of many observers in Germany, whose hopes are that the Dutch model might be transferred to Germany, saving them from an all-out deregulation in the Anglo-Saxon image.[7]

However, the prima facie similarities hide an important set of differences that are extremely significant in considering the applicability of the Dutch strategy to Germany. The first of these has to do with *economic structure*. The Dutch manufacturing sector is very small in comparison with that of Germany: in 1993, it accounted for 18% of GDP and 24% of employment. In Germany the figures were 25% and 39%, and in some of the German Länder the role of manufacturing is even considerably higher: North Rhine-Westphalia, for example, employs, with roughly the same total population as the Netherlands, over three times more people in industry.

This difference is important because *employment growth* in the Netherlands has been primarily a service sector phenomenon. Between 1988 and 1994, the average growth rate of employment was slightly negative in industry (-0.03%) and 2.58% in the services. Furthermore, much of it resulted directly from the redistribution of work through the generalised introduction of part-time work (see also Schmid and Helmer, Chapter 3 in this volume). Between 1985 and 1990, 75% of new service sector jobs were part-time. In 1997, fully one third of Dutch employees worked part-time. Thus the Dutch employment miracle appears to

---

[7] See, among others, Schmid and Helmer, Chapter 3 in this volume and *Wirtschaftswoche*, 20 February 1997. Remarkably, *Manager Magazin* (May 1997) ran a very intelligent piece warning for this love of foreign models: they do not work nearly as well as all think, it said, and they can most probably not be transferred anyway.

have far more to teach us about strategies for creating service sector employment, than methods of addressing the current crisis in the German industrial sector.

Table 2.1 Comparison of German and Dutch economic performance for selected variables, 1974-1993

	Manufacturing gross profit shares (%)		Employment growth (%)		Unemployment (%)		Wage inflation (%)	
	Germany	Netherlands	Germany	Netherlands	Germany	Netherlands	Germany	Netherlands
1974-78	25.6	23.2	-0.92	0.6	3.5	4.2	7.5[1]	10.0[1]
1979-83	21.6	21.8	0.51	-0.8	5.1	9.4	5.3	5.3
1984-88	24.2	30.9	0.76	1.6	7.7	12.7	3.4	1.4
1989-93	22.0	33.9	6.4[2]	2.1	7.1	7.0	5.3	3.2
1994	17.5[3]	33.6	-1.1	0.6	9.4	8.1[3]	3.7	1.7

[1] Figures cover the period 1970-1978.
[2] This employment growth is a direct result of German unification.
[3] 1993.
Source: OECD and Glyn 1995.

However, in spite of its much smaller significance to the economy as a whole, the Dutch manufacturing sector has also out-performed its more dominant German counterpart in terms of manufacturing *profitability*. While profitability is very low in Germany, and has been so since the mid-1980s, profitability in the Netherlands is among the highest in the OECD. In large measure, this follows directly from a policy of wage restraint that labour unions have accepted since the early 1980s. Table 2.1 above shows that wage inflation in the Netherlands has been less than half of that in Germany in the early 1990s. Again this outcome has attracted attention in Germany where the goal of wage restraint has become increasingly critical and elusive.

Some observers attribute the high level of wage restraint to the Dutch culture and tradition of consensual decision-making between unions, employers and the government. Whereas "*Tarifautonomie*" is the guiding principle of labour negotiations in Germany, the Dutch government plays an active role in setting the national level framework accords for wage negotiations. This tradition of *tripartite negotiation* over wages and working conditions has enabled the Netherlands to achieve wage restraint at times when German unions and employers have failed (see Visser 1996; Van de Meerendonk, Chapter 4 in this volume). Others maintain, however, that the Dutch outcomes really represent government enforcement of wage restraint upon weak unions. Unions are extremely poorly implanted at the local level in the Netherlands, and they are therefore unable to impose costs on employers who want to reorganise companies in order to restructure internal labour markets. Moreover, the Netherlands rank (with France) among the countries with the lowest rates of unionisation. In 1988, unionisation of the workforce in the Netherlands was below 20%, compared to about 35% in Germany (see OECD 1991). Unionisation rate may not be the only relevant variable in measuring union power, but it is critical in at least one respect: low union participation implies among other things that workplace representation through works councils often revolves around issues that are relatively distant from traditional union concerns.[8] In any case, it seems unlikely that powerful German unions with high coverage and local strength would accept to tolerate a strong government presence in collective bargaining.

The relative weakness of the Dutch unions has also been an important factor in allowing the *flexibilisation of individual labour* contracts which has occurred in the Netherlands over the last decade. While rejecting the wide-scale deregulation of wages and working conditions imposed in the United Kingdom, the Dutch 'work-sharing' strategy has involved the introduction of a wide range of new working time arrangements and flexible contracts — which remove many of the restrictions on hiring and firing.[9]

We have already outlined the potentially damaging effects of labour market deregulation on the HQII production strategy so critical to German industry. Dutch industry, by contrast, does not rely on the innovative capacity of workers for incremental product innovation. Most innovations are driven by high-level technicians and engineers. Flexible labour contracts for lower-skilled workers therefore do not undermine *industry innovation* in the Netherlands because their knowledge is not integral to the innovation process. In Germany, however, the workers' skills and engineers' knowledge are tightly integrated in the innovation process. In this context, flexible contracts risk to sever the long-term ties between worker and company that are so crucial to the innovation process. In sum, importing the deregulatory elements of the Dutch political-economic model to Germany would impose the same threats to the German HQII strategy as the Anglo-Saxon model.

The final dissimilarity between the Dutch and German economies which calls the applicability of the Dutch model to Germany into question relates to their relative positions in the European economy. As a small country, the Netherlands has been able to follow a strategy based on *labour costs*. Under the fixed exchange rate system that we know in Europe since the late 1970s – known consecutively as the Exchange Rate Mechanism (ERM) and the EMS – a small country can obtain beneficial economic results by cutting real wages. Because of the high level of exports as a proportion of GDP – for most small European countries ranging between 25 and 35% – lower real wage costs are, in a fixed exchange rate regime, the equivalent of a competitive devaluation, since they lower export prices of goods and services. Growth, and employment expansion as a result of that, follows simply from the export strategy.

---

[8] This position is argued in Hancké and Slomp 1997 forthcoming.

[9] See Wijgaerts 1985 for a contemporary discussion of these new labour contract models.

The Netherlands export far more than most other small countries — around 50% of its GDP, most of which goes to Germany; the Dutch guilder has followed the Deutschmark closely since 1980; and after the serious crisis of 1982 in the Netherlands and the 'Wassenaar Agreement' of that year, real wage costs have dropped by 1.2% on average a year.[10] As a result, exports boomed, and the economy grew on that expansionary wave. By lowering real wages, the Dutch managed to do exactly what the British and the Italians did during the currency crisis of September 1992, and for which they were rewarded with higher growth: a competitive devaluation.

Imagining what would happen if Germany did the same, reveals the problem. At first sight, if wages in the German export sector fell by a substantial proportion, it too could reap the benefits of this as it is transmitted through the exchange rate system. But Germany is not a small country. It is the most powerful European economy and home of the currency that all other European currencies have to follow: diversions from German interest rates is swiftly *punished by financial markets*. This central role of the German economy and its currency is precisely what makes a 'Dutch' macroeconomic strategy – pursuing the equivalent of a competitive devaluation through lower real wages – impossible. As soon as the German collective bargaining partners would negotiate such a settlement, all trading partners would rapidly follow, which would neutralise the effect – or worse, a downward wage spiral might ensue when all adopt the same competitive wage behaviour. In other words, macroeconomic options that are open to a small country like the Netherlands, are, in the current European set-up, simply not available for a large country like Germany.

2.6 Options for Germany

Germany in the mid-1990s faces a dual problem of deflationary macroeconomic policy and an extremely low profitability rate of its exporting industry. The first is related to the hard currency policy of the Bundesbank, which stymies growth in Germany and its main trading partners. The second is in addition a result of the structure and strategies of the partners in the wage bargaining system.

The central position of Germany in the European economy precludes competitive devaluations: the Bundesbank is unwilling, at least for the time being, to 'soften' the Deutschmark against its European partners, while an equivalent strategy, which lowers real wages, would lead to a competitive downward spiral as the other countries in the Deutschmark-zone move rapidly to adjust their wage levels.

The Anglo-Saxon deregulatory road is, for all practical purposes, a dangerous one, since it would upset the system of careful microeconomic balances at the

[10] For this discussion and a presentation of most relevant data, see Visser 1996.

heart of German companies that are central to German export success. It severs the ties between the skilled workers (and probably the engineers as well) and the companies – in short the German high-quality incremental innovation strategy. The Dutch option appears more favourable, but creates some similar microeconomic tensions; and the basic dissimilarities between the two political economies – economic significance of the service sector, union power, industrial production strategies and position in the European economic order – call into question the applicability of the Dutch model in the German case.

Within these constraints, three scenarios seem possible for Germany to find its way out of the current crisis. The first is a straightforward revision of monetary policy to create the basis for macroeconomic expansion. Since the Bundesbank's restrictive macroeconomic policy hampers economic growth in Germany and abroad, a more *expansionary policy* would have the immediate effect of pulling Germany and Europe out of the deflationary cycle it is stuck in today and thus generate employment. However, recent events in Germany demonstrate, to put it mildly, that this is a very unlikely scenario. In preparation of EMU the Bundesbank has, if anything, persisted in reaffirming its commitment to the hard Deutschmark and demonstrating its independence vis-à-vis the political decision-makers. Furthermore, the discussions between the potential Euro-members over the situation after its introduction in 1999 are directed toward harder rather than softer currencies.

This profoundly changes the character of the options available to Germany. If a Europe-wide expansion is impossible, at least in the short run, two other options are available. The first is to lower the relative level of semi- and unskilled worker wages corresponding to their relative abundance in the labour market. This *wage dispersion* needs to be large enough to restore profitability in the manufacturing sector without hurting either aggregate consumption or the employment rates of semi- and unskilled workers. Accepting wage dispersion as a policy option may, however, be the first step down a slippery slope to deregulated labour markets. It might, for example, undercut the attractiveness to young people of investing in lower-level apprenticeships, thus increasing the pool of low-paid unskilled labour in the economy.

The final option thus appears to be the most viable. Its core is to bring unions and employers around the table in order to negotiate *wage restraint.* While a reduction in real wages may not be a viable export strategy because of the interdependence of the European economies, it could, alternatively be used to restore corporate profitability, which supports investment and thus employment growth.

This idea is close to the '*Bündnis für Arbeit*' proposed by IG Metall in November of 1995, in which the union offered wage restraint in exchange for a commitment by the employers association Gesamtmetall to increase employment. The problem with this proposal, and most likely the main reason for its failure, is that export companies cannot credibly commit to increasing their employment levels. Government participation might help in principle, but it is unclear if this will work in the German setting, with its emphasis on the freedom of collective bargaining.

The restoration of profitability levels, which both in historical and in comparative perspective have been extremely low in the Germany of the 1990s, offers the intermediate step for the strategy to succeed. Careful analysis of the links between profitability, investment, economic growth and, as a result, employment growth, suggests that this redefined strategy may help the German political economy pull itself out of the deflation without jeopardising the careful microeconomic balances that have been at the basis of German export success in the past decades (see Glyn 1995).

References

Berghahn, V.R. and D. Karsten (1987), *Industrial Relations in West Germany*, Berg, Oxford.

Carlin, W. and D. Soskice (1997), Shocks to the system: the German political economy under stress, *National Institute Economic Review*, 159 (1), pp. 57-76.

Glyn, A. (1995), Does profitability really matter?, *Discussion Paper FS I 95-306*, Wissenschaftszentrum Berlin für Sozialforschung, Berlin.

Hall, P. (1994), Central bank independence and coordinated wage bargaining: Their interaction in Germany and Europe, *German Politics and Society*, (31).

Hancké, B. and H. Slomp (1997 forthcoming), A small difference with large consequences: local and national unions in postwar Belgium and the Netherlands, in: R. Locke and K. Thelen (eds.) *The Shifting Boundaries of Labor Politics: New Directions for Comparative Research Theory*, MIT Press, Cambridge (MA).

Matraves, C. (1997), German industrial structure in comparative perspective, *Industry and Innovation*, 4 (1), pp. 37-52.

OECD (1991), *Employment Outlook*, Organisation for Economic Cooperation and Development, Paris.

Soskice, D. (1997), German technology policy, innovation and national institutional frameworks, *Industry and Innovation*, 4 (1), pp. 75-96.

Streeck, W. (1984), Neo-corporatist industrial relations and the economic crisis in West Germany, in: J. H. Goldthorpe (ed.) *Order and Conflict in Contemporary Capitalism. Studies in the Political Economy of Western European Nations*, Oxford University Press, New York, pp. 291-314.

Visser, J. (1996), *Two Cheers for Corporatism, One for the Market. Industrial Relations, Unions, Wages and Labour Markets in the Netherlands*, Max Planck Institut für Gesellschaftsforschung, Köln, manuscript.

Wijgaerts, D. (1985), Flexibilisering en deregulering: naar een individualisering van de arbeidsverhoudingen? *Tijdschrift voor Arbeidsvraagstukken*, 1 (4), pp. 41-56 (in Dutch).

3 The Dutch Employment Miracle? A Comparison of Employment Systems in the Netherlands and Germany[1]

Günther Schmid in collaboration with Maja Helmer
Wissenschaftszentrum Berlin für Sozialforschung, Germany

3.1 Introduction

The Netherlands are attracting increasing admiration. There are many good reasons why this should be so. However, the one that concerns us here is the country's recent successes in the labour market. In the 1980s, the unemployment rate in the Netherlands was still one of the highest in the European Community, and the Federal Republic of Germany had one of the lowest. Today, the positions have been reversed. Why is this? Is there such a thing as a Dutch employment miracle? What contribution has labour market policy made to this state of affairs? Can we learn anything from the Netherlands or does the German model, once so highly praised, still retain a certain charm?

The following attempt to answer these questions is divided into seven stages. First in Section 3.1, the problems facing modern industrial societies are described and an analytical framework for comparing employment systems developed. The performance of the two labour markets (Section 3.2) and economies (Section 3.3) is then measured and the role of labour market policy in the process of adjusting to structural change investigated (Section 3.4). Comparative assessment of the two employment systems in Section 3.5 shows that an interesting new situation is emerging in the Netherlands, in which flexible, high-quality production is combined with labour market mobility and social welfare. A fundamental shortcoming of both employment systems, however, is the extremely passive nature of employment redistribution; transitional labour markets, in which long-term social considerations could be combined with economic efficiency, would be a more suitable strategy for redistributing employment (Section 3.6). In general

[1] We are grateful to Jacqueline O'Reilly for her detailed comments and suggestions on an earlier draft, and to Christoph Hilbert for his assistance in the calculations for Tables 3.2 and 3.3. Thanks are also due to Lei Delsen for providing material on the Netherlands, and to Andrew Wilson for translating the German version of this essay.

terms, however, developments in the Netherlands point more clearly than those in Germany to the direction in which the European model might move (Section 3.7).

3.2 Employment Systems in the Modernisation Process

Employment systems in advanced industrial societies are faced with a dual problem of adjustment: they have, on the one hand, to struggle against the increasingly chill wind of globalisation and, on the other hand, to cope with increased social differentiation and ever greater individualisation. What exactly does this mean?

The oil price shocks of the middle and late 1970s, and the recessions that followed, heralded dramatic changes in the world economy and in international politics.[2] While restrictions on capital flows and financial transactions have been gradually lifted, new technologies, information systems and organisational methods provide the means for the flexible, real-time management and coordination of activities, regardless of geographical boundaries. As a result, there has been an exponential increase in transnational trading, production and financial relationships. A network of some 39,000 multinational companies, with 270,000 foreign subsidiaries, has now spread throughout the entire global economy (UNCTAD 1996). Irrespective of the extent to which prophecies of transnational companies and virtual factories are already a reality and whether or not it is really possible to speak of a single world market, the powerful trend towards *globalisation* is a reality and determines the discourse throughout the world.[3]

Neither economic actors nor national governments can escape this integrative dynamic. Success in world markets requires new economic and political management skills in order to survive in the increasingly tough competitive environment

---

[2] For example, all controls on the movement of capital were gradually removed from the beginning of the 1970s onwards, in order to underpin the liquidity of the oil-importing economies and to finance government budgets. The deregulation of financial markets that began in the 1970s was intended to extend governments' scope for manoeuvre in adjusting financial policy to deal with the 'stagflation' crisis; in the long term, however, the massive increase in capital mobility began to undermine the economic autonomy of nation states. The opening up of capital markets is reflected in various indicators, including the growth in private transnational financial transactions, the ratio of national savings rates to the volume of domestic investment, the removal of restrictions on capital movements and also the growing interdependence of national interest rates (Garrett and Lange 1995). On the liberalisation of capital markets since the 1950s, see Helleiner 1989 and Strange 1986 (see also Hoogduin and Huisman, Chapter 5 in this volume).

[3] There is space here for only a few selected references to the literature on the globalisation debate: Albert 1992; Altvater and Mahnkopf 1996; Crouch and Streeck 1995; Dörre 1996; Dunning 1992; Esping-Andersen 1996; Giddens 1995; Ohmae 1996; Ruigrok and Van Tulder 1995; Thurow 1996.

of the global economy. The more mobile capital is and the smaller the differences in competitive factors become, through increasing similarities in infrastructure or the availability of skilled labour, for example, the more important the remaining differences between employment regimes become. Among other things, but not least of all, these include labour costs, both wage and non-wage. These costs must either tend towards convergence or acquire renewed justification through innovation and consequent differences in productivity. No economy can escape from price competition unless it has a 'vanguard' whose innovations can be disseminated to many other firms that are suppliers and customers of the pioneering elite.

However, consideration should also be given to another major trend, one that is usually ignored in the often very ideological debate on international competitiveness, namely increasing social differentiation, possibly even a renewed drive towards individualisation. The associated change in family and demographic structures creates new challenges for the employment systems in modern industrial societies that are at least as dramatic as the changes in the global economy. The historical phases of civilisation, rationalisation and differentiation[4] are now being followed by a new element of modernisation, namely individualisation: individuals are increasingly seeing themselves as the creators of their own, non-collective life plans. This phenomenon has always existed in individual cases. However, the early 1970s saw a significant shift in this direction. It has been possible since then to talk of a phase of *individualisation*, in which a critical mass of separate individual interests, not only of men, but also of women and children, is defined and put into practice not only in the face of the state and the church, of local communities and kin but even of individuals' families (see among others, Beck 1986; Huinink 1995; Van de Loo and Van Reijen 1992; Miegel and Wahl 1993; Mayer 1996).

The consequences can only be intimated with the aid of a few key terms: an endogenous trend towards increasing female participation in the labour market, rising divorce rates, increasing numbers of single parents and declining birth rates. The process of individualisation is further reinforced by demographic trends. Between the end of the working life and eventual death there is now an increasingly long period of independent living that can be organised according

---

[4] *Civilisation* denotes the process of exerting control over the exterior and, above all, the interior nature of human beings as part of the monopolisation of power by the state (Elias 1976 [1936]). *Rationalisation* denotes, on the one hand, the "demystification of the world": not the increasing general awareness of the conditions under which one lives but rather the knowledge or the belief "that, in theory at least, *one could control* all things if one only *wanted to*" (Weber 1992 [1917], p. 87; thus the rationalisation of society denotes a belief in the increasing intellectual mastery of living conditions *and* the concomitant trust in or reliance on the appropriate experts. On the other hand, rationalisation also denotes the pluralisation of value systems and the scientific search for the means to put them into practice (Weber 1992 [1917], p. 103). *Differentiation* denotes the defining of various spheres of action and their individual participation in several fields of action (Durkheim 1977).

to individual taste. Thus individualisation also denotes a society in which life expectancy is long and increasingly long periods of people's lives can be organised to suit individual wishes. The consequence is a shift in the age structure, which in turn has an effect on the conditions under which the labour market operates. Until now, for every 100 economically active individuals aged between 20 and 60, there were about 35 pensioners; soon there will be 70 or more (see among others, Baltes and Mantada 1996; Deutsche Gesellschaft der Vereinten Nationen 1994; Enquête-Kommission Demographischer Wandel 1994; Harrison 1994; Hof 1993; Klose 1996).

As far as the employment systems of modern industrial societies are concerned, the process of individualisation and longer life expectancy create two major problems. First, the notion of full employment can no longer be sustained: work for all[5], eight hours per day, five days per week, 46 to 48 weeks per year, 40 to 50 years per individual life, is both outdated and unachievable. Second, the growing number of pensioners, or more precisely the increasing number of older people not burdened by paid work, is becoming a drain on the social security system. The old-age pension system can no longer be financed primarily by those in work (through social security contributions and income tax); other sources of finance or subsistence must be institutionalised. Employment systems have to adjust to these major trends, and current mass employment can be interpreted as an expression of the inability to adapt to these trends. But what does the ability to adjust consist of? This question, a classic one in comparisons of different systems, will be addressed in what follows.

Employment systems are understood here as the set of institutions and policies affecting them that simultaneously determine the level of unemployment and of employment (for a more detailed exposition see Schmid 1997). These institutions act as filters, suggesting certain reactions to external shocks or challenges and more or less excluding other, theoretically possible ones.[6] In turn, employment systems are characterised by the interaction of two subsystems: the production system and the labour market system. It is in the *production system* that decisions on production are taken. These decisions depend on interest and exchange rates, technological innovations, actual demand and the cost of production factors. Changes in these parameters are determined by actors whose decisions are, in turn, made within a framework of institutionalised rules: by central banks, (Schumpeterian) entrepreneurs, private households, treasury officials, bodies representing various interests and executive authorities. From this point of view, unemployment can be seen as the result of unrealised or uncompetitive production.

Viewed from this angle, the long-term rising trend in unemployment can be readily explained. In the 1970s and 1980s, growth rates fell by half in virtually

---

[5] For ideological reasons, of course, restricted to (usually male) heads of households.

[6] On the significance of institutions see, among others, Garrett and Lange 1995; North 1991; Schmid et al. 1992; Schmid 1994.

all industrialised countries, with the exception of Japan. Industries with the highest productivity increase are no longer those in which employment is expanding, as was the case in the 1950s and 1960s. On the contrary: in many industries in which employment levels have hitherto been high, the price elasticity of demand is declining because saturation points have been reached. In consequence, investment to serve larger markets is not worthwhile and large numbers of jobs are lost. International price competition worsens the situation, and there is not yet any sign of a new long-term (Kondratief Cycle) economic cycle in which jobs will be created over a sustained period through the application of new information and communications technologies (see Appelbaum and Schettkat 1993; for a somewhat more optimistic view, see Freeman and Soete 1994).

Why, however, has Europe's position worsened dramatically in comparison with competitors who are subject to the same trend? Since there is virtually no difference in quantitative rates of growth between the United States of America (USA) and Europe, this is clearly not where the essence of the matter lies. However, there are indications that Europe has a qualitative growth problem. European production systems seem to be less innovative than the American one. In any event, Europe is lagging behind in several new growth areas (see for example, OECD 1994a; Freeman and Soete 1994; Lehner 1996). Moreover, there are also signs that monetary and financial policy is not sufficiently well coordinated. Money deposits still earn higher returns than real investments, and labour is taxed too highly relative to consumption and wealth (see among others, Dornbusch 1994; European Commission 1993). It will not be possible to investigate this side of the employment regime in greater detail here. However, these brief remarks were made because there is a current tendency to focus solely on the labour market in the search for a scapegoat for the desperate employment situation in Europe.

If we now turn to the other side of the employment regimes, then decisions on employment do not necessarily follow those on production. These decisions are made in the labour market. The rules and incentives that lead to employment decisions constitute what we term the *labour market system*. From this perspective, unemployment can be seen as the result of unrealised or misplaced employment. At least four institutions play a role in such decisions, and all of them interact with each other:

- first, the private *household system*, which offers alternatives to paid employment, shapes cultural attitudes towards work and places constraints on the volume of time available for paid work;
- second, the *industrial relations system*, in which the conflicting interests of the various labour market actors come up against each other and whose rules and power relationships determine, in particular, the level and structure of wages;
- third, the *education system*, which produces general knowledge, learning skills and vocational qualifications and determines the limits of occupational mobility and flexibility;

- fourth, the *social security system*, which affects employment decisions in a variety of different ways: a) through the state as employer, which can offer alternative employment in social spheres outside the market; b) through the largely state-regulated benefit system, which offers alternatives to earned income for workers in certain risk situations (unemployment, sickness, old age); c) through the regulation of certain aspects of the employment relationship, such as dismissal protection, fixed-term contracts and working-time arrangements.

Labour market policy can influence employment decisions through all four of these institutional channels: by providing systematic information and advice (job placement); by subsidising wage costs; by eliminating skills shortages; by creating publicly-funded 'bridges' into employment or altering the level and duration of benefit payments and, finally, by deregulating or re-regulating employment relationships.

Thus employment systems are very complex institutional arrangements. Their very complexity rules out one-dimensional theories of unemployment; equally, however, they cannot be regarded as an arbitrary conglomeration of possible institutional factors. They usually form a coherent functional framework, in other words, an employment policy configuration or *employment regime*, that has developed over time and has regional and national characteristics. There seems to be something akin to institutional hegemony at work, ensuring that this overall coherence is preserved in the multitude of everyday interactions between individual members of society.

One such configuration, for example, is often referred to as *competitive capitalism*, which denotes the predominance of market mechanisms in decisions on production and employment, as exemplified by the United States. Another is known as *coordinated capitalism*, which refers to the close coordination between state and business in decisions on production and employment that characterises Japan, for example. A third configuration is commonly referred to as *welfare capitalism*, which alludes to the important role played by social security systems in decisions on production and employment in most European countries. The competition that used to exist between capitalism and socialism has now been replaced by competition between these variants of capitalism.

There are considerable differences in this respect within the European Union (EU). Not only are these differences more visible because of the competition between the various regimes, but they are also relevant to the question of whether a new, independent and successful European model will emerge from this competition. Will that model develop more in the direction of that of the Netherlands or more in that of Germany? Or, expressed in normative terms, what factors are there in favour of the one direction, and what in favour of the other? Let us turn first to the empirical evidence and ask how the two employment systems have reacted to the major trends outlined above.

3.3 Performance of the German and Dutch Labour Markets

We shall begin with a few simple indicators of labour market performance. The one that most obviously suggests itself, the *unemployment rate*, has already been mentioned. In 1970, unemployment in both countries was about 1%, a situation of full employment of which we dare not even dream today (see Figure 3.1). The gap then widened to the disadvantage of the Netherlands. The two recessions of 1974/75 and 1980/81 were a considerably greater shock to the Netherlands than to the former West Germany. In the mid-1980s, however – before German unification – the tables began to turn. The gap began to close, initially among men, then among women as well, and since the beginning of the 1990s, the gap has been widening again, this time to the disadvantage of Germany (see also Arthur van de Meerendonk, Chapter 4 in this volume for a comparison of labour market performance).

Figure 3.1 Unemployment rates in Germany and the Netherlands, 1970-1995

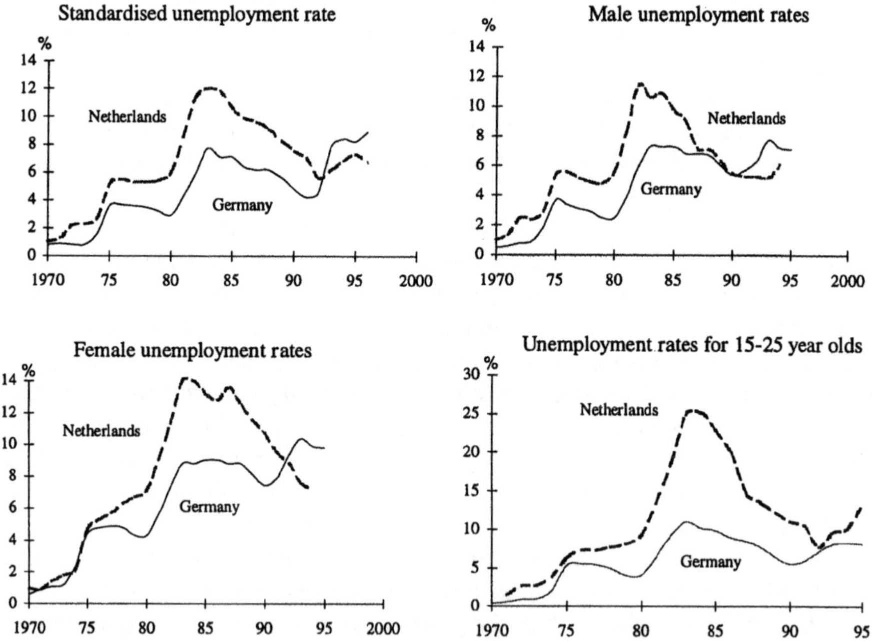

The labour market situation in the Netherlands has improved, particularly for older and younger workers, while unemployment rates among ethnic minorities remain high, and are above the corresponding rates in Germany (see Table 3.1). The deterioration in the labour market situation in Germany has been mainly at the expense of low-skilled and older workers. In both countries, long-term unemployment is high, although the trend is improving in the Netherlands and deteriorating in Germany.

Table 3.1 Structure of unemployment in Germany and the Netherlands, 1983 and 1995

	Germany		Netherlands	
	1983	1995	1983	1995
Overall unemployment rates[1]	7.7	8.2	12.0	6.5
Older workers (55-64)	8.9	11.6	13.4	3.0
Young workers (15-24)	11.0	8.5	24.9	12.8
Women	8.8	9.7	14.0	9.1
Low-skill workers[2]	11.9	19.7	19.8	15.7
Foreigners[3]	12.3	16.6	19.3[b]	18.3[a]
Long-term unemployed[4]	41.6	48.3	47.8	43.2

[1]Standardised; [2]without vocational qualification; [3]ethnic minorities in the Netherlands; [4]share in all unemployed; [a] = 1993; [b] = 1987; [c] = 1991.
Source: OECD *Employment Outlook*, July 1996; Jahrbuch StBA Strukturanalyse.

What initiated the turn-round in the Netherlands in the mid-1980s? The first (and often the only) explanation that occurs to economists is wages. It is indeed the case that *unit wage costs* have been rising less rapidly in the Netherlands than in Germany since the middle of the 1980s. However, this does not apply across the board, and in any case the difference has been less marked in the 1990s (see Figure 3.2).

Figure 3.2 Annual increase in unit wage costs in Germany and the Netherlands, 1980-1995, in %

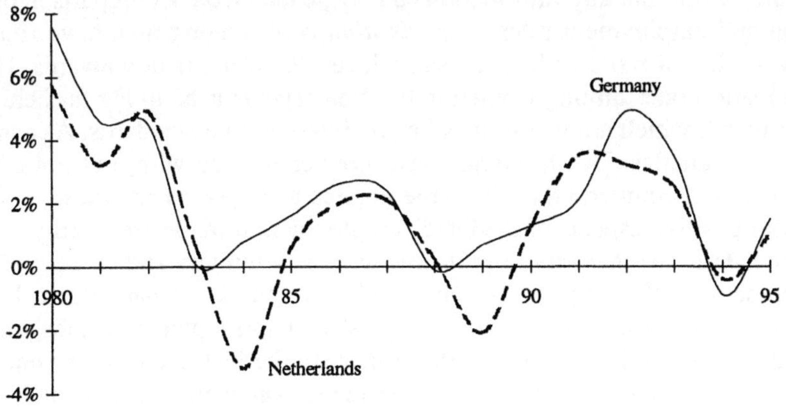

Source: OECD, *Employment Outlook*, July 1996.

Thus the key to the Dutch employment miracle cannot be found in pay policy alone. Are there differences in the wage structures? Wage differentials are comparatively low in both countries and have scarcely changed. In Germany, however, there has been an above-average increase in the real wages of low-paid workers. The consequences can be seen in the dispersion of wages in the low-pay sector. Whereas the ratio of the middle (D5) to the lowest decile (D1) in the Netherlands has remained more or less constant at 1.55, it fell in the former Federal Republic from 1.65 to 1.44 between 1983 and 1993.[7] In the light of these wage structures, neo-classical economists would again ask: does this not have negative consequences for *employment*?

This is clearly not the case in the Netherlands, at least not at first sight. Between 1971 and 1991, the number of employees rose from 4.8 to 6.5 million, or by no less than 36%. Even in the United States, the rise was lower (33%), and in West Germany during the same period, the employment level rose by only 8% (IAB 1994). The Dutch employment miracle is also reflected in the high level of *employment elasticity*. Between 1974 and 1995, one percentage point of economic growth in the Netherlands produced an increase in employment of 0.41%; the corresponding figure for the United States was 0.75%, but for West Germany it was only 0.23%.

However, more detailed analysis reveals a somewhat different picture. By far the greatest share of the Dutch job miracle is attributable to the creation of *part-time jobs*. No other OECD country currently has such a high level of part-time employment as the Netherlands. Over a period of 25 years, and particularly in the 1980s, the overall rate of part-time work rose from about 5 to 35%, and for women from 15 to no less than 65% (see Figure 3.3). The rise in part-time work in Germany was considerably lower, and has now reached an overall level of 18%; the figure for women is about 33%, that for men only 3.3%.

Further illuminating information can be gleaned from a comparison of participation and employment rates. *Participation rates* among men have run parallel to each other at more or less the same level; the trend is downwards. However, participation rates among women in the Netherlands used to lag far behind those in Germany, which are themselves low by international standards. As can be seen from the statistics, Dutch women have now caught up with, but not overtaken, their German counterparts. The same applies to *employment rates*.

Four positive aspects of the Dutch employment miracle are worthy of particular note. The vast majority of part-time work is voluntary and clearly reflects the preferences of the employees concerned. Two thirds of part-timers have high levels of education, which would suggest that most part-time jobs make high demands of those holding them. Part-timers in the Netherlands also enjoy better social security cover than those in Germany, since the entitlement thresholds have been reduced (see Den Broeder 1995, p. 301, and the bibliographical refer-

---

[7] Wage dispersion in the low-pay sector fell particularly sharply among women; among men, the fall was only slight (see OECD 1996b, Table 3.1, pp. 61-62).

Figure 3.3 Part-time rates in Germany and the Netherlands, 1983-1995

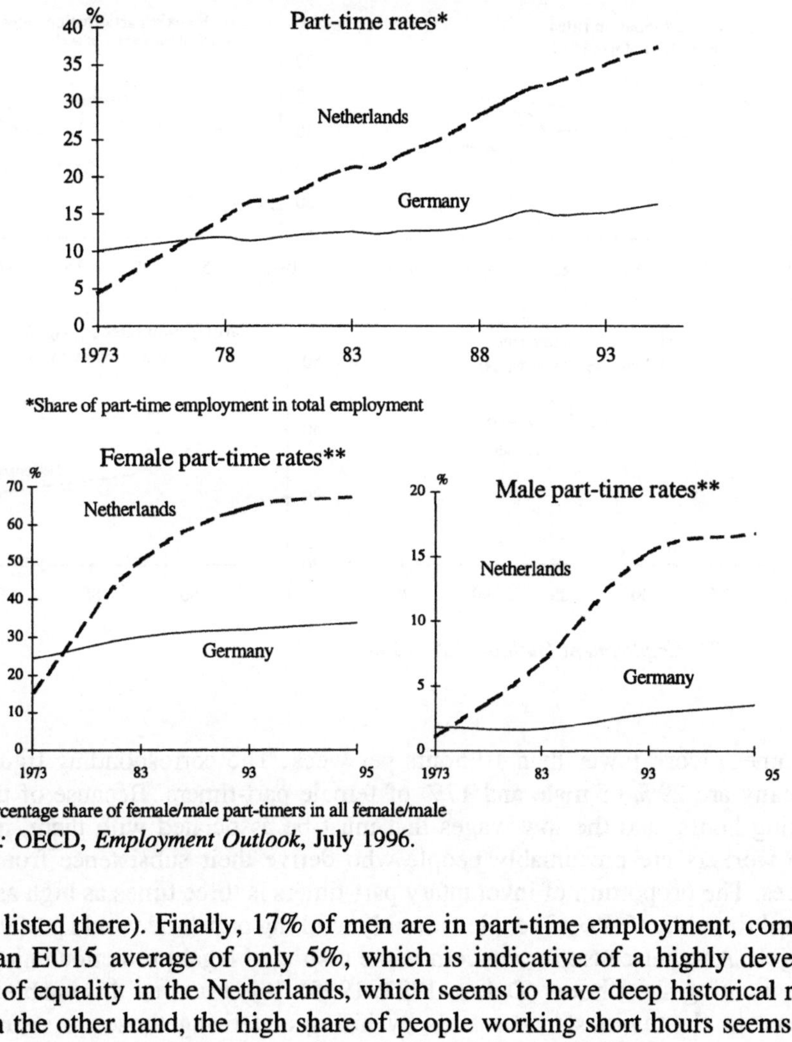

Source: OECD, *Employment Outlook*, July 1996.

ences listed there). Finally, 17% of men are in part-time employment, compared with an EU15 average of only 5%, which is indicative of a highly developed sense of equality in the Netherlands, which seems to have deep historical roots.[8]

On the other hand, the high share of people working short hours seems to be a cause for concern: 35% of part-timers in the Netherlands (43% of men, and 32%

---

[8] Unfortunately, I cannot go into this in greater detail here, although it would be very tempting to do so. However, the following cheering quotation, taken from a government document intended to initiate visitors to the Netherlands into the Dutch way of life, may provide further support for this thesis of cultural difference: "Great attempts were made in the Republic to create greater equality between the sexes. The contemporary fashion of sitting men and women alternately at the dining table originated in the Netherlands in the seventeenth century. ... In England at that time, wife-beating was still a popular sport; but it was different in the Netherlands ... [and] the Dutch were one of the first nations to provide commercial education for both boys and girls ... which ... was one of the main reasons for their great success as a trading nation" (Huggett 1982, pp. 57-59).

Figure 3.4 Participation rates in Germany and the Netherlands, 1970-1995

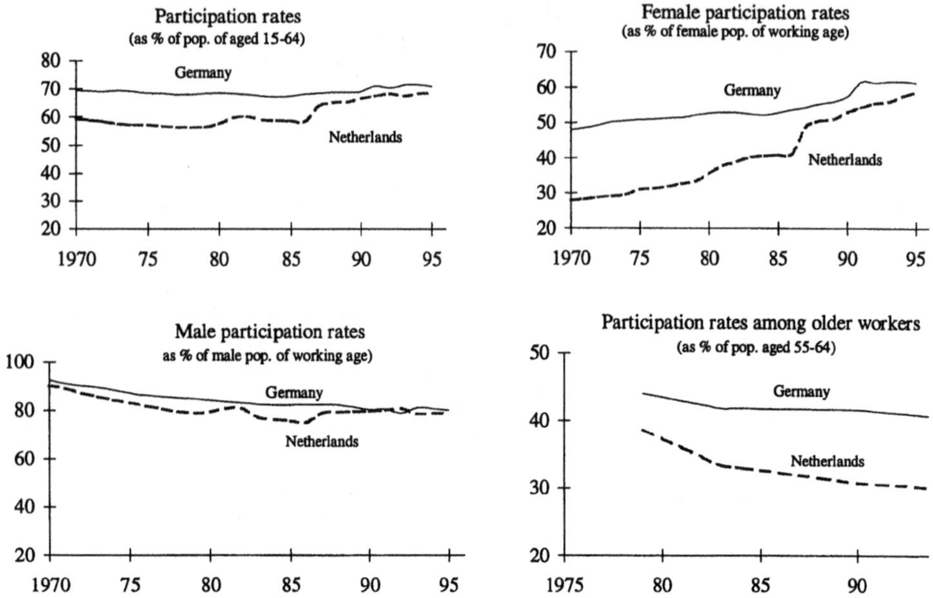

Source: OECD, *Employment Outlook*, July 1996.

of women) work fewer than 10 hours per week. The corresponding figures for Germany are 29% of male and 17% of female part-timers. Because of the low working hours, and the low wages that must be associated with them, most of these workers are presumably people who derive their subsistence from other sources. The proportion of involuntary part-timers is three times as high as in the Federal Republic: 5.5% of people currently working part-time would prefer a full-time job. Another cause for concern is the restricted legal protection enjoyed by those working short hours (Delsen 1993; 1995). It is true that this enables firms to react to fluctuations in demands by hiring and firing those on short-hours contracts, but equally, it could hinder the sustainable integration of young people, female returners or workers on fixed-term contracts into the regular labour market.

However, deregulation of this kind can also lead to higher turnover rates, thereby increasing the chances of integration for those workers with a competitive advantage in the labour market. The balance can be determined only by detailed studies of work histories and income distribution. Thus a recent study found that 50% of those in 'flexible jobs' in 1988 (fixed-term contracts, temporary work, short hours) were in 'regular employment' three years later. On the other hand, only 4.5% of those in 'regular jobs' had been in non-standard employment three years earlier. The Netherlands have the highest rate of part-time work among young people in Europe (25%) which would suggest that entry into the labour market is commonly effected through part-time jobs (Muffels et al. 1996).

Admiration for the Dutch job miracle is further diminished by the knowledge that the volume of work declined in the 1980s, despite the growth in the number of people in work, and did not return to the 1970 level until 1993. Rising numbers of people in work with static or even declining volumes of work can mean only one thing: there has been a massive redistribution of work, with a corresponding redistribution of earnings. We will return later to the question of how such a redistribution of work is to be judged in economic terms.

However, part-time work (in newly created jobs) is only one of the elements in the Dutch model of employment redistribution. The second element is (or was) the early retirement of large numbers of older or handicapped workers. As a result, employment rates among older people in the Netherlands are the lowest in the world (see Figure 3.4). If all forms of exclusion from the labour market, together with participation in labour market programmes and highly subsidised types of employment, are added together, the result is the so-called 'broad unemployment rate'. The latest OECD report on the Netherlands puts this at 27.1%, an order of magnitude that brings the Netherlands close in this respect to Eastern Germany. However, the exclusion strategy has also been adopted in Germany, albeit in a moderated form, and the 'broad unemployment rate' in Germany, at about 22%, is considerably lower (see Figure 3.5), despite the greater numbers involved in active labour market policy measures (see below).

Sceptics may object that such a strategy impairs economic efficiency and competitiveness. Whether such scepticism is justified will be examined in the next section.

3.4 The Macroeconomic Performance of the German and Dutch Employment Systems

The economic effect of the institutional economic filters can be seen in the level and dynamic of national income and in the contribution of the individual components that make up value added. *Disaggregation* of the various components of per capita Gross Domestic Product (GDP) into separate figures for labour productivity, working hours per person employed and participation rate is well suited to the purpose. Whereas labour productivity can be used as an indicator of labour market efficiency, working time per person employed will serve as an indicator not only of the degree of employment and income redistribution but also of individual control of time management and flexibility; the participation rate, for its part, serves as an indicator of the degree of social integration.

Table 3.2 shows that, measured in terms of GDP per capita (in purchasing power parity terms), the United States enjoyed the highest level of economic well-being, followed by Japan and Germany and with the Netherlands trailing all three countries in this respect. Whether national income per capita is still the right criterion for measuring economic well-being is another question, to which we shall return at the end.

Figure 3.5 Broad unemployment rates in Germany and the Netherlands, 1970-1996

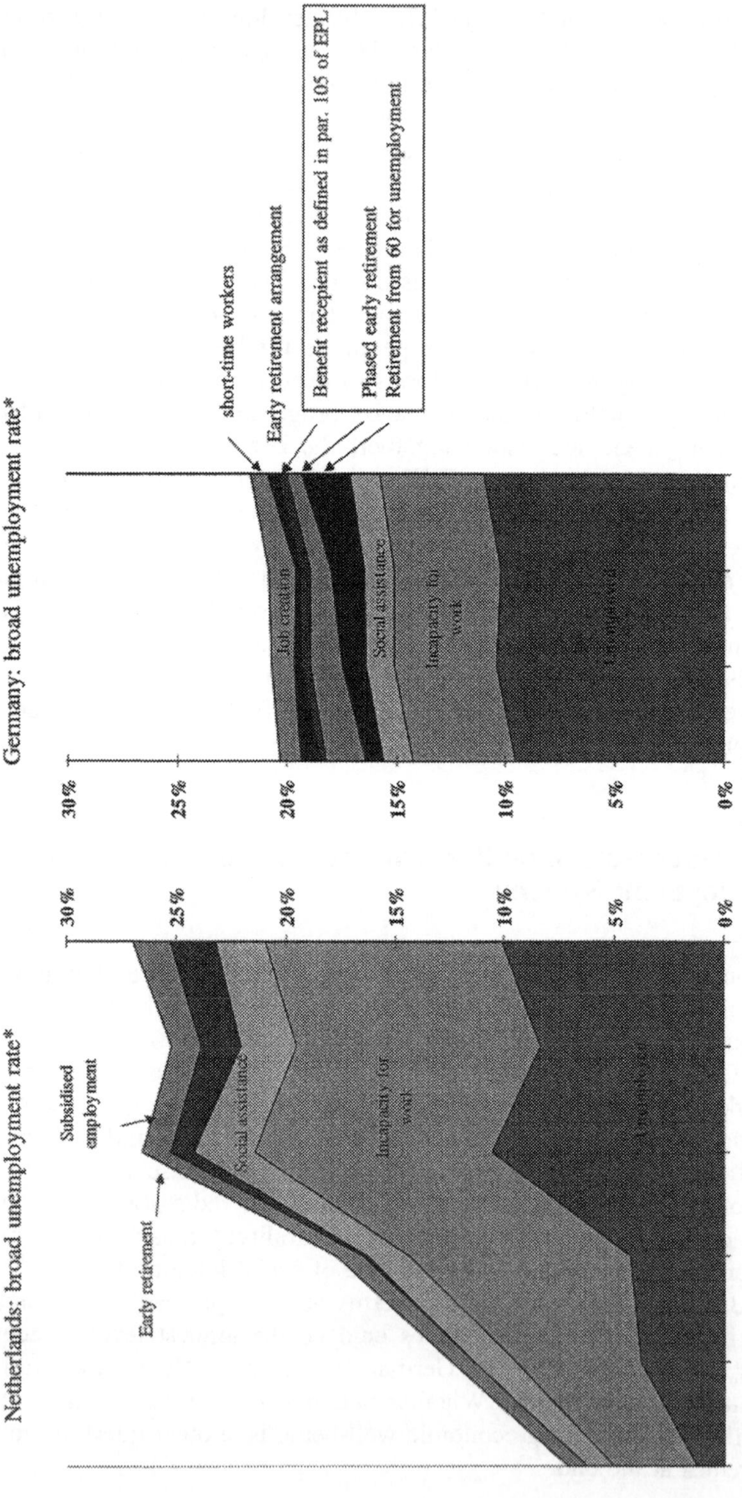

*% of economically active population, full-time equivalents.
Source: OECD Labour Force Survey Netherlands 94; StJB 96; VDR; IAB-Kurzberichte; Arbeit+Beruf 2/96; Schmid, 1995b.

As far as the *indicator of efficiency* (i.e. hourly productivity) is concerned, however, the rank order is quite different. The Netherlands and (by some distance) Germany head the table, followed by the United States and Japan. The Netherlands also lead the pack when it comes to the indicator of *employment redistribution* and *individual control of time management*: the Dutch have the lowest average working time per person employed, followed by Germany, with Japan and, surprisingly, the United States, bringing up the rear.

Table 3.2 Disaggregation of GDP per capita into indicators of efficiency, employment redistribution and integration (1994 and in ECUs)

	GDP/POP	=	GDP/h	*	h/E	*	E/POP
United States	19,364	=	21.09	*	1,945	*	0.47
Japan	15,735	=	16.07	*	1,898	*	0.52
Germany	14,933	=	21.50	*	1,575	*	0.44
Netherlands	14,109	=	23.43	*	1,397	*	0.43

GDP/POP = Gross domestic product per capita; h = actual hours worked per year (i.e. the volume of work); E = economically active employed person; h/E = actual hours worked per year per person; E/POP = employed persons/total population (i.e. employment participation rate).
Source: Own calculations; data on GDP from OECD 1996c (Basic Statistics, International Comparison) and conversion of data given there in US $ into ECU at a rate of 0.759; data on hours worked from OECD 1996a (Table C, p. 190); data on economically active population from OECD 1996c (Basic Statistics, Total Civilian Employment); population data ditto.

It will be no great surprise, finally, that the rank order for the indicator of the degree of *social integration* in the labour market is different again. Japan has the highest degree of integration, followed by the United States, with the Netherlands trailing behind Germany. This breakdown of GDP into its various components reveals more clearly the reason why the Netherlands has a relatively low GDP per capita, despite having the highest ranking for efficiency. It is due mainly to the low level of employment, which is the result of the early retirement strategy that has been pursued over a long period and has not been fully redressed even by the creation of large numbers of part-time jobs. If the Dutch are to stick to the strategy of redistributing work and reducing average working time (over the working life), then ways have to be sought of raising the general employment level further. Germany is faced with a similar problem, although with a somewhat different emphasis: there is still scope for a further redistribution of work in the interests of job creation, and the degree of labour market integration could also be improved.

However, before we bid a premature farewell to the Dutch model, we should take a quick look at the dynamic of economic well-being. Has the dynamic of growth in the Netherlands deteriorated in relative terms as a result of the massive redistribution of work and income, as the received wisdom of neoclassical economists and of classical Keynesians would lead us to suppose? Far from it. A breakdown of annual average rates of growth in per capita GDP between 1983 and 1994 into separate figures for labour productivity, work redistribution and labour market integration produces the following picture (see Table 3.3):

Table 3.3 Disaggregation of economic growth into indicators of efficiency, employment redistribution and integration (1983-1994)

	Annual average growth rates						
	ΔGDP/POP	=	ΔGDP/h	+	Δh/E	+	ΔE/POP
United States	2.0		0.8		0.3		0.9
Japan	3.0		3.2		- 0.9		0.7
Germany (West)	1.8		0.3		- 0.9		2.4
Netherlands	2.0		0.8		- 0.8		2.1

Source: OECD Employment Outlook; OECD National Account, OECD Economic Outlook; Statistisches Jahrbuch; UN Demographic Yearbook; own calculations. Because of 'noise' in the basic data and rounding errors caused by failure to extend decimal places to the full, the sum of the various components does not always produce the exact figure for GDP/POP.

A breakdown of the increase in national income per capita over the last decade reveals an astonishing picture. The dynamic of growth in the Netherlands is the same as in the United States, while West Germany actually comes out slightly worse. Only Japan performed better. The relatively low rate of growth in the (former) Federal Republic is probably attributable to the enormous transfer payments made to the new *Länder* of former East Germany in the years following unification.

However, the composition of this growth differs widely from country to country. Just about half of the growth in the United States is derived from labour productivity and from the increase in labour market participation. If the increase in average working time per person employed is taken into account, then the employment regime in the United States can be described as one of extensive growth. Japan, on the other hand, is the high-productivity regime par excellence: labour productivity exceeds growth, and the relative employment rate could be increased only by reducing individual working time (albeit from a very high starting level).

What is surprising is the extent of the contribution made by the integration factor in Germany and in the Netherlands. At first sight, this result completely contradicts what might have been expected on the basis of other indicators, which suggest that exclusion is rising and that economic growth is producing little in the way of new jobs. However, the contradiction is resolved if account is taken of the drastic reduction in individual working time relative to growth. True, this has reduced potential growth by almost 50%, but the effect in both cases on job creation and work redistribution has clearly been positive. In the

Netherlands, this effect was achieved by the creation of part-time jobs and the early retirement policy, as already outlined above; in Germany, it was achieved largely by reducing weekly working time and through early retirement programmes.[9]

If it is assumed that the early retirement policy can no longer be sustained and that considerable scope for a policy of employment redistribution through increased part-time working still exists only in Germany, then the question to be answered is what policy is capable of encouraging employment-intensive growth.[10] It should not be forgotten (see Section 3.1) that the employment level depends primarily on decisions taken in the production system, i.e. on monetary and financial policy and on the extent to which structural policy is conducive to innovation. However, it is labour market institutions – the private household, education, industrial relations and social security systems – that determine whether production decisions are converted into jobs. Labour market policy is an important intermediary factor, having a catalytic and coordinating function in improving the interfaces between the various labour market institutions. So we shall pursue our comparative study and investigate the role of labour market policy in the Dutch and German employment systems.

3.5 Labour Market Policy in Germany and in the Netherlands

Despite lower unemployment, the Netherlands spend a higher share of GDP on *passive labour market policy* than Germany in 1995; this was true in absolute as well as in relative terms. Whereas the Dutch spent a good 3% of GDP on providing for the unemployed, the corresponding figure in Germany was 'only' 2%. In other words, for each unemployed person, the Dutch pay out an average of 19,329 ECUs per year, compared with 'only' 12,057 ECUs in Germany (see Figure 3.6).

Thus the social security provision for unemployed people in the Netherlands is considerably more generous than in Germany. This can also be seen in the wage replacement rates. The wage replacement rate (before tax) in the Netherlands for

[9] Furthermore, the growth in employment in the United States is due, to a much greater extent than in the Netherlands or in Germany, to the increase in the population of working age. In other words, the American jobs miracle has less to do with the soundness of the employment regime than with demographics: 75 to 80% of the growth in employment can be explained by the increase in the number of people of working age (Houseman 1995). It may be that the declining ratio of the population of working age to total population in the United States further relieved the strain on the labour market (1983: 66.3; 1994: 65.2), whereas the same ratio increased slightly in Germany and the Netherlands, and is considerably higher than in the United States (West Germany 1983: 69; 1994: 67.2; Netherlands 1983: 67.5; 1994: 68.6)

[10] There is still scope in the Netherlands for a redistribution of employment between men and women, although this would of course be employment neutral in overall terms.

Figure 3.6 Expenditure on labour market policy in Germany and the Netherlands, 1985-1995

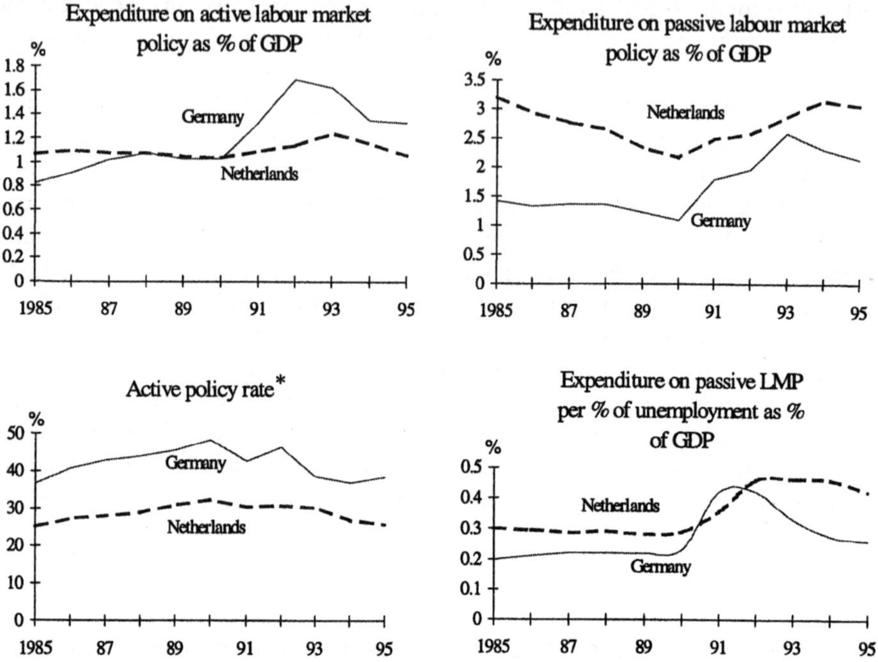

*Active policy rate share of expenditure on active labour market policy in total expenditure on labour market policy.
Source: OECD, *Employment Outlook*, July 1996.

a single person on average pay is 70% in the first month of unemployment, compared with 37% in Germany. The net wage replacement rate (after tax, including transfer payments) is 77% for a married couple without children, compared with 60% in Germany; the corresponding figures for a married couple with two children are 84 and 78%. Even the maximum period of entitlement, which mainly applies only to older employees with a long employment history, is considerably longer in the Netherlands than in Germany – 54 months compared with 32. Once the period of entitlement has expired, unemployment benefit is replaced by means-tested unemployment or social assistance. In the case of a person who has been unemployed for 60 months, who is entitled to claim, who is married and also has two children, the net wage replacement rate in the Netherlands is still 80%, compared with 71% in Germany; these figures are even higher for low-earners[11] (see also Van de Meerendonk, Chapter 4 in this volume).

On the other hand, *active labour market policy* has a higher profile in Germany than in the Netherlands. In 1995, Germany spent a total of 1.33% of GDP

[11] All figures taken from OECD 1996a, Table 2.1, pp. 31-32.

on employment promotion measures, the Netherlands 'only' 1.06%. However, activity in this area in Germany is still distorted by the extraordinary situation in Eastern Germany, where an above-average number of programmes are still running, since there is virtually no other alternative to high unemployment. The structure of the measures is also very different. The main focus in Germany is on further training and job creation programmes, while 50% of expenditure in the Netherlands goes on employment promotion schemes for handicapped people. One striking difference is in the use of labour market policy as an instrument for smoothing out cyclical fluctuations in demand: short-time allowances play a considerably smaller role in the Netherlands than in Germany. And the option of using the short-time allowance for structural adjustments, introduced in Germany at the beginning of the 1990s, is not available in the Netherlands (Den Broeder 1995). It is also noticeable that no expenditure on occupational rehabilitation is listed in the Netherlands, whereas it plays an important role in Germany. Finally, German labour market policy seeks, to a greater extent than in the Netherlands, to place unemployed people in regular employment in the private sector by subsidising wage costs or providing support for those setting up their own businesses (see Table 3.4).

Table 3.4 Expenditure on (as % of GDP) and participants in (as % of total labour force) labour market policy measures in Germany and the Netherlands, 1992 and 1995

	Germany		Netherlands	
	1992	1995	1992	1995
Expenditure on passive LMP	1.96	2.14	2.58	3.06
Expenditure on active LMP	1.69	1.33	1.14	1.06
Employment service	0.24	0.23	0.16	0.17
Training and further training	0.65	0.38	0.23	0.16
Youth programmes	0.06	0.06	0.06	0.09
Wage cost subsidies	0.07	0.07	0.03	0.01
Business start-ups	–	0.02	–	–
Job creation schemes	0.43	0.31	0.05	0.09
Occupational rehabilitation	0.14	0.13	–	–
Programmes for the disabled	0.11	0.13	0.61	0.54
Entries into	6.3	4.2	2.9	2.5
Training and further training	4.1	2.0	1.6	1.2
Youth programmes	0.6	0.7	0.8	0.7
Subsidised employment	0.2	0.2	0.2	0.2
New business start-ups	0.1	0.2	–	–
Job creation schemes	1.0	0.9	0.2	0.2
Occupational rehabilitation	0.3	0.3	–	–
Workshops for the disabled	n.d.	n.d.	0.1	0.2

Source: OECD, *Employment Outlook*, July 1996, Table T.

The structure of expenditure is reflected in the numbers of *participants in labour market programmes*: in 1995, 4.2% of the economically active population in Germany was involved in such programmes, almost twice as many as in the Netherlands (2.5%). Once again, however, this difference is largely a result of the extraordinary situation in the new *Länder* of Eastern Germany. The greatest differences are in the further training and job creation programmes that were initially more part of social than of labour market policy in Eastern Germany. These differences are diminishing over time, as a result both of cuts in funding and the gradual process of normalisation taking place in Germany. It also seems that the resources allowed per person are used more effectively in the Netherlands than in Germany.[12] It is noticeable, however, that the Netherlands devote considerably fewer resources to wage-cost subsidies but succeed in returning as many people to the regular labour market as Germany.

The *active policy rate*, which measures the share of expenditure on active labour market policy in the total labour market budget, is correspondingly lower in the Netherlands than in Germany; only about a quarter of the Dutch budget is devoted to employment promotion measures, compared with a good third in Germany. These shares have remained virtually unchanged over the past ten years. What is to be concluded from this?

First, a high active policy rate is better than a low one, provided that the outcomes of the employment promotion programmes thus financed are not wholly negative. Even if the marginal productivity of German labour market policy is declining, most programmes can still be given a positive assessment. This applies at least to a high proportion of the further-training programmes, to the assistance given to unemployed people seeking to establish their own businesses, to the short-time allowance and to the wage subsidies that form part of structural policy.[13] In these respect, the Netherlands have something to learn from Germany. This is particularly true in the sphere of training, which is where the gap between Dutch and German labour market policy is greatest in quantitative terms. This statement is supported by a comparative analysis of human capital supplies, which reveals the Netherlands' relative disadvantage compared with Germany in the sphere of medium-level skills (De Jager 1995).

On the other hand, Germany can learn something from the modernisation of the Dutch employment service. Of particular interest here is the placement service for the long-term unemployed, who under normal conditions have virtually no chance of finding employment again. Some new ideas have already been introduced, for example the START and MAATWERK concepts.[14] Other

---

[12] Comparison of the annual average numbers of participants has not been possible to date, although it would be essential for any attempt to make a rough comparison of cost-effectiveness. For more detailed comparisons, the rate of success in placing participants in permanent work would also have to be taken into account; unfortunately, there are no data on this either.

[13] On the evaluation of German labour market policy, see, among others, Arbeitskreis 1994; Bach et al. 1993; Blaschke and Nagel 1995; Schmid and Schömann 1994; Schmid et al. 1996.

[14] START is the name given to non-profit-making employment agencies whose main task

forward-looking measures include cooperation agreements between employment offices and key actors at regional level, and attempts to allocate resources to programmes with a proven record of success.[15] However, the low level of active labour market policy measures in both countries would suggest that there are still considerable untapped resources that could be used for productive employment promotion measures. We shall return to this question later.

It is now time to take stock provisionally. As far as unemployment is concerned, the situation in the Netherlands is more favourable than that in Germany, and the gap is currently widening to the further disadvantage of Germany. As far as the structure of unemployment is concerned, both countries still face the unresolved problem of long-term unemployment, although the situation in the Netherlands seems to be easing slowly, while that in Germany is deteriorating at the same time as the number of people unemployed continues to rise. On the other hand, the position of the young unemployed and of ethnic minorities is more serious in the Netherlands than in Germany, where it is older workers, and those with few skills, who are increasingly threatened by permanent exclusion from the labour market.

As far as employment growth is concerned, however, the Netherlands are the undisputed European champion. This success is the result of an aggressive strategy of employment and income redistribution, which has involved the trade unions and been supported by a rigorous policy of wage moderation. Despite this, hourly productivity in the Netherlands is one of the highest in the world. In international terms, Germany is also a high-productivity country, although to a lesser extent than the Netherlands. However, this performance indicator should be interpreted with caution in both countries, since in part it merely reflects the extremely low average working times and the low degree of social integration in the labour market.

The Dutch success in this field is also tarnished by the high number of precarious part-time jobs involving short hours. And despite the jobs miracle, the employment level in the Netherlands is not (yet) anything to write home about, and has just about reached the level in Germany. Even in Germany, however, the

---

is to find work for the long-term unemployed who are otherwise difficult to place. This model, Dutch in origin, is currently being adapted for use throughout the German *Land* of North Rhine-Westphalia (see Weinkopf 1996). MAATWERK, which literally means 'tailor-made work', is now also being tested in Hamburg, for example. Employment agencies located in the immediate vicinity of benefit offices send applicants capable of work immediately to 'Maatwerk' as well, on the assumption that a high proportion of vacancies (estimated at about 70% in the Netherlands) are neither notified to employment offices nor advertised in the press. Such vacancies are tracked down by contacting employers directly. If a benefit recipient stays in the new job for longer than six months, the benefit office pays Maatwerk 4000 German marks per person placed in work. The department of social security in Hamburg estimates that, for every 300 claimants placed in work in this way, savings of 3.8 million German marks can be made in the benefits budget. This model is also attractive for the long-term unemployed.

[15] For an assessment of Dutch labour market policy see Dercksen and De Koning 1996; Moraal 1994; Schmid 1995a.

potential for employment (unemployment aside) is far from fully exploited in international terms.

Whereas German labour market policy has used short-time working (coupled in part with further training), occupational rehabilitation, wage subsidies and further vocational training to provide considerable and, for the most part, successful support for the process of adjustment to structural change, Dutch labour market policy is still to a large extent rooted in passive social security. The target groups for active labour market policy measures in the Netherlands tend to be the most needy; basically all that is provided for the 'average' unemployed person is a placement service.

To what are these differences to be attributed? The answer is to be found in the labour market institutions outlined at the beginning. The next section focuses on the interaction between industrial relations, social security and labour market policy, which is of decisive importance in converting decisions taken in the productive system into employment.[16]

3.6 Employment Systems in Comparative Perspective

The starting point for such a comparison is not uninfluenced by the fact that the Netherlands are an extremely open economy, one that is becoming ever more open and is more dependent than virtually any other country in the world on its ability to compete in international trade. Exports of goods and services accounted for 51% of GDP in 1994, compared with 43% in 1970; the corresponding figure for Germany was only 23% (1970: 21%), although that is still considerably higher than Japan (9.5%) and the United States (11%).

These differences offer a preliminary explanation of why the Netherlands was initially clearly harder hit by external trends than the Federal Republic of Germany. A good indicator of this is the government *budget deficit*, which rose to over 6% in the 1980s in the Netherlands, whereas the German national budget was slowly stabilised over the course of the same decade (see Figure 3.7). In the 1990s, on the other hand, German fiscal policy was rocked by the shock of unification, while the Dutch national budget began slowly to stabilise and now easily meets the Maastricht criteria. It is difficult to predict how the (West) German economy would have evolved without unification. In any event, it should be noted that the Dutch success in job creation was not bought at the expense of increased state indebtedness, whereas the employment and fiscal situation in the German economy has deteriorated, particularly recently.[17]

---

[16] For a comparison of the education systems see De Jager 1995. The general political situation in the 1980s was at least comparable, with both countries seeing a shift in 1982 from a social democratic/liberal to a conservative/liberal coalition government.

[17] It would be appropriate at this point to examine the monetary, fiscal and structural policy measures put in place in the Dutch and German productive systems in order to support the

Figure 3.7 Unemployment rate and budget deficit in Germany and the Netherlands, 1970-1995

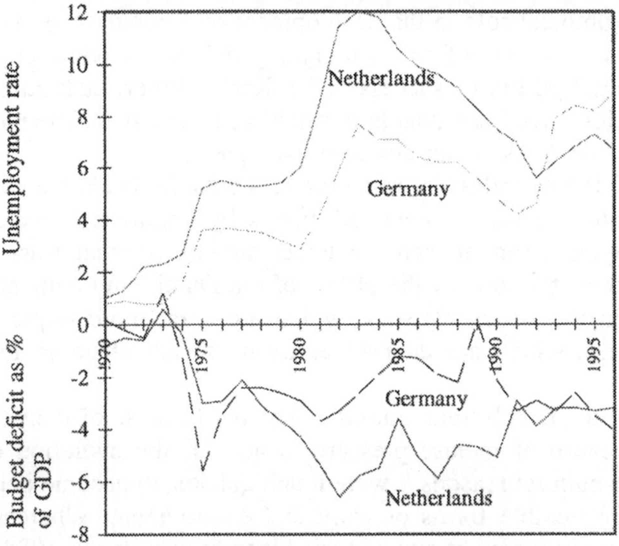

Source: OECD, Economic Outlook 1996.

What might the Dutch labour market system have contributed to this success? Let us begin with the industrial relations system (see also Soskice et al., Chapter 2 and Van de Meerendonk, Chapter 4 in this volume). A distinction is made in comparative research on social systems between liberal and social corporatism.[18] The Netherlands tend to be regarded as belonging to the former, with Germany generally allocated to the latter category. The trade unions in the Netherlands are more fragmented than in Germany, and have lost both density and power. The decentralisation of the public employment service, which gave the social partners greater rights of codetermination in the implementation of regional labour market policy, did little to alter this situation. On the other hand, employers in the Netherlands are considerably better organised than their German counterparts, and maintain close links with the political decision-making elites. Moreover, the Netherlands have always had many of the characteristics of a consensual democracy[19], and these were further strengthened during the 1980s and 1990s. Finally,

essential process of adjusting the economy to structural change. However, such an undertaking lies outside the scope of this article. Nevertheless, there are signs that structural policy in the Netherlands was considerably more active than in Germany – see, among others, Ministry of Economic Affairs 1996.

[18] The characteristics of liberal corporatism include fragmented trade unions and a strong conservative alliance, whereas social corporatism is characterised by strong and largely centralised trade unions and a weak conservative alliance; see the thesis of Werner Eichhorst 1995, which provides an excellent survey of research into corporatism.

[19] The term denotes a democracy in which the political elites cooperate at the highest level

there are several consultative institutions at central level in the Netherlands (the Social and Economic Council and, in particular, the Central Planning Bureau) that play a prominent role in the development of a common strategy, or at least of a common diagnosis of the country's problems. In Germany, in contrast, despite an initial period of success under Karl Schiller, institutions engaged in concerted action have been unable to establish themselves. The recent failure of the 'Alliance for Work' is an eloquent example.

In general terms, industrial relations in the Netherlands are even more consensual than in Germany. Concerted efforts by employers' associations, trade unions and government to achieve understanding, mutual trust and common standpoints constitute one of the pillars of the Dutch employment system. This is reflected in the strike statistics, which are even more impressive than the German figures, which are themselves by no means shaming in international terms.[20]

Moreover, the Dutch trade unions – whether because of their (looming) loss of power, because of intense pressure to act (cf. the evolution of the budget deficit) or for cultural reasons – were much quicker to become persuaded of the need for more flexible forms of work and employment. Whereas the German engineering workers fought one of their bitterest disputes in 1984 in support of their claim for a 35-hour week with full wage compensation, the social partners in the Netherlands had agreed as early as 1982 on a social pact, in which wage moderation was accepted in exchange for jobs, albeit part-time ones for the most part, and the retention of social security cover for the unemployed and those taking early retirement. It is known from many studies that the employment effect of working-time reductions is all the smaller the narrower the gap is between full-time working and the reduced hours, since work intensification and rationalisation effects predominate if the gap is small. This is why the Dutch strategy was converted more quickly and effectively into jobs than the German one. Whereas the German unions still feared part-time work as much as the Devil fears holy water, the Dutch unions clearly came to terms with this form of flexible working time at an early stage, and sought to regulate and control it.[21]

Does *labour market policy* make a difference? To what extent can active labour market policy have any influence at all on the level and structure of employment?

The theoretical response to these questions is important, not least because the empirical evidence for the effectiveness of the forms of active labour market policy used to date is as scanty as it is contradictory.

---

in order to further the common good, irrespective of religious or ethnic differences. Japan is regarded as the best example of a consensual democracy.

[20] In the period between 1980 and 1994, the Netherlands lost an average of 18 days' work to strikes each year for every 1,000 dependent employees; the figure for Germany is 29 days (Bertelsmann Stiftung 1996, p. 252).

[21] The precise forms taken by this social pact are still to a large extent a mystery to outsiders.

Active labour market policy[22] can initially increase competition on the labour supply side: if the *labour market competitiveness of unemployed people* is increased through training, those still in work will moderate their wage demands, so that the demand for labour increases. However, this effect can be cancelled out if those at risk of unemployment come to rely to such support (*moral hazard*). As a result, the risks associated with unemployment are diminished, particularly since participation in labour market policy programmes is often more lucrative than claiming unemployment benefit. Moreover, the *search for work* comes to a halt or is neglected for the duration of such programmes, so that re-entry into the regular labour market is delayed.

The *negative effects* can, however, be mitigated by making the payment of unemployment money dependent on a claimant's willingness to take part in constructive programmes and by ensuring that all possible steps are taken while the programmes are running to find a new job, for example through the acquisition of relevant practical skills or periods of work experience with potential employers. Arrangements of this kind require both a powerful and effective public employment service and close coordination of active and passive labour market policy. Both of these conditions seem to be met more satisfactorily in Germany than in the Netherlands, where passive and active labour market policies are administered by separate organisations (see Dercksen and De Koning 1996; Moraal 1994; Schmid 1995a).

Active labour market policy can also improve the *matching process*. If the labour market can be made more transparent by improving the supply of information and knowledge, then employers should no longer be forced to attract the workers they want by offering high wages; this will encourage them to register more vacancies, which it will be quicker and cheaper to fill.

Increasing the productivity of unemployed people through training reduces the marginal costs of labour, thereby increasing demand for labour. However, a positive employment effect will not be achieved unless product demand is price elastic. In the case of mass consumer goods, where saturation limits have more or less been reached in Europe, this is not the case. Moreover, the fast-developing nations are incomparably cheap in these areas. Thus training programmes are most worthwhile in those sectors that are largely protected from international competition; these include education, health, environmental projects and local crafts, as well as the new mass consumption sectors such as media and communications and tourism.

However, shortcomings in policy design and implementation may make labour market policy damaging, or at best merely ineffective. Employers may simply take advantage of certain measures, for example by accepting wage subsidies to

[22] The term 'active labour policy' is taken to denote measures intended directly to promote employment; these include job placement, further vocational training, job creation programmes and wage subsidies for employers recruiting unemployed people or to preserve jobs (e.g. through the short-time allowance). Passive labour market policy includes wage replacement benefits for the unemployed, and in some cases also early retirement programmes.

hire workers they would have recruited anyway (*dead-weight* effect or *windfall profit*); moreover, labour market programmes may simply *displace* other manufacturers or service-providers, as when new companies set up by unemployed people with government subsidies squeeze other self-employed workers out of the free market. Job creation programmes can also produce similar substitution effects, if local authorities, for example, use participants in such programmes to fulfil their statutory obligations. And finally, there may be *substitution effects* if subsidies are used to hire long-term unemployed workers who then squeeze out other unemployed people not in receipt of subsidies, or if subsidised cereal production squeezes non-subsidised potato production out of the market.

Thus it should be clear from this that more does not necessarily mean better. High and rising expenditure on active labour market policy may actually lead to higher unemployment, just as there are good arguments to support of the view that active labour market policy can have a positive effect not only on the structure but also on the level of employment. Thus the outcome depends on the type, mix and implementation of policies. For this reason, it is not a simple matter to conduct a comparative assessment of Dutch and German labour market policy. In general terms, however, the theoretical benefits listed here are confirmation that, in a well-defined, targeted and implemented labour market policy, there is considerable room for manoeuvre which, in the light of the enormous sums devoted to passive labour market measures, particularly in the Netherlands, seems to be far from fully exploited. The direction that the new active labour market policy should take will be outlined later.

Finally, mention should be made briefly of the effects of *social security systems*. In both countries, but more particularly in the Netherlands, the social security systems have, to date at least, offered both the unemployed and those taking early retirement decent compensation for the loss of their jobs. Any assessment of such a large-scale exclusion strategy is necessarily complex. In social policy terms, such a strategy is extremely dubious if paid work is a powerful force for social (and possibly also political) integration; on the other hand, if leisure or, more accurately, free time is highly preferred, then such a policy will be judged more positively. Free time is particularly highly preferred among older workers, and it would seem that these preferences are culturally more marked among the Dutch than among the Germans.[23]

One economic advantage of the early retirement policy is that older, less efficient workers can be replaced by more efficient, more highly skilled younger workers. *Ceteris paribus*, therefore, productivity is improved. Moreover, if wage structures are rigid and based on seniority and if pay differentials are low (both of which apply to the Dutch and German labour markets), then early retirement also becomes an instrument of wage flexibilisation. *Ceteris paribus*, this will have a favourable effect on employment and earnings.

---

[23] There is no verifiable empirical evidence to support this statement, but further research would be worthwhile.

On the other hand, social security expenditure is rising. The social security budgets in Germany and, even more so, the Netherlands are thus very high. If this expenditure is financed out of earnings-related contributions or taxation, then the 'tax and contributions wedge' (i.e. the difference between gross and net pay) increases. The greater the wedge becomes, the higher labour costs are and the lower the incentives to work. And when the wedge is high and rising, then it is difficult for trade unions to support a moderate wage policy. All these factors have a negative effect on employment and earnings. As far as the tax and contributions wedge is concerned, the Netherlands has succeeded in reversing the upward trend; the same cannot be said of Germany, where a high proportion of the transfer payments to the new *Länder* had to be financed out of increased contributions and income tax (see Figure 3.8) (see also Van de Meerendonk, Chapter 4 in this volume).

Figure 3.8 The evolution of the tax and contributions wedge in Germany and the Netherlands, 1979-1992

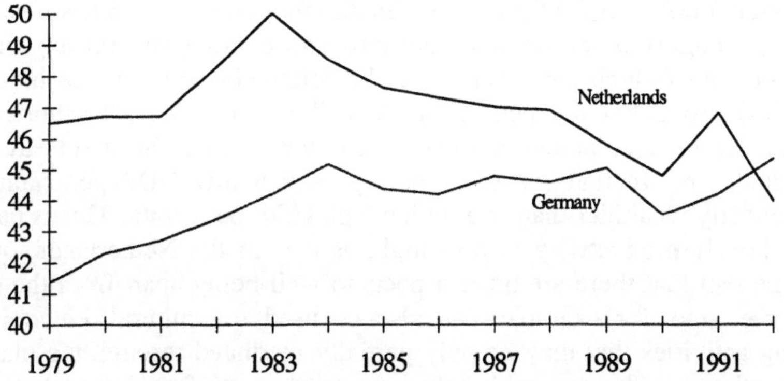

*Tax and contributions wedge = income tax, employers' and employees' contributions as % of gross pay.
Source: OECD, *OECD Economic Surveys, the Netherlands* 1994, 1996, Paris; OECD, *OECD Economic Surveys, Germany 1995/1996*, Paris.

The final balance between the positive and negative effects of a strategy of employment redistribution has to be determined empirically. Indeed, the evidence initially confirmed the sceptical view that the general economic outcome is slighter if increasingly few people are employed in the labour market. This is no longer even offset by the resultant high productivity. On the other hand, the sceptical view was countered by the finding that, in the Netherlands in particular, the dynamic of growth has not suffered and that therefore the gap between that country and the other three compared here has not increased (see Tables 3.2 and 3.3).

However, in the light of the changes in technical, economic and social structures that we described in broad outlines in our introduction, is the national product still an up-to-date yardstick? It may reasonably be asked whether *GDP per capita* is still an appropriate *indicator of economic well-being*. It is indeed appropriate only to the extent that it measures transactions mediated through the market. This of course also includes transactions that merely rectify damage, such as the repair of accident or hurricane damage and the cleaning-up of environmental pollution, although they do absolutely nothing at all to increase economic well-being. On the other hand, GDP per capita does not measure the additional economic well-being that is created without market transactions. Examples include do-it-yourself work in the house or garden, but above all child-rearing and other housework, most of which is still 'contributed' by women, who remain unpaid for their efforts.[24] Not to mention the informal economy. According to the most recent calculations, the goods and services produced in the informal economy are equivalent in value to 13.9% of GDP in the Netherlands, 13.1% in Germany, but only 8.6% in the United States (see Schneider 1994 and 1996).

One important precondition, finally, for productive independent work is the availability of own capital or assets to supplement current income when it is reduced as a result of part-time work or retirement, whether early or not. The employment policy role of policy on the distribution of wealth has not even been properly recognised yet, let alone put into action. However, for any given level of technology (which can assumed to be relatively equal in the industrialised countries), productive independent work is all the more likely the shorter working time in the official labour market is and the greater the assets available to individuals are. In that sense, a country with a low GDP per capita can be economically wealthier than one with a high GDP per capita. This is particularly true if hourly productivity is very high, as it is in the Netherlands, quite apart from the fact that there are other aspects to well-being apart from the economic one. Free time, for example, can also be used for cultural, entertainment or sporting activities that may be only partially mediated through the market, if at all. In other words, and with reference to the interface between the private *household system and the labour market*: an egalitarian distribution of wealth on a broad basis encourages a redistribution of work that will have a positive employment effect.[25]

---

[24] Without undermining our essentially academic approach, we can allow ourselves the indulgence of injecting a romantic note into the proceedings at this point by thinking, for example, of the (not virtual, but real) experience of catching crayfish in a remote Swedish lake, cooking them with mushrooms one has gathered oneself and washing them down with a bottle of Australian Chardonnay. This whole event takes up time, of course, but gives (not for every character type of course) more pleasure (although little or no employment) than an expensive meal in one of the so-called international metropolises.

[25] The Dutch model seems to have advantages over the German one in this respect as well. Anecdotal evidence would seem to suggest, for example, that private house ownership is much more broadly based in the Netherlands than in Germany; income from assets also seems to play a greater role in household income. However, these and other aspects require more detailed empirical evidence.

The reverse side of this redistribution of work and income, however, is the threat it poses to competitiveness. A high degree of wage moderation and pay differentials that take little account of performance relieve the pressure on firms to innovate and give workers little incentive to acquire new skills (Kleinknecht 1996). And, as the most recent pay agreements show, particularly at the transnational company Philips, acceptance of lasting wage cuts is also limited.[26] Furthermore, strict wage moderation and the exclusion of less efficient people from the labour market reduce purchasing power. Finally, if high social security expenditure is financed primarily from individual contributions and taxation, which are a burden on earned income, rather than from taxes on consumption, energy and wealth, then incentives to work and ability to invest are also undermined.

Thus both countries are faced with the question of whether there are approaches to the distribution of work that do not threaten productivity and competitiveness in the long term and encourage better social integration in the labour market.

3.7 Transitional Labour Markets as a Strategy for the Productive Redistribution of Work

One answer to this question might lie in the stronger institutionalisation of transitional labour markets. In metaphorical terms, *transitional labour markets* are institutional 'bridges' between unemployment and the regular labour market that allow a choice permanently to be made between various employment forms. As already outlined in the first section, current trends require a major advance in optional or even virtual employment forms. The traditional social contract underpinning the social-security system devised by Lord Beveridge in Britain is now outmoded: to provide continuous, full-time employment for all – in the past self-evidently male – heads of households would not only be an unrealistically utopian goal, but also backward looking. A 30-hour week for all, men and women alike, would be a more realistic target figure. However, in view of the changed economic and social conditions, this would have to be an average figure achieved over the course of the working life. Actual working time would fluctuate widely around the 30-hour mark, depending on the phase of the life cycle and economic needs. In extreme cases, this model would allow for periods of transitional unemployment as well as periods of extremely intensive work; even in normal cases, however, increasing use would be made of hybrid employment

[26] In the spring of 1996, Philips and its 44,000 employees concluded a two-year collective agreement that provides for a 6% pay increase but does not meet the unions' objective of the 36-hour week; moreover, the agreement alters the pension entitlement of all new recruits, who in future will receive 70% of average pay in the company as a whole rather than 70% of their final salary (IRES – *Chronique Internationale*, no. 41, July 1996, pp. 7-9).

forms combining part-time work and training or dependent employment and self-employment.

Transitional labour markets are characterised by the following principles:

- in organisational terms, by a combination of paid work with other socially useful activities, such as further training, retraining, child-rearing, creative or cultural work, political activity, voluntary work or self-employment;
- in terms of income policy, by a combination of earned income with transfer payments from social security funds or tax credits or with income from self-employment and assets;
- in social policy terms, by the acquisition of entitlement to the periodic use of institutionalised 'bridges', under conditions that are laid down in company or collective agreements or in legislation and are therefore enforceable;
- in fiscal policy terms, by the financing of employment or other useful activity with money that would otherwise be used to support the unemployed.

There is space here merely to indicate, with the aid of a few examples, the ways in which a cooperative rather than an interventionist active labour market policy might support such transitional labour markets in future:

- first, instead of redundancies, company agreements providing for fixed-term part-time work for all, possibly combined with further training, could be concluded; the four-day week at Volkswagen is an example;
- second, the employment of unemployed people in socially important areas, such as environmental, social and infrastructure activities, could be encouraged by long-term, degressive wage subsidies; generous support for those setting up on their own who then go on to develop their businesses into small firms is also part of such a policy of structural wage subsidies. The regional authorities should have a great deal of latitude in defining those employment structures worth supporting;
- third, large-scale 'rotation' models along Danish and Swedish lines could be promoted, in which employees on training leave are replaced by unemployed people hired on fixed-term contracts;
- fourth, again following the Danish model, the right to take sabbaticals could be established in collective agreements or in law; during such sabbaticals, cost-neutral wage replacement payments could be made if the temporary vacancies are filled by unemployed people, or the sabbaticals could be financed by savings on wages, along the lines of the Berlin system of sabbaticals for teachers;
- fifth, phased early retirement systems could be implemented on a wider scale, in other words, part-time working for older workers could be encouraged instead of full early retirement, which is socially questionable and economically very costly.[27]

---

[27] For a more detailed study of the theory and practice of transitional labour markets in the Federal Republic of Germany, see Schmid 1994 and Schmid 1995c.

3.8 Summary

This chapter has sought to 'explain' the Dutch jobs miracle by comparing the employment systems in the Federal Republic of Germany and the Netherlands. An analytical framework has been developed that provides a basis for meaningful comparisons of employment systems, which have to be able to meet the new challenges of globalisation and individualisation. An important part of this process was making a distinction within the employment system as a whole between the production system and the labour market system. The institutional arrangements that constitute the production system influence and filter decisions on production, and it is in inadequate coordination within that system that initial explanations for Europe's competitive disadvantage must be sought. However, production decisions are merely a necessary, not a sufficient condition for a high and balanced level of employment. Decisions on employment are taken in the labour market, which has the task of coordinating a range of different institutions, including private households and the industrial relations, education and social security systems.

One cause of the 'European sickness' is obviously the inability to transform production decisions into employment decisions. The Netherlands seem to be an exception. However, the country's success in increasing employment in quantitative terms, which is also reflected in relatively low unemployment figures, must also be subjected to a qualitative test. A more complex diagnosis of this kind does indeed take some of the shine out of the Dutch model. Nevertheless, the Dutch employment strategy of redistributing work and income on a massive scale must, initially at least, be judged a success. Sceptics may object that a strategy of this kind impairs economic efficiency. It is indeed true that GDP per capita in the Netherlands is lower than in comparable countries, but there are no signs that the dynamic of growth is flagging.

Nevertheless, it must be asked whether the current approach to redistribution, namely the exclusion of older and less efficient workers from the labour market, can be sustained. In this respect, Dutch labour market policy, which to date has done little to enlarge the economically active population, will have to change direction. However, this also applies to Germany labour market policy, which is only a few lengths ahead of the Netherlands in terms of participation levels. Our comparative assessment of the two countries has shown that an interesting new configuration is emerging in the Dutch employment system that combines in an effective way the advantages of competitive and consensus capitalism with a modernised welfare state.

One new element that should be highlighted is that the new active labour market policy can no longer focus solely on the interfaces between the social security (unemployment insurance), education (further and continuing training) and industrial relations (wage subsidies) systems, but must concentrate to a greater extent than hitherto, and to a certain extent also in a completely new way, on the interface between the labour market and private households. In addition to making available options for flexible working time, it must also include an active policy on the distribution of wealth in order to reduce individual dependence on the labour market and thus widen the scope for making up reductions in earned income caused by part-time working, frictional unemployment, short-time working or further training.

One fundamental shortcoming of both employment systems, however, is the extremely passive way in which work has been redistributed to date. A more suitable strategy for the redistribution of work would be one based on transitional labour markets, which combine temporary reductions in working time with non-market but nevertheless productive activities such as training, voluntary work, child-rearing and creative and cultural activities. The consequent temporary reduction in earned income should be offset partly by transfer payments, which could be financed predominantly from the resources that would otherwise be devoted to unemployment benefit and social assistance.

Moreover, the linking of reduced dependency on wage work to new entrepreneurial activities will be a forward-looking element of transitional labour markets.

In general terms, the Dutch employment system is evolving in a direction that seems better suited to meeting the twin challenge of globalisation and individualisation than the German system. However, there is no empirical or normative reason why the German system should go down the same path in adapting to meet that challenge. The specific characteristics of national employment systems will endure, and should provide an incentive to initiate institutional innovations in keeping with those characteristics.

References

Albert, M. (1992), *Kapitalismus contra Kapitalismus*, Frankfurt/M (in German).

Altvater, E. and B. Mahnkopf (1996), *Grenzen der Globalisierung. Ökonomie, Ökologie und Politik in der Weltgesellschaft*, Münster (in German).

Appelbaum, E. and R. Schettkat (1993), Employment developments in industrialized economies: Explaining common and diverging trends, *Discussion Paper FS I 93-313*, Wissenschaftszentrum Berlin für Sozialforschung, Berlin.

Arbeitskreis AFG-Reform (Hrsg.) (1994), *Memorandum für ein neues Arbeitsförderungsgesetz*, Druckerei Johannes Plum, Düsseldorf (in German).

Bach, U., D. Blaschke, H. Leikeb, E. Spitznagel and U. Walwei (1993), Wirkungsforschung zur Arbeitsmarktpolitik, in: Friedrich Buttler (Hg.), *Arbeitsmarkt- und Berufsforschung*, Stuttgart et al.: Kohlhammer Verlag, 2., neubearb. Aufl., pp. 204-220 (in German).

Baltes, M. and L. Mantada (Hrsg.) (1996), *Produktives Leben im Alter*, Frankfurt (in German).

Beck, U. (1986), *Risikogesellschaft. Auf dem Weg in eine andere Moderne*, Frankfurt/M (in German).

Bertelsmann-Stiftung (Hrsg.) (1996), *Internationales Beschäftigungs-Ranking 1996*, Verlag Bertelsmann Stiftung, Gütersloh (Authors: Jörg Schröder, Ulrich van Suntum) (in German).

Blaschke, D. and E. Nagel (1995), Beschäftigungssituation von Teilnehmern an AFG-finanzierter beruflicher Weiterbildung, in: *Mitteilungen aus der Arbeitsmarkt- und Berufsforschung*, 25 (2), pp. 195-213 (in German).

Braun D. (1989), *Grenzen politischer Regulierung. Der Weg in die Massenarbeitslosigkeit*, Deutscher Universitätsverlag, Wiesbaden (in German).

Broeder, C. den (1995), A comparative analysis of labour market flexibility in Germany and the Netherlands, in: *De Nederlandse Arbeidsmarktdag 1995*, Centraal Bureau voor de Statistiek, Voorburg/Heerlen, pp. 287-309.

Calmfors, L. and P. Skedinger (1995), Does active labour-market policy increase employment? Theoretical considerations and some empirical evidence from Sweden, *Oxford Review of Economic Policy*, 11 (1), pp. 91-109.

Crouch, C. and W. Streeck (eds.) (1995), *Modern Capitalism or Modern Capitalisms?* Sage Publications, London.

Delsen, L. (1993), Atypical employment and industrial relations in the Netherlands, *Economic and Industrial Democracy*, Vol.14, pp. 589-602.

Delsen, L. (1995), *Atypical Employment: An International Perspective, Causes, Consequences and Policy*, Wolters-Noordhoff, Groningen.

Dercksen, W.J. and J. de Koning (1996), The new public employment service in the Netherlands (1991-1994), *Discussion Paper FS I 96-201*, Wissenschaftszentrum Berlin für Sozialforschung, Berlin.

Deutsche Gesellschaft für die Vereinten Nationen und Deutsche Stiftung Weltbevölkerung (Hrsg.) (1994), *Weltbevölkerung und Entwicklung – Die Herausforderung des globalen Bevölkerungswachstums*, Bonn and Hannover (in German).

Dörre, K. (1996), Globalstrategien von Unternehmen – ein Desintegrationsphänomen? Zu den Auswirkungen grenzüberschreitender Unternehmensaktivitäten auf die industriellen Beziehungen, *SOFI-Mitteilungen*, Nr. 24, pp. 15-27 (in German).

Dornbusch, R. (1994), Is there a role for demand policy?, *Swedish Economic Policy Review*, 1 (1-2), pp. 155-177.

Dunning, J. (1992), *Multinational Enterprises and the Global Economy*, Wokingham.

Durkheim, E. (1977), *Über die Teilung der sozialen Arbeit*, Frankfurt/M (in German).

Eichhorst, W. (1995), *Institutionelle, politische und situative Bestimmungsfaktoren der Arbeitslosigkeit in vier kleinen offenen Volkswirtschaften*, Diplomarbeit, Universität Konstanz (in German).

Elias, N. (1976, 1936), *Über den Prozeß der Zivilisation. Soziogenetische und psychogenetische Untersuchungen.* (2. Bde.), Frankfurt/M (in German).

Enquête-Kommission Demographischer Wandel (1994), *Herausforderungen unserer älter werdenden Gesellschaft an den Einzelnen und die Politik. Zwischenbericht*, Deutscher Bundestag, 12. Wahlperiode, 12/7876, Bonn (in German).

Esping-Andersen (ed.) (1996), *Welfare States in Transition. National Adaptions in Global Economies*, Sage Publications, London.

European Commission (1993), *Growth, Competitiveness, Employment. The Challenges and Ways Forward Into the 21st Century* (*White Paper*), Supplement 6/93 of the Bulletin of the European Communities, Office for Official Publications of the European Communities, Luxemburg.

Freeman, Ch. and L. Soete (1994), *Work for all or Mass Unemployment? Computerised Technical Change into the 21st Century*, Pinter Publishers, London.

Garrett, G. and P. Lange (1995), Internationalization, institutions and political change, *International Organization* 49(4) Autumn, pp. 627-655.

Giddens, A. (1995), *Konsequenzen der Moderne*, Frankfurt/M (in German).

Harrison, P. (1994), *Die dritte Revolution – Antworten auf Bevölkerungsexplosion und Umweltzerstörung*, Heidelberg (in German).

Helleiner, E. (1989), *The Internationalization of Private Finance and the Changing Postwar Order*, Paper prepared for ISA/BISA Conference in London, March 28-April 1.

Hof, B. (1993), *Europa im Zeichen der Migration – Bevölkerungs- und Arbeitsmarktentwicklung in der Europäischen Gemeinschaft*, Köln (in German).

Houseman, S.N. (1995), Job growth and the quality of jobs in the U.S. economy, *Labour*, S93-S124.

Huggett, F.E. (1982), *The Dutch Connection*, The Hague.
Huinink, J. (1995), *Warum noch Familie? Zur Attraktivität von Partnerschaft und Elternschaft in unserer Gesellschaft*, Frankfurt/M (in German).
Jager, N.E.M. de (1995), A comparative analysis of current and future human capital in Germany and the Netherlands, in: *De Nederlandse Arbeidsmarktdag 1995*, Centraal Bureau voor de Statistiek, Voorburg/Heerlen, pp. 310-331.
Kleinknecht, A. (1996), Is labour market flexibility harmful to innovation?, *Discussion Paper TI 96-37/6*, Tinbergen Institute, Vrije Universiteit, Amsterdam.
Klose, H.-U. (1996), *Revolution auf leisen Sohlen. Politische Schlußfolgerungen aus dem demographischen Wandel*, Forum Demographie und Politik, Bonn (in German).
Kohli, M. (1988), Normalbiographie und Individualität, in: H.-G. Brose und B. Hildenbrand (Hrsg.), *Vom Ende des Individuums zur Individualität ohne Ende*, Opladen (in German).
Lehner, F. (1996), Innovative Antworten auf Strukturbrüche: Kurswechsel für Wettbewerbsfähigkeit, Beschäftigung und Umwelt, in: Institut Arbeit und Technik (Hg.), *Jahrbuch 1995*, Gelsenkirchen, pp. 14-29 (in German).
Loo, M.-J. van de, and W. van Reijen (1992), *Modernisierung, Projekt und Paradox*, München (in German).
Mayer, K.U. (1996), Erklärung und Folgen der Bevölkerungsentwicklung, Anmerkungen zu dem Buch von Meinhard Miegel und Stefanie Wahl: Das Ende des Individualismus, in: Friedrich Ebert Stiftung (Hg.), *Gesellschaft des langen Lebens: Sozialgeschichte und Gesellschaftspolitik* [Gesprächskreis Arbeit und Soziales Nr. 68], Bonn, pp. 57-75 (in German).
Miegel, M. and St. Wahl (1993), *Das Ende des Individualismus*, München/Landsberg (in German).
Ministry of Social Affairs and Employment (1995), *Summary of the 1995 Social Memorandum*, Directorate for International Affairs, The Hague.
Ministry of Economic Affairs (1996), *Benchmarking the Netherlands. Test of Dutch Competitiveness*, Ministry of Economic Affairs, The Hague.
Moraal, D. (1994), Reorganisation der Arbeitsmarktpolitik. Weiterbildung für Arbeitslose in den Niederlanden, *Discussion Paper FS I 94-204*, Wissenschaftszentrum Berlin für Sozialforschung, Berlin (in German).
Muffels, R., R. Dekker and E. Stancanelli (1996), *Moving Into and Out of Flexible and Permanent Jobs: An Empirical Analysis of Labour Market Mobility Patterns in the Netherlands Using Dutch Panel Data*, Paper for the Annual Conference of the European Association of Labour Economics (EALE) held at Crete, Chania, 19-22 September.
North, D.C. (1991), Institutions, *Journal of Economic Perspectives*, 5 (1), pp. 97-112.
OECD (1994a), *The OECD Jobs Study. Facts, Analysis, Strategies*, Organisation for Economic Co-operation and Development, Paris.
OECD (1994b), *The OECD Jobs Study. Evidence and Explanations. Part I: Labour Market Trends and Underlying Forces of Change; Part II: The Adjustment Potential of the Labour Market*, Organisation for Economic Co-operation and Development, Paris.
OECD (1996a), *Employment Outlook*, Organisation for Economic Co-operation and Development, Paris.
OECD (1996b), *Economic Outlook*, Organisation for Economic Co-operation and Development, Paris.
OECD (1996c), *OECD Economic Surveys 1995-1996, Netherlands*, Organisation for Economic Co-operation and Development, Paris.
Ohmae, K. (1996), *Der neue Weltmarkt*, Hamburg (in German).
Ruigrok, W. and R. van Tulder (1995), *The Logic of International Restructuring*, Routledge, London.
Schmid, G. (1994), Übergänge in die Vollbeschäftigung. Perspektiven einer zukunftsgerechten Arbeitsmarktpolitik, in: *Aus Politik und Zeitgeschichte B 12-13* (Beilage zur Wochenzeitung Das Parlament), pp. 9-23 (in German).
Schmid, G. (1995a), Reorganisation der Arbeitsmarktpolitik. Märkte, Politische Steuerung und

Netzwerke der Weiterbildung für Arbeitslose in der Europäischen Union, *Discussion Paper FS I 94-213*, Wissenschaftszentrum Berlin für Sozialforschung, Berlin (in German).
Schmid, G. (1995b), Europas Arbeitsmärkte im Wandel. Institutionelle Integration oder Vielfalt?, in: K. Bentele, B. Reissert and R. Schettkat (Hg.), *Die Reformfähigkeit von Industriegesellschaften*. Fritz W. Scharpf zu seinem 60. Geburtstag, Campus Verlag, Frankfurt/New York, pp. 250-276 (in German).
Schmid, G. (1995c), Is full employment still possible? Transitional labour markets as a new strategy of labour market policy, *Economic and Industrial Democracy*, 16 (3), pp. 429-456.
Schmid, G. (1997), Arbeitslosigkeit und Beschäftigung in Europa. Ansätze zu einer Theorie der Beschäftigungsregimes, *Discussion Paper FS I 97-207*, Wissenschaftszentrum Berlin für Sozialforschung, forthcoming (in German).
Schmid, G., B. Reissert and G. Bruche (1992), *Unemployment Insurance and Active Labour Market Policy. Financing Systems in International Comparison*, Wayne State University Press, Detroit.
Schmid, G. and K. Schömann (1994), Institutional choice and flexible coordination: A socioeconomic evaluation of labor market policy in Europe, in: G. Schmid (ed.), *Labor Market Institutions in Europe. A Socioeconomic Evaluation of Performance*, M.E. Sharpe, Armonk, New York, pp. 9-58.
Schmid, G., J. O'Reilly and K. Schömann (eds.) (1996), *International Handbook of Labour Market Policy and Evaluation*, Edward Elgar, Cheltenham.
Schneider, F. (1994), Determinanten der Steuerhinterziehung der Schwarzarbeit im internationalen Vergleich, in: Ch. Smekal and E. Theurl (Hrsg.), *Stand und Entwicklung der Finanzpsychologie*, Nomos, Baden-Baden, pp. 247-288 (in German).
Schneider, F. (1996), *Aktuelle Ergebnisse über die Schattenwirtschaft (Pfusch) in Österreich*, Manuskript, Institut für Volkswirtschaftslehre, Johannes Kepler Universität Linz (in German).
Strange, S. (1986), *Casino Capitalism*. Blackwell, Oxford.
Thurow, L. (1996), *Die Zukunft des Kapitalismus*, Düsseldorf (in German).
UNCTAD (1996), *Word Investment Report*, New York.
Visser, J. (1992), The Netherlands: The end of an era and the end of a system, in: Ferner, A. and R. Hyman (eds.) *Industrial Relations in the New Europe*, Blackwell, Oxford, pp. 323-356.
Walwei, U. (1997), Are part-time jobs better jobs than no jobs?, in: C. Fagan and J. O'Reilly (eds.), *Prospects and Paradoxes of Part-Time Work*, Routledge, London forthcoming.
Weber, M. (1992), *Wissenschaft als Beruf [1917/1919], Politik als Beruf [1919]*, hrsg. von W.J. Mommsen and W. Schluchter, J.C.B. Mohr (Paul Siebeck), Tübingen (in German).
Weinkopf, C. (1996), *Arbeitskräftepools*, Rainer Hampp Verlag, München and Meering (in German).
Werner, H. (1994), Beschäftigungsboom in den Niederlanden – ein Phänomen wird entschlüsselt, *IAB Kurzbericht* Nr. 9, 24.6.1994 (in German).

4 Benchmarking the German and Dutch Welfare States

Arthur van de Meerendonk[1]

4.1 Introduction

Several times a year competitiveness reports are published in which countries are ranked according to their economic performances. These reports as a rule conceive welfare state institutions to be improductive and detrimental to the growth potential of economies. The incidence of institutions, such as a large share of public expenditure on social security, statutory minimum wages and a centralised bargaining structure in industrial relations, in these reports is subtracted from economic performance on, what is basically no more than an *assumption* that it is a competitive disadvantage (see, for example, Sachs and Warner 1996). Yet, this has left observers of the sound economic performance of extensive welfare states in the past and the present puzzled. The Dutch Ministry of Social Affairs and Employment has published a competitiveness report in 1996 that explicitly focuses on the impact of the welfare state on economic performance. This chapter draws primarily on this report. It will address two questions: i) to what extent are economic performances determined by welfare state institutions? and, more specificly ii) are there differences in German and Dutch institutions that explain the current diverging economic performances of both economies? To examine these questions the Federal Republic of Germany and the Netherlands are compared with two liberal market economies: the United States of America and the United Kingdom, and another welfare state: Sweden.

The methodology used throughout this chapter is the *structure – conduct – performances* framework (SZW 1996). The institutional structure determines the opportunities and restrictions that economic agents (individuals or, for example, trade unions) face and thus influences their conduct. Trade unions in liberal market economies will use different communication channels and different

[1] The author is indebted to Dick Hagoort, Wolter Hassink, Jan Koeman, Adri Moons, Wouter Roorda, Anthony Stigter and Coen Teulings for useful comments on a previous version.

instruments to achieve their objectives than trade unions in corporatist economies. Their objectives may differ as well. The institutional order also determines the adjustment potential of an economy to structural trends such as internationalisation and technological change, and hence the competitiveness of economies. This methodological framework aims at explaining why some economies will adjust *differently* (using other channels; but not necessarily adjusting *more* or *less*) than others.

The setup of this chapter is as follows. Section 4.2 explores the economic performances of the Federal Republic of Germany and the Netherlands and compares the economic track-records of both with the United States, the United Kingdom and Sweden. That section also discusses the policies of Germany and the Netherlands in the past one-and-a-half decade. Section 4.3 maps the institutional infrastructure. Several similarities and disparities in German and Dutch industrial relations, social security and health care will be discussed. Section 4.4 describes some of the mechanisms (the conduct of economic agents) through which the institutional infrastructure determines economic outcomes. It also generalises some of the findings from the limited sample of five countries, to an analysis of the impact of the *welfare state* on economic performance. Section 4.5 provides some conclusions.

4.2 Economic Performances

4.2.1 Macroeconomic and Labour Market Performance

The perception of a poor competitiveness of the German and Dutch economies is widespread.[2] However, it is not very instructive, as is often done, just to compare wage levels per hour with Poland, the Czech-Republic or South East Asian countries. This may indeed point at high wage costs in Germany and the Netherlands but, apart from absolute wage costs, a proper assessment of competitiveness should include a wider set of indicators such as the schooling level of the labour force, the social and political climate and several other factors that determine the overall level of productivity. This, in turn, is reflected in unit wage costs which is a better measure for competitiveness than wage costs per hour. Moreover, there are numerous conditions in the transition economies in Eastern

---

[2] A 1995 DIW-report *Hat Westdeutschland ein Standortproblem?* (Wochenbericht 38/95, Deutsches Institut für Wirtschaftsforschung) in this respect poses the question whether "... die deutsche Wirtschaft" is wedged "mehr und mehr zwischen die Mühlsteine der Niedriglohnländer einerseits und der Hochtechnologieländer Japan und USA andererseits"; in the Netherlands the perception of poor competitiveness is mainly communicated through the domestic press: see for example J.F. Hoogervorst in *Het Financieele Dagblad*, 3 September 1996; Van Wijnbergen in *Trouw*, 26 June 1996. In observing the performance of the Dutch 'model' the foreign press as a rule is much more positive.

Europe or the new industrialised countries in the Far East that are fundamentally different. Hence, to assess the performance of the German and Dutch economies, it makes more sense to benchmark with countries that are at a similar stage of industrialisation. This section elaborates on this and compares the German and Dutch labour market performances with those of Sweden, the United Kingdom and the United States of America.

Table 4.1 Relative GDP per capita growth, employment and net labour participation growth, 1970-1994

	Relative GDP per capita[1]				Employment	Net labour participation[2]	
	1970	1980	1990	1994	1995 (1970=100)	1983	1994
Germany	94.5	98.9	99.9	105.5	107	60	55
Netherlands	103.9	102.9	99.7	99.7	119	44	50
Sweden	114.9	108.8	106.3	93.4	103	63	60
United Kingdom	97.7	94.6	99.2	94.7	103		63
United States	147.7	139.9	137.3	136.8	159	66	72

[1] At current prices using current purchasing power parities; the OECD average = 100.
[2] In standardised labour years of 1800 hours; as a percentage of the population between 15-64 years.
Source: OECD 1997, p. 124; Franzmeyer et al. 1996, p. 14; SZW 1996, p. 78.

Competitiveness has been defined as the ability of a national economy to achieve sustained high rates of economic growth, measured by the growth of *Gross Domestic Product* (GDP) per capita (Hu and Sachs 1996, p. 19). As Table 4.1 illustrates, German per capita income relative to other OECD countries has risen. The four other countries in the table have experienced a modest (the Netherlands and the United Kingdom) or even a strong (Sweden and the United States) decline in their per capita income, relative to the OECD average. On the other hand, the United States of America (USA) are still leading and the gap with the other countries remains considerable. Furthermore, the USA during the past quarter century have had an outstanding employment record. The performance of the European economies is rather bleak in this respect, although the Netherlands have managed to increase employment substantially in the past decade.

Net labour participation rates are moderate both in Germany and the Netherlands. As a percentage of the population between 15 and 64 years 63% of the Germans and 64% of the Dutch were employed in 1994. This is modest compared with for example Sweden (70%) and the United States (73%). Calculated in standardised labour years to control for differences in average working hours, the Netherlands have a participation rate of 50% and Germany of 55%. Sweden has a rate of 60 and the USA of 72%. The gap between German and Dutch labour participation has narrowed down approximately ten percentage-points over the past decade.

It appears that Germany, relative to other OECD countries, has been successful in raising per capita income. This holds true also for the period after 1990. The Netherlands have lost some ground in the 1980s but have managed to stabilise their position in the past ten years. The USA have experienced a stagnant real income growth but a large employment growth. The German performance is more or less the opposite of this: a large rise in real income but a rather modest employment growth. The Dutch track record appears to be somewhere in the middle. However, the modest German and Dutch net participation rates point at some underutilisation of their capacities. The remainder of this subsection will explore the labour market situation of both countries: it subsequently will compare unemployment, the composition of unemployment (the proportion of long-term unemployed and of low-skilled unemployed in total unemployment) and labour costs (both wages and non-wage labour costs) (see also Schmid and Helmer, Chapter 3 in this volume).

Table 4.2 Standardised unemployment (percentage of the labour force), 1995

	Level 1995	Average 1990-1995
Germany	8.2	6.4
Netherlands	6.5	6.6
Sweden	9.2	6.6
United Kingdom	8.7	9.1
United States	5.5	6.4

Source: OECD 1996d, p. A25.

Table 4.2 gives the *unemployment rates* of Germany, the Netherlands, the United Kingdom, United States and Sweden over the period 1990-1995. The United Kingdom (UK) seems to be recovering from high unemployment rates in the early nineties. The USA have had a relatively modest rate of unemployment throughout the period. Unemployment in Sweden has boosted from 1990 onwards. It is currently at some 10%. The same, more recently, goes for Germany. Unemployment in Germany has risen to a level of 9.4% in 1995 and has since then moved steeply upwards to 10.3% currently. In Eastern Germany the rate was 15.5% in May 1996; in the Western part of the Federal Republic the rate at that time was 9%. The overall German unemployment rate is projected to stabilise in 1997 at a level of 10.4% (OECD 1996d, p. 56; the projection for 1998 is 10.1%). The Netherlands have managed to diminish unemployment. The figures in the table are part of a more prolonged downward trend, initiating in the mid 1980s. At 6.5% the Dutch unemployment rate is currently one of the lowest in the OECD area (OECD 1996b, p. 35).

Another indicator for the functioning of the labour market is the persistence of unemployment: the level of *long-term unemployment*. Table 4.3 shows that both Germany and the Netherlands have high proportions of long-term unemployed in total unemployment. The UK has both a high share and a high absolute percentage of long-term unemployed. Long-term unemployment is particularly harmful because it leads to a destruction of human capital. Skills are lost and knowledge becomes outdated.

Table 4.3 Long-term unemployment (percentage of the labour force), 1995

	Perc. unemployed longer than 1 year	Proportion of long-term in total unemployment
Germany	4.0	48.3
Netherlands	2.8	43.2
Sweden	1.4	15.7
United Kingdom	3.8	43.5
United States	0.5	9.7

Source: calculated from OECD 1996c, Statistical Annex, Tables L and Q.

In all the countries benchmarked unemployment is concentrated in the *low skill segment* of the labour market. It is striking though, that this is in particular the case in the Anglo-Saxon countries. Table 4.4 shows that the USA and the UK have unemployment rates among the low skilled that exceed 12%. Germany and the Netherlands take intermediate positions respectively with 9% and 8%. Sweden comes off best.

Table 4.4 Low-skilled and high-skilled unemployed (percentage of the relevant labour force), 1992

	Unemployment low-skilled	Unemployment high-skilled
Germany	8.9	3.7
Netherlands	8.0	3.9
Sweden	4.6	2.0
United Kingdom	12.3	3.6
United States	13.5	2.9

Source: SZW 1996, p. 109.

The United States, Germany and Sweden all have high shares of the population between 25 and 64 years that have at least finished upper secondary *education*. In this respect the Netherlands and the United Kingdom fall behind. Due to a low participation of less educated people in the Netherlands however, the educational record of the Dutch employed is close to Germany and the USA, as Table 4.5 shows. As far as reliable evidence is available, a comparison of the *quality* of the educational systems turns out relatively favourable for the Netherlands and Germany compared with the USA and Sweden (SZW 1996, p. 89).

Table 4.5 Educational level of working persons 25-59 years, 1993

	Secondary		Tertiary
	Lower	Upper	
Germany[1]	13	55	24
Netherlands	16	58	26
United Kingdom[2]	43	31	24
United States	10	62	28

[1, 2] 8% is unknown for Germany and 2% for the UK.
Source: SZW 1996, p. 87.

Initial education however does not tell the whole story. Post-initial or vocational education is an important factor in upgrading the skill level so as to keep pace with technological progress. Vocational education has several merits, one of which is the enhancement of the adaptability to changing conditions, a greater receptiveness for innovations in the production process. The report on the *Dutch welfare state* shows a good performance of Germany and Sweden, with some distance followed by the Netherlands. The Anglo-Saxon countries have low scores in this respect (SZW 1996, p. 90; Schröder and Van Suntum 1996, p. 81). Vocational training and industrial relations are connected. Bipartite or tripartite agreements on training, often compulsory for entire branches of industry, are practice both in Germany and the Netherlands (SZW 1996, pp. 59-60). This stimulates employers to invest in skill enhancement in stead of just buying skilled labour away of their competitors which is not very efficient from a macro point of view (see also Soskice et al., Chapter 2 in this volume).

Table 4.6 Wage costs per hour in manufacturing, 1994

	Level in 1994	% Change 1980-1994	
	(in DM)	(in DM)	(in nat.currency)
Germany	43.97	102.4	102.4
Netherlands	34.87	57.5	61.6
Sweden	31.00	34.1	174.0
United Kingdom	22.06	83.1	211.8
United States	27.97	68.3	88.5

Source: SZW 1996, pp. 38-39; Roorda and Vogels 1997, p. 52.

Table 4.6 compares *wage costs* per hour in manufacturing in five countries in 1994. Average wage costs are high in Germany; the Netherlands, Sweden and the United States take an intermediate position and the United Kingdom has relatively low wage costs per hour. Table 4.6 further reveals a relatively moderate *increase* in labour costs per hour (if measured in German marks) in Sweden and in the Netherlands in the last one-and-a-half decade whereas Germany again takes the least favourable position.

Table 4.7 Unit wage costs in manufacturing, index 1994 (Germany = 100)

Germany	100
Netherlands	89
Sweden	94
United Kingdom	106
United States	99

Source: SZW 1996, pp. 38-39.

Labour costs per hour must be assessed however, in combination with productivity. This is expressed in Table 4.7 where the same five countries are compared in terms of differences in the level of *unit wage costs.* Due to its relatively high labour productivity German unit wage costs in manufacturing are close to those of the USA. The UK now ranks last with the highest unit wage costs despite its favourable record on wage costs per hour. Sweden and the Netherlands have relatively low unit wage costs.

A final, but important, indicator with respect to the economic performance of the welfare state is the *wedge*: the differential between the costs of labour (to the employer) and net earned wages. High indirect labour costs are generally assumed to drive up labour costs and unemployment. The performance of the labour market may be inhibited when indirect labour costs are high. Labour may accept a decrease in net wages (Franzmeyer et al. 1996, p. 21) but this may subsequently lead to a reduction of labour supply and entail a lower participation rate. Through a high wedge, the welfare state may have a negative impact on the operation of the labour market.

Table 4.8 gives the average and marginal wedges of different income categories in four countries. The figures are calculated for 1993 by the CPB Netherlands Bureau for Economic Policy Analysis and take account for various subsidies e.g. for housing costs. The *average* wedge in the Netherlands is relatively high compared with Germany. Only at APW-level (i.e. the earnings of an average production worker) the average wedges of both countries are in the same range. The United Kingdom has a negative average wedge at the minimum wage level due to the application of *in-work benefits*, supplementary benefits which are included in the wedge. Remarkable is that the level of the United States (New York) is close to the German level.

Table 4.8 Average and marginal wedges as a percentage of labour costs for different income categories, 1993

	Average wedge			Marginal wedge		
	Minimum	APW[1]	Double APW	Minimum	APW	Double APW
Germany	20.1	41.4	41.7	49.9	52.6	35.6
Netherlands	31.9	44.0	48.4	58.6	53.9	59.7
United Kingdom	-15.8	28.8	32.8	74.3	40.2	43.9
United States[2]	18.7	37.3	40.7	41.6	39.1	51.0

[1] APW = Average Production Worker.
[2] The figures apply to the State New York.
Source: SZW 1996, pp. 98-99.

The Dutch *marginal* wedge again is high compared with Germany, although not at APW-level. Particularly striking is the relatively low German marginal wedge for higher earnings (double APW-level). In general the OECD concludes that high marginal wedges are unlikely to distort labour market behaviour as long as they exist only for a short range of earnings (OECD 1996c, p. 45). This clearly applies to the UK. The high marginal rate for the UK at the minimum wage level is related to the incidence of in-work benefits at that level. These supplementary benefits are withdrawn as soon as earnings rise above 77% of APW-level. On grounds of cost and because the effects of a high marginal wedge on work incentives, the benefit must, according to the OECD, be withdrawn from earnings which are received by the bulk of the working population (OECD 1996c, p. 48).

4.2.2 Social Security and Health Care

The previous subsection provided some data on unemployment rates. A poor labour market performance however will not be put on the stage if unemployment to a substantial extent remains hidden in other social security schemes, such as disability insurance and early retirement schemes. Both Germany and the Netherlands have poor records on this. The OECD reports for the Netherlands for instance a *broad unemployment rate*, in full time equivalents, of 27.1% in 1994 (this broad unemployment rate, that includes disability, early retirement, social assistance and subsidised employment, was already 26.6% in 1985; see OECD 1996b, p. 41). A comparable figure for Germany is 22% (see Figure 3.5, Chapter 3 by Schmid and Helmer in this volume).

A more comprehensive measure of labour market slack is the *inactivity/activity-ratio* (i/a-ratio). The numerator of this ratio displays the number of beneficiaries of the various social security schemes (the total number of benefit years); the denominator consists of all employed persons of working age (the number of labour years). Table 4.9 gives the i/a-ratio in several countries for persons below pensionable age (15-64 years). Germany and especially the Netherlands have higher i/a-ratios than for example the United Kingdom. Yet, Germany and the Netherlands are the only two countries out of six European countries where the i/a-ratio has decreased since 1985 (De Voogd et al. 1996, p. 33). In the UK the i/a-ratio has considerably risen in the same period.

Table 4.9 Inactivity/activity-ratios persons 15-64 years, 1992

	1992 Level	Perc. change 1985-1992
Germany	38.1[1]	-5.4
Netherlands	42.2	-2.1
United Kingdom	34.3	5.6

[1] An alternative calculation gives a level of 44.7 (see De Voogd et al. 1996 for the details).
Source: SZW 1996, p. 156, p. 167.

The extent to which welfare states redistribute income by means of social security and provide public services, such as health care and education, is expressed by the share of *social expenditure* in GDP. Usually the share of *public* social expenditure is taken; Table 4.10 gives the figures for gross public expenditure in several countries. The United States (15%) spend substantially less than the European countries. Differences within the European countries are substantive too: the UK spends a little over 23% whereas Sweden spends 38%. Germany (28.7%) and the Netherlands (30.6%) are more or less in the middle. The picture changes however, if account is taken of differences in various countries in the taxation of benefits. In the Netherlands, Sweden and to a lesser extent Germany, large differences exist between *net* and gross public expenditure. The variance in *net* public expenditure between the UK (21.8%), the Netherlands (22.4%) and Germany (24.0%) is relatively small, as the second column of Table 4.10 reveals.

Table 4.10 Share of public and private social expenditure in GDP, 1993

	Public		Private[2]	Total
	Gross (11)	Net[1] (2)	(3)	(4)
Germany	28.66	23.97	4.23	28.20
Netherlands	30.64	22.39	2.47	24.86
Sweden	38.25	29.24	3.54	32.78
United Kingdom	23.41	21.28	3.40	24.68
United States	15.04	15.64	9.41	24.95

[1] Gross expenditure minus direct taxes and social contributions paid on transfers and minus indirect taxes and plus social/fiscal measures on public and private social expenditure.
[2] Net current mandatory private social expenditure plus social/fiscal measures on old-age cash benefits plus pensions under administrative extension plus non-public health expenditure.
Source: Adema et al. 1996, p. 34.

In the United States however, apart from publicly financed social protection an extensive private insurance market exists that covers income and health risks. When private social expenditure (including private outlays on health care) is included in the picture the figure for the USA (25.0%) equals that of the UK (24.7%) and the Netherlands (24.9%) and comes close to Germany (28.2%) and even the difference with Sweden (32.8%) has been reduced substantially. Column four in Table 4.10 gives the results; Section 4 will submit this topic to further analysis.

The share of *health care expenditure* in GDP is particularly high in the United States: 14% in 1992. Germany and the Netherlands spend 8.7 respectively 8.6% of their GDP on health care. Sweden (7.9%) and the United Kingdom (7.1%) manage to keep expenditure under the 8% (all figures relate to 1992; SZW 1996, p. 187).

To control for country specific definitions of the health care package a *common comparable package* (CCP) has been constructed. This CCP consists of 83% (80%) of the German (Dutch) cure sector and of 17% (20%) of long-term care provisions in Germany (the Netherlands). Still, the differences between Germany and the Netherlands remain minor: this mutually comparable package of health care provisions 'costs' 4.1% of GDP in Germany and 4.3% in the Netherlands (the figures relate to 1992; see VWS 1996, Annex pp. 34-35).

4.2.3 Current Economic Performances in a Brief Historical Perspective

In order to assess the current German economic situation, the developments in the 1980s, the unification and the subsequent years have to be taken into account. Porter (1990) has argued that competitiveness is about the aim to support high wages and command premium prices in international markets. The performance of German manufacturing in the 1960s and 1970s stands out as an example. This was the period of corporatist wage bargaining, reflecting a large consensus over industrial modernisation, where high wages and shorter working hours were considered as perfectly compatible with a competitive position on world markets (Lehmbruch 1996). Or in the words of Streeck: "the same set of institutions that constituted a prohibitive liability in price-competitive markets served as a competitive asset – with what would be *debilitating rigidities* for firms trying to compete on price, offering *enabling flexibilities* to firms pursuing quality-competitiveness through upgrading and customization of products" (Streeck 1995, p. 13, his italics). However, in the outset of the 1980s internationalisation and technological change increasingly challenged German manufacturings' stronghold in two respects. First, there was the emergence of high tech industries. And second, there was the increased ability of third countries to compete German manufacturing on German quality standards. Since German industry became less in a position to command premium prices in world markets, production costs had to adjust. On top of this in 1981 the economies of the industrialised countries had turned into a recession that constrained private profitability and public finance. In 1982 the newly elected German government set out to cut public expenditure and reduce the budget deficit. Wage moderation throughout the 1980s improved the rate of return on investment. This, together with an enormous expansion of the US economy, contributed to an economic recovery in the second half of the decade. The fall in unit wage costs although, was not enough to prevent a deterioration of profitability in the exposed sector (CPB 1996, pp. 268-277): German manufacturers had to lower their prices in order to maintain their international market share (see also Soskice et al., Chapter 2 in this volume). Others point at high real interest rates during the recovery period reflecting the shift towards restrictive fiscal and monetary policies in Europe (Franzmeyer et al. 1996, p. 104). In any case, investment failed to pick up sufficiently and unemployment continued to rise.

The initial results of the *German unification* in 1990 were accelerating GDP and employment growth rates. Germany (West Germany) managed to avoid the recession that hit other European countries in the early 1990s, due to a prolonged unification-boom. The upturn did not last, however. And currently Germany faces a severe downturn. Economic growth has decelerated from over 5% in 1990-1 to an average of slightly more than 1.5% since. The consequence of the unification has been a deteriorating labour market performance and posed a drawback on the existing West German social protection infrastructure initiating a large amount of public transfers eastbound. Wages in the Eastern part of the country were allowed to increase rapidly, reflecting a widely held view at the time that the East German economy should not compete as a low wage territory but on the basis of a fast and thorough industrial modernisation (Lehmbruch 1996). Or, as Streeck has put it: "Unification was conceived and executed as a giant exercise in *Institutionentransfer*: a wholesale transplantation of the entire array of West German institutions to the former East Germany" (Streeck 1995, pp. 20-21). As the markets for East German products collapsed, this caused a massive job loss: from 9.8 million jobs in 1990 to 6.2 million in 1993 (OECD 1996a, p. 107). Wage moderation in the 1993-4 wage-rounds was not sustained in 1995 contributing to a renewed downturn (OECD 1996a, pp. 7-8). After a large employment growth in 1990 and 1991, from 1992 onwards employment declined considerably with more than 1% on average per year. At the end of 1996 the government deficit exceeds the Maastricht target and social security expenditure and unemployment are on the rise. The OECD in its *Economic Outlook* of December 1996 expects 1996 to be the turning point: employment in Germany is projected to rise at a modest rate of 0.2% and 0.7% in 1997 and 1998.

The foundations for the current Dutch employment performance were led in 1982 when in the Netherlands a new government took office. At that time unemployment exceeded 10%, the fiscal deficit was close to 6% of GDP and, due to a rapid expansion of welfare state outlays in the 1970s, public expenditure was up to 60% of GDP. Institutionalised adjustment mechanisms in public and private wage formation had turned out to be built-in *de*stabilisers (Hemerijck 1992). The government implemented a retrenchment programme and sustained this throughout the 1980s and beyond. This programme consisted of a reduction in the fiscal deficit and in public expenditure by keeping wage increases in the public sector below that of the market sector and by freezing social security benefits. A prolonged period of wage moderation up to the end of the decade contributed to a recovery of profitability in the exposed sector. In the early 1990s ill-timed wage claims accompanied by the recession constituted a temporary drawback in the recovery process. This forced the government to implement substantial additional expenditure cuts and provoked a debate on the sustainability of several social security schemes. The current Dutch government, at the time it resumed office in 1994, set a ceiling in real terms in public spending and deliberately used a very modest GDP growth forecast in estimating revenues out of taxes and social security contributions, both in order to make *fiscal policy* less dependent of the business cycle. Moreover, the government undertook several reform measures in social security (see Section 3). Evaluating Dutch fiscal policy, we may conclude that it has turned out to be successful in meeting both the fiscal and employment targets. A larger than estimated GDP growth rate has facilitated reductions in taxes and social security contributions that have in turn been favourable to employment. The Netherlands managed to increase *employment* substantially in the period 1989-1995 and even outperform the USA in employment growth measured in persons: 1.6% annually in the Netherlands against 1.5% in the USA. For the Netherlands, the OECD projects an increase of 1.8 and 1.9% in 1997/98 (OECD 1996d, p. A23).

It is perhaps a little premature to draw *conclusions* at this stage. In benchmarking the German and Dutch economic performances with those of Sweden, the United States and the United Kingdom, a low participation rate, high share of long-term unemployment and high inactivity-activity-ratio stand out as negative features. The other side of the coin is that Germany, the Netherlands and Sweden have in common a relatively educated work force and a relatively modest rate of unemployment of low skilled, compared with the Anglo-Saxon countries. On the other hand, the unfavourable German and Dutch inactivity/activity-ratios suggest that a substantial component of low-skilled unemployment may well be hidden in social security schemes (for example disability in the Netherlands). Germany performs well, compared with the Netherlands, on the educational attainment of the work force (especially in vocational training) and the magnitude of the *wedge*. The Netherlands have a better record than Germany on employment growth, wage costs and the rate of *un*employment. The German labour market did not benefit from the recovery in the late 1980s and subsequently, in the early 1990s in the face of a strong but temporary upswing, rises in German unit wage costs have inhibited the competitiveness of the exposed sector (an exception being 1993-4).

The next section will address the socio-economic infrastructure underlying these performances.

4.3 Employment and Social Policies and Institutions

4.3.1 Similarities in Policy and Institutions

4.3.1.1 Concerted Economies

Three categories of organisation in the advanced economies can be distinguished (Van Waarden 1997). The first is the liberal market economy. Here, the coordination of economic transactions and the allocation of productive resources is established first and foremost through the market. The government merely provides the institutional framework for the market mechanism to operate with as least constraints as possible. The United States, Australia, Canada and the United Kingdom are all notably liberal market economies. In the second type, the emphasis is on central planning by the government bureaucracy. France stands out as an example in this etatist tradition. In the third type, labeled as *concerted economies*, an elaborate and institutionalised network of intermediary organisations exists. These organisations take part in economic governance. A key feature of these intermediary organisations is that they have developed from being merely narrow interest organisations to more comprehensive or 'public regarding' associations. Van Waarden describes this as follows: "... comprehensive associations can less easily seek rents for special interests at the costs of others. As such organizations have to aggregate a greater variety of interests, their policies tend to become more moderate and to gravitate to the centre of the political spectrum, just as usually is the case for political parties as they grow bigger." (Van Waarden 1997, p. 15). Austria, Germany, the Netherlands and the Scandinavian countries fall into this category of concerted or neo-corporatist economies.

Hence Germany and the Netherlands are both neo-corporatist economies. They form the heartland of what has been named 'The Rhineland model' (Albert 1992). Lehmbruch (1996) however, has emphasised that corporatism in Germany is the product of extensive historical learning processes. He situates the emergence of corporatist patterns of interest representation in the process of state formation in the 16th and 17th centuries. Likewise, Hemerijck (1992) contends that Dutch corporatism goes back to the Dutch Republic of the Seven United Provinces in the 16th century. Essential, both for the German and the Dutch case, has been that the central state was not capable of exerting hierarchical control over the constituent territories. The state issued the principle of joint representation and institutionalised an equilibrium of the interest positions of the territories. In the case of the Dutch Republic this was the institution of the States General that, for example, signed alliances or agreements with foreign powers and in which each of the seven provinces had one vote (Israel 1995, p. 292). The autonomous legislative and fiscal position of the Länder in the contemporary German Federal Republic can be perceived as an outcome of these historical processes, as Lehmbruch (1995) has argued. The German federal government finds itself in complex institutional constraints. First, it has no hierarchical administrative authority over the Länder; for example with respect to fiscal and economic structural policies. Second, since the principles of joint representation and autonomous administration (*Selbstverwaltung*) have been constituted in the social insurance infrastructure (Lehmbruch 1995), the federal government shares political space with the peak associations of employers and organised labour. Lehmbruch (1995) argues that the corporatist elements of the German institutional heritage in combination with the federal tradition encourage conflict management by bargaining between powerful, and partially autonomous, corporate social actors.

Hemerijck distinguishes between corporatism as an institutional structure and corporatism as a strategy (Hemerijck 1992, p. 96). The institutional structure will channel the conduct of trade unions, to take an example. In corporatist countries trade unions will fall back on corporatist strategies; they will be more prone to consultation and coordination. As trade unions take part in economic governance their objectives will differ as well: they may be less inclined to *rent-seeking* behaviour than trade unions in liberal market economies. However, structures evolve and this applies in particular to corporatist structures. Hemerijck (1992) argues that corporatism in the Netherlands has altered several times during the relatively short time span of the post Second World War decades. Corporatist structures respond to shifts in economic or cultural preconditions. Dutch corporatism was conducive for economic growth and the pursuit of full employment in the 1960s. It had become adversarial just one decade later: preconditions had changed and the conduct of corporate agents changed as a result. This points to a conclusion that the perception of a Rhineland model is not very instructive since it cannot account for the diversity in institutional constellations in different countries on different points of time.

The next two subsections address first industrial relations and labour market legislation and second social security and health care.

4.3.1.2 Industrial Relations and Labour Market Legislation

Germany and the Netherlands have a number of important institutions in industrial relations in common: the Collective Labour Agreement, the administrative extension that declares these collective agreements generally binding ('Algemeinverbindlichkeit', 'Algemeen Verbindend Verklaring') and various forms of labour protection legislation. In the report *The Dutch welfare state* an elaborate description is given of the advantages and disadvantages of these institutions (SZW 1996, pp. 61-70). The key argument against institutions is that they reduce dynamic efficiency, the capacity to adapt and modernise and that institutions entail rent-seeking behaviour. An argument in favour of institutions is the reduction of transaction costs: collective agreements lay down various procedural rules and render the bulk of individual bargaining obsolete. In addition, collective agreements facilitate schooling and other skill-upgrading arrangements. Collective agreements initiate a medium or long-term commitment between employer and workers and provide a solution for what is known as the hold-up problem (Teulings 1995, p. 12)[3] (see also Soskice et al., Chapter 2 in this volume).

---

[3] Eichengreen (1994) argues that institutions were formed in the decades after the Second

Both in Germany and in the Netherlands *collective negotiations* are concentrated at a sectoral level. The two countries take an intermediate position in this respect. In the Anglo-Saxon countries the enterprise is the dominant level. In most countries however, a long-term tendency towards decentralisation is observable. In Sweden, for example, the central level was predominant but since 1983 the trend has been towards bargaining at the industry and enterprise level (OECD 1997, p. 84). In the Netherlands, and to a lesser extent in Germany too, negotiations at an enterprise-level gain importance (Den Broeder 1996, pp. 77-78). The coverage rate of collective agreements is high in Germany and the Netherlands as is the case in the Scandinavian countries. In the latter countries this is due to trade union density rates of over 80%. In Germany and in the Netherlands density rates are only 32% and 25% respectively. The high coverage rate in both countries (around 90%, SZW 1996, p. 62) is due to the widespread affiliation of employers in associations and the administrative extension of collective agreements.

On top of this, the *coordination* of collective bargaining is high in Germany and in the Netherlands. Trade unions tend to use guidelines from their peak-organisations as an input in sectoral negotiations. Employers' associations support collective bargaining and coordinate positions of affiliated employers. Finally, in the Netherlands employers' and workers' associations consult frequently at the central level in the so called *Stichting van de Arbeid* (The Foundation for Labour). A similar central platform for consultation does not exist in Germany and Den Broeder (1996, p. 75) concludes from this that coordination is less explicit ('less overt') in Germany.

In the Anglo-Saxon countries established structures for consultation and negotiation at a sectoral or central level do not exist. This entails that the government cannot exert influence on wage formation. The other extreme is Sweden where government interference in industrial relations is paramount (Lindbeck et al. 1994). In the Netherlands the government takes a more active stance in wage formation than in Germany where employers and workers have established *Tarifautonomie*, in which the state is granted no power to intervene in industrial relations (Lehmbruch 1996). This discrepancy in government interference may be an important element in an explanation of the diverging wage-performance of both countries during the 1980s and 1990s.

In the United States *employment protection* is largely effectuated through jurisprudence. In the European countries the emphasis is more on labour legislation. Both Germany and the Netherlands have, compared with the Anglo-Saxon countries, extensive dismissal procedures. On the other hand, in the Netherlands the restrictions on temporary labour are lenient. This is not the case in Germany and Sweden. The statutory maximum number of working hours both in Germany

---

World War to overcome the problem of 'dynamic inconsistency'. Wage restraint from the part of the workers was traded off against the precommitment on the employers' side to reinvest the revenues and hence further increase employment and prospected (future) real wage growth.

and the Netherlands is 48 hours per week. The UK until recently had no statutory maximum. In the USA the maximum is 44 hours. The differences between these four countries in regular, that is actual, full time working hours are only minor. In an overall ranking of eight countries the USA has the least regulation, followed by Denmark and the UK. The Netherlands occupy rank five followed by Sweden on six and Germany on rank seven (SZW 1996, p. 114).

An important aspect is the *enforcement* of legislation. Van Waarden (1997, p. 9) points to a difference between European countries such as the United Kingdom, Sweden and the Netherlands vis-à-vis the United States. American authorities are found to be less flexible in rule enforcement than authorities in several European countries. An example of different practices within the European countries is found in occupational health and safety (OHS) legislation. The British inspectorate uses OHS data on damages (workers compensation) to concentrate on those firms that have a high loss of labour: the grave offenders. In the UK the number of convictions is high in relation to the number of established offences: in 1993 for instance, 1793 inspectorate warrants resulted in 1507 convictions. The German inspectorate is relatively large (ten times as large as in the USA) and it carries out relatively many inspections (e.g. one-and-a-half times as many as in the Netherlands). In Germany also data on OHS-damages is used to select the firms to be inspected. Yet, in the number of convictions with respect to the number of established offences Germany falls far short to the United Kingdom. In the Netherlands likewise, the number of effective sanctions is low compared with the United Kingdom (SZW 1996, p. 136). The British thus manage to operate efficiently with a relatively small inspectorate.

A report of the Union of Industrial and Employers' Confederations of Europe reveals support for a strict supervision of clearly formulated rules (UNICE 1995, pp. 39-40). However, this supervision must focus on fundamental health and safety risks. In this respect the United Kingdom, Germany and the Netherlands all perform better than the USA (SZW 1996, p. 138).

4.3.1.3 Social Security

The social insurance model was initiated in late nineteenth century Germany and was explicitly designed to precommit the labour movement and the manufacturers to the interests of the nation state. On top of this, the aim to consolidate pre-existing distinctions in social stratification, has resulted in a multitude of specific insurance schemes (De Swaan 1989; Esping-Andersen 1990). In the Netherlands the Occupational Accidents Act came into effect in 1901. The establishment of a comprehensive framework of public social insurance and assistance schemes however, took more than half a century. The Unemployment Insurance Act (1952), General Old Age Pensions Act (1956), Income Support Act (1963) and Incapacity Insurance Act (1967) were established well after the Second World War. Both in the past and the present, the German and the Dutch public social insurance schemes use economic incentives for employers and workers for purposes of cost-containment. From the outset, the emphasis in social insurance in both countries has been on contribution-based financing and the schemes were largely administered by the social partners. In the Netherlands in the recent years some major policy reforms have been implemented. The level of benefits was left intact but eligibility criteria were tightened. Furthermore the administrative governance has been reformed in order to separate the *execution* of the social security schemes from employers' and workers' responsibilities and decentralise it to local administrative bodies. Moreover, sickness benefits have been privatised, the only restriction thereby being the entitlement of the workers to receive 70% of earnings and the maintenance of the public scheme as a safety net for vulnerable groups. The current reforms among others in the incapacity insurance scheme aim at the enhancement of competition among public insurers and an introduction of experience rating for employers. This subsection describes some features of the main income replacement schemes in Germany, the Netherlands, Sweden, the UK and the USA.

In the UK, as is typical for the Anglo-Saxon countries, social-security benefits are first and foremost targeted to those living on subsistence level. In *social assistance* (not in social insurance) means testing is common in Germany and the Netherlands as well. Benefit levels in social assistance schemes in these countries are rather generous as compared with the Anglo-Saxon countries. Table 4.11 reveals this. In the Netherlands the social assistance for single persons and couples without children in particular, are higher than in other countries. In Sweden and Germany benefits for (single parent) families with children are higher than in the Netherlands. Benefit levels in the UK and the USA are low compared with the continental European countries.

Table 4.11 Net social assistance benefit payments (after living expenses) in purchasing power parities ($US, 1994, net sums including subsidies)

	Single person	Couple no children	Couple two children	Single parent two children
Germany	3,360	6,073	10,069	8,685
Netherlands	4,173	7,362	8,764	7,900
Sweden	3,852	6,376	10,427	7,903
United Kingdom	2,819	4,515	8,038	6,484
United States[1]	2,952	4,596	7,788	6,908

[1] There are large differences across the American states. These amounts are the maximum benefit payments; the minimum figures for the four categories in the table are: -2,112, -2,388, 2,052 and 612 respectively. So, some states even pay negative benefits (calculated after subtracting living expenses).
Source: SZW 1996, p. 178.

The same picture is found in the *unemployment benefit* schemes. This is illustrated in Table 4.12. Germany and especially the Netherlands have high replacement rates for various categories of households, both for minimum wage earners and for average wage earners. The replacement rate is the ratio of the net benefit to the net earned wage. In comparison with Germany and the Netherlands the replacement rates for different types of households are much lower in the UK and in the USA. The incentive in those countries for benefit recipients to take a job therefore may be higher than in Germany and the Netherlands. In Germany and the Netherlands however, replacement rates decrease after some time which is clearly not the case for instance in California.

Table 4.12 Replacement rates of unemployment benefits, 1993

	Minimum wage earners				Average wage earners			
	Single-earner households with children		Single persons		Single-earner households with children		Single persons	
	start	5 yrs	start	5 yrs	start	5 yrs	start	5 yrs
Germany	111.8	111.8	78.6	78.6	74.0	68.6	61.1	54.8
Netherlands	99.5	99.5	84.8	84.8	81.5	76.6	74.2	56.8
United Kingdom	86.1	86.1	79.7	79.0	69.8	69.8	41.4	41.1
United States[1]								
NewYork	104.2	91.7	50.4	68.8	48.6	57.3	53.4	30.4
Texas	36.7	47.5	50.2	16.9	46.5	27.3	51.8	6.7
California	72.0	92.0	47.8	60.9	36.6	53.5	40.5	25.4

[1] Figures differ across states, therefore the figures of three states are given.
Source: SZW 1996, pp. 153-154.

Table 4.13 Eligibility criteria in unemployment benefits schemes, 1994

	Qualifying conditions[1]	Duration 1st period
Germany	52 of 3	0.5-2.67 years
Netherlands	208 of 5[2]	0.5-5 years
Sweden	13 of 1	up to pensionable age[3]
United Kingdom	50 of 2	0.5 year

[1] x of y; x number of weeks worked during the last y years.
[2] Plus 26 of the last 39 weeks for an earnings related benefit.
[3] The official duration is 14 months but after finishing a training program qualification is renewed.
Source: SZW 1996, p. 170.

The above picture of relatively generous German and Dutch replacement rates changes when *eligibility criteria* are taken into consideration. Figures for four countries are recorded in Table 4.13. In the Netherlands, the requirements for entry into the wage related benefit are relatively strict. One has to have worked for four out of five years and 26 out of the last 39 weeks. If one only meets the latter requirement, one receives a benefit of 70% of the minimum wage for six months. In Germany the requirement is one out of three years, in the UK it is one out of two years. In Sweden the required working time is 13 weeks in the last year. Both in Germany and the Netherlands the duration of the unemployment benefit depends on age and employment history. The maximum duration in Germany is 2.65 years; in the Netherlands this is 5 years. The duration in the UK and USA is 6 months, in Sweden it is one year and two months but the duration may be extended up to pensionable age because of job offers and training.

In the Netherlands and in the UK employers have to continue wage payments during absence due to *sickness* of their workers for a considerable period of time (see column one of Table 4.14). In the Netherlands this period recently has been extended and is now 52 weeks, in the UK it is 28 weeks. In Germany the employers have to continue payment for 6 weeks, in Sweden for 2 weeks. In the United States only five states have local statutory regulations; elsewhere employers are free to make agreements with their workers concerning the continuation of payment. In Germany and in the Netherlands the employers do not have to pay the full wage during sickness. In both countries however, full wage payment is collectively agreed upon by the majority of workers and employers.

Table 4.14 Some characteristics of the sickness and disability schemes

	Sickness			Disability		
	Employers risk[1]	Benefit level[2]	Med. certif.[3]	Qualifying conditions[4]	Min. % of disability	Benefit level[2]
Germany	6	100	yes	36 of 5	50	15-80
Netherlands	52	70	no	none	15	20-70
Sweden	2	75	yes	none	25	up to 65
United Kingdom	28	up to 85	yes	6 of 1		flat rate

[1] The statutory number of weeks the employer continues wage-payment during sickness.
[2] As a percentage of last earnings (the figures for sickness refer to the mid 1996 situation (for Germany it is now less than 100%); for disability they refer to the 1991 situation).
[3] Requirement of a medical certificate.
[4] x of y; x number of months worked in y years.
Source: SZW 1996, p. 140, p. 175.

In *disability* (as far as not covered by occupational accidents insurance) Germany has far less lenient conditions of entry than the Netherlands (Table 4.14, column four). The Netherlands in this respect are comparable with Sweden: no reference period is required and the minimum level of disability is set at 15% (the Netherlands) and 25% (Sweden) respectively. In Germany one has to have worked for three out of five years and a minimum reduction of one half of one's earnings capacity is required. A Reform Bill however has passed the Dutch Parliament in the spring of 1997 and reform measures will be implemented at the start of 1998. The reforms will entail a considerable enhancement of the employers risk in the case of disablement. Table 4.14 provides an overview of sickness and disability schemes in five countries. It shows the present state of affairs; future reforms are not included.

Germany, the United Kingdom and Sweden all have public *occupational accidents and diseases insurance schemes.* In Germany and to a lesser extent in Sweden the insurers put considerable effort into prevention and re-integration of sick employees. In the UK this is not the case. The same is true for the USA where occupational accidents insurance is a private market. The Netherlands do not have a separate occupational accidents and diseases insurance scheme at all.[4]

In the Netherlands we observe a significant increase in the number of liability claims, presumably due to the recent and forthcoming reforms in the sickness and disability legislature (SZW 1996, p. 141). The Anglo-Saxon countries traditionally have a claims culture whereas liability claims in Sweden and in Germany still are relatively rare. The incentives for employers in these two countries appear therefore to be more directed at the maintenance and restoration of favourable working conditions. The emphasis is more on commitment whereas in the Netherlands, as in the USA and UK, it is perhaps more on financial compensation after an accident has occurred, or employees have become ill.

4.3.2 Disparities in Policy and Institutions

Related to *industrial relations* differences in German and Dutch policy and institutions are found first and foremost in the involvement of the government in wage formation. Geelhoed (1996, pp. 22-29) emphasises this point. The German authorities ever since 1949 have abstained from compulsive intervention in wage formation. Government interference is considered only legitimate in extreme economic circumstances. The autonomy of the social partners is embedded in the Constitution (Lehmbruch 1996).

In the Netherlands in the decades after the Second World War the government determined wages. In the 1960s economic growth and a short labour supply led to a gradual liberalisation that became materialised in the 1970 Wage Determination Act. Government interventions in wage formation remained frequent although, at least up to 1982. Hemerijck has coined the term 'immobile corporatism' to characterise the nature of Dutch corporatism in the 1970s (Hemerijck 1992, p. 164). Controlling public expenditure came to depend on wage moderation. This was due to two mechanisms that were institutionalised in the 1970s. One was the indexation of social minimum standards and public sector salaries to the contractual (market) wage increases. The other mechanism was the practice of indexing contractual wages to inflation (the automatism of cost-of-living adjustments). These 'built-in fiscal destabilisers' captured the government in a

---

[4] The Occupational Accidents Act was replaced by the Incapacity Insurance Act of 1967.

corporatist deadlock (Hemerijck 1992, pp. 168-171). In 1982 the emphasis in the governments position shifted from tripartite concertation to a more technocratic stance. The new centre-right government sidetracked the corporatist institutions by implementing an austerity policy without consulting the tripartite Social and Economic Council (Hemerijck 1992, p. 184). The institutional 'built-in destabilisers' were called off in order to restore government control over public expenditure. The government position from then onwards was that institutional indexation of social minimum standards and public sector salaries was rested on private sector wage moderation. And, as Hemerijck (1992, p. 185) puts it: "By disengaging the coupling mechanism, it not only endowed the state with renewed autonomy over the public budget, ironically, in addition, it also granted the government more control over the private sector. Surprisingly, the public sector now became the trend-setter for the private sector, rather than the other way round." This in turn, put considerable pressure on the social partners to reach a bi-partite agreement. The November 1982 bi-partite 'Wassenaar-agreement' initiated an extensive wage moderation process. The Dutch government has refrained from intervention in private sector wage formation from 1983 onwards.

In *health care* one difference between Germany and the Netherlands stands out in particular. This is the relatively large market-share of *private* health care *insurers* in the Netherlands compared with Germany. In Germany 8% of the population is privately insured; in the Netherlands this is 37%. This is still relatively minor as compared with the United States where 64% is privately insured. Only 20% of Americans is publicly insured (Medicare and Medicaid) and 16% of the population has no insurance at all (White 1995, p. 36). The private health insurance sector has a considerable stake in health care reform policies. Schut (1995) in this respect points at the deficiencies in the Dutch corporatist model with respect to health care. Interest organisations of health care providers and health insurers are rather pluralist and less inclined to engage in compromises. This has been reflected in the experiences with health care reform in the Netherlands in the early 1990s. Health care reform proposals in the USA and the Netherlands were blocked to a large extent because the proposals did not fit in with the interests of private health insurers (see for the USA: White 1995, pp. 254-255; and for the Netherlands: Schut 1995, pp. 78-81).

In German public health insurance there is no *Tarifautonomie*. The legal bargaining framework is self-administration supervised by the government (Lehmbruch 1996). In a sequential process the government from the late 1980s onwards has incorporated medical providers in this framework, that consists of an aggregate budget-cap that leaves the various categories of medical providers with the problem of distributing revenues. The final step, the incorporation of the hospital sector, is currently prepared. Lehmbruch (1996, p. 6) comments on this as follows: "All in all, the corporatist repertoire in the system of public health insurance (including strong monitoring by government) has been steadily expanding in the last decade, and while this development fuelled distributional conflicts within the different groups of medical providers, the system as such has remained fairly effective as long as the state proves capable to act."

4.4 The Impact of the Welfare State on Competitiveness

4.4.1 Introduction

The previous sections have shed a light on several disparities and similarities in German and Dutch economic performances and in welfare state institutions. In the introduction I have posed two questions: i) to what extent are economic performances determined by welfare state institutions?, and ii) are there differences in German and Dutch institutions that explain the current diverging economic performances of both economies? We are now better equiped to address these questions. This section proposes to take a closer look into the mechanisms (the conduct of economic agents) through which the institutional infrastructure determines economic outcomes.

The plan of this section is as follows. Subsection 4.4.2 examines wage formation in industrial relations. With respect to the conduct of trade unions, there is a distinction between the two liberal market economies (the UK and USA) and the three concerted economies (Germany, the Netherlands and Sweden); but there are differences within the three concerted economies as well. Dutch trade unions, in exerting modest wage demands, have been rather responsive to the macroeconomic situation. German trade unions have exerted less restraint, in particular in the early 1990s and in 1995. In Subsection 4.4.2.1 I will argue that the extensive Dutch bargaining coordination and in particular the role of the government in creating conducive macroeconomic conditions marks the difference between the Netherlands on one hand, and Germany and for example Sweden on the other. Subsection 4.4.2.2 covers persistent unemployment. This has been ascribed to the existence of labour market rigidities. Indeed there is evidence that institutions in continental Europe have an effect on the earnings distribution. I will explore whether this affects labour market outcomes. The point of reference will be the employment opportunities for the low-skilled. Subsection 4.4.3 addresses the impact of the welfare state on household income inequality. I will assess first whether welfare state programmes of a different signature are equally effective in serving equity objectives. Subsequently I will discuss the efficiency of welfare state institutions.

4.4.2 Wage Flexibility

4.4.2.1 Macroeconomic Wage Flexibility and Collective Bargaining

Wages react to events such as inflation, unemployment, shifts in the terms of trade (e.g. an oil-price shock) and productivity growth. In the long term wages adjust but in the short and medium term they may do so at more or less speed: in the first case wages are flexible, in the second they are sticky. Apart from the events mentioned in the first line, the occurrence of persistent unemployment may diminish downward adjustments in the wage level. This issue will be taken up in the next subsection.

In general wage flexibility has to be large. However, the direction of the adjustment matters as well. This may not be self-evident but can be illustrated with an example. Suppose a deterioration in the terms of trade due to a boost in oil-prices. Then, a quick upward adjustment of the wage level to compensate for the negative terms-of-trade effect would easily induce an inflationary process. This has been the case in most industrialised countries during the period following the first oil-crisis in 1974 (Franzmeyer et al. 1996, p. 29). On the other hand, the current low inflation environment in several OECD countries requires some downward adjustment potential of real wages. Otherwise, a deceleration of inflation would ceteris paribus lead to an automatic rise in real wages.

Empirical research points to a level of *wage flexibility* in both Germany and the Netherlands that is comparable with the USA. Blanchflower and Oswald for example, find little variance in *real* wage flexibility: they report an elasticity of wages with respect to unemployment of -0.08 in the UK, -0.10 in the USA, -0,13 in Germany and -0,18 in the Netherlands (Blanchflower and Oswald 1995). Layard et al. (1990, p. 58) report a rather high nominal wage rigidity in the USA partly because of the prevalence of long-term contracts.[5] Apparently wages in Germany and the Netherlands have responded reasonably to fluctuations in the unemployment rate and seem to have adjusted to the reduced inflation level in the past 1½ decade. An exception is the early 1990s period when unit labour costs in Germany, and to a lesser extent in the Netherlands too, have risen considerably (OECD 1996d, p. A16). In a longer time perspective however, unit labour costs have risen only slightly in the Netherlands: 9.2% during the period 1980-1994. The USA and Germany take mid-range positions: 27.3% and 41.9% respectively. In the UK (70.4%) and Sweden (79%) unit labour costs have risen much steeper in the past 1½ decade (Roorda and Vogels 1997, p. 53).

These results challenge the *hump-shape* argument put forward by Calmfors and Driffill 1988. They have argued that the impact of increasing centralisation on wages depends on two forces which work in opposite directions: bargaining power and the effect of wages on prices. More centralised unions acquire greater bargaining power and hence will be able to command higher wages. Yet, when the scope of bargaining extends beyond the industry level, the effect of nominal wages on the aggregate price level will become more important. Hence, the real wage gains of a given nominal wage increase are limited. Calmfors 1993 has entered several caveats with respect to the argument. Account must be taken of historical traditions and structural characteristics: "different wage-setting institutions may contribute to good macroeconomic performance in different places" (Calmfors 1993, p. 182). Next, the openness of economies to foreign competitors will force wage restraint in bargaining at industry level and at firm level alike. Moreover, Calmfors argues that cooperative and coordinated wage setting can take different forms. It may or may not entail multi-level bargaining. And last but not least, pattern bargaining (in which certain industries act as wage leaders) can be regarded as a method of informal cooperation (Calmfors 1993, p. 171).

---

[5] The evidence is mixed; the OECD for example, reports with respect to the USA that it "does not seem to display much downward rigidity" (OECD 1996e, p. 93).

The empirical results above indicate that those countries in our sample with trade unions operating at an intermediate level (Germany and the Netherlands) do not perform worse on aggregate real wage flexibility than countries where unions operate at enterprise level (USA and UK) or at a central level (Sweden, until the mid 1980s). Moreover, Germany and the Netherlands have good records on the subject of *industrial conflicts*. In the period 1982-1993 the Netherlands lost an average per year of 17 days per thousand workers, Germany an average of 19 days. The United States (78 days), Sweden (97 days) and the United Kingdom (109 days) on average lose far more working days in conflicts. On first sight there seems to be no strong connection between strike intensity and the development of wages (as revealed in Section 4.2.1). Sweden for instance has had a moderate wage increase, when measured in German marks, despite a relatively large number of strikes. The reverse goes for Germany. In Germany however, an upward trend in industrial conflicts in the 1990s has been observed (Schröder and Van Suntum 1996). On top of this, the wage increase in Sweden measured in Swedish currency: in Krona (the third column in Table 4.6), by far exceeds the wage increase in German marks. The Swedish trade unions therefore, like the German, do appear to have been successful in forcing wage increases. The OECD (1994, p. 11, 18) reports for Germany and the Nordic countries that sectoral or central bargaining often sets wage floors that are subsequently added to at lower levels. Since the exchange rate of the Swedish Krona has deteriorated considerably in the same period, for the Swedish workers this has been merely a Pyrrhic victory (Lindbeck et al. 1994).

Streeck 1995 and Lehmbruch 1996 describe the erosion of the German corporatist model, which they perceive to be the outcome of globalisation and the crisis that emerged in the aftermath of the unification. Discontented employers have challenged the corporatist high wage strategy that all parties until recently adhered to. The president of the Federation of German Industries (BDI) has called for the abandonment of traditional centralised bargaining in favour of firm-level bargaining (Lehmbruch 1996; Soskice et al., Chapter 2 in this volume). Hence to conclude that German industrial relations currently appear to be in serious disarray, probably will not be wide beside the mark.

However, in order to assess the diagnosis and proposed solutions it may prove worthwhile to take account of the Dutch track-record. The Netherlands in fact, has had both a moderate wage development (both in German marks and in Dutch guilders) and a low strike intensity. In the Netherlands, trade unions have shown a considerable restraint in their wage demands in the 1980s and from 1992 onwards. Part of the explanation is the traditional high exposure of the Dutch economy to foreign competition, rendering it less vulnerable to the current internationalisation process. The core of the explanation however, lies in the wage-formation framework. The Dutch government throughout the 1980s and in the 1990s has supported wage moderation with parallel public expenditure policies (as described in the previous sections). On top of this, wage drift at a more decentralised level generally did not occur due to a high degree of vertical bargaining coordination.

The growth in employment in the centralised Nordic countries, if any, has been caused by a sharp expansion in public employment. In Sweden a substantial increase in public employment has just offset the decline in private employment. In the United States both public and private employment expanded strongly in the period 1970-1995. In the Netherlands the more recent employment growth has occurred in the private sector as well, whereas in Germany the increase over the same period largely has taken place in the public sector (Franzmeyer et al. 1996, p. 14). These figures, combined with those concerning the wage increases in the past, point to the positive impact of real wage restraint on employment growth (as argued for example in OECD 1994, p. 20).

4.4.2.2 Structural Unemployment and Labour Market Adjustment

The high shares of long-term unemployment in total unemployment in Germany and the Netherlands indicate that structural unemployment does not exert much downward pressure on wage levels in both countries. This calls for an explanation. The low proportion of long-term unemployed in the United States and Sweden points to a better performing adjustment mechanism. According to Table 4.15 in Sweden wages respond strongly to the level of unemployment. In the USA this is much less the case but there geographic mobility is more important as a mechanism to bring back unemployment to its long-term equilibrium level (OECD 1994, p. 67).

Table 4.15 Econometric estimates of wage effects of long-term unemployment (1970-1991)

	Estimated effect	(t-value)
Germany	-1.26	(8.4)
Netherlands	-0.99	(9.3)
Sweden	-1.59	(3.9)
United Kingdom	-0.54	(6.0)
United States	-0.60	(5.0)

Source: OECD 1993, p. 94.

The OECD has come up with an institutional explanation for the persistence of unemployment in several continental European countries, pointing to rigidities in (i) the wage formation process, (ii) employment protection legislation and (iii) social security schemes (OECD 1994, Ch. 5). The OECD admits that changes in institutions from the 1980s onwards have not likely aggravated rigidities; if any, they would have alleviated rigidities; still, the increase in the structural rate of unemployment may have been related to changes in the institutional arrangements in the 1970s (OECD 1994, p. 4). However, some have argued that, since the level of unemployment in Europe appears to be path-dependent (*hysteresis*), the timing of macroeconomic policy is extremely important as well (Franzmeyer et al. 1996). Still, the mere existence of rigidities may be sufficient to turn macroeconomic shocks into permanent unemployment. The adjustment potential of labour markets in Europe at the outset of the 1980s was less than in the USA. On top of this, US fiscal and monetary policies in the mid-1980s have provided more leeway for expansion, than policies in Europe at the same time did. A recent International Labour Office Report has submitted some evidence that growth oriented policies do indeed matter (ILO 1996). This subsection will not elaborate on this; instead it will explore the differences in labour market outcomes of the liberal market economies (the USA and UK) and the neo-corporatist economies (Germany, the Netherlands and Sweden). This, in order to assess whether liberal market economies perform better, different or perhaps even worse than neo-corporatist ones.

Table 4.16 Trends in earnings dispersion, 1985-1995

	D9/D5		D5/D1	
	1985	1995	1985	1995
Germany[1]	1.65	1.61	1.59	1.44
Netherlands[2]	1.62	1.66	1.55	1.56
Sweden[1]	1.59	1.59	1.30	1.30
United Kingdom	1.77	1.87	1.73	1.81
United States[3]	1.84	2.04	2.03	2.13

D1 and D9 refer to the upper limits of respectively, the first and ninth decile of employees ranked in order of their earnings from lowest to highest, i.e. 10% of employees earn less than the D1 earnings limit and 90% earn less than the D9 earnings limit. D5 is defined similarly and corresponds to the median earnings.

[1] Last year is 1993.
[2] Last year is 1994.
[3] Data refer to male earners.

Source: OECD 1996c, pp. 61-62.

The internationalisation of trade, structural economic change (the emerging services sector) and technological change are generally assumed to determine the widening of *wage differentials* in several countries, such as the USA and the UK (Atkinson et al. 1995, p. 83). Some credit internationalisation, others emphasise structural and technological change. In any case, these factors of influence are difficult to disentangle (OECD 1996d, p. 39) and we observe widening wage differentials in some countries, notably the United States and the United Kingdom, whereas we do not observe a widening of the wage spread in other countries as, for instance, Sweden and Germany (Charts 3.1 and 3.2 in OECD 1996c, pp. 64-65 are instructive). Table 4.16 gives some results. In Germany since 1985 the D9/D5 ratio (the spread in high earnings) was stable; the D5/D1 ratio (the spread in low earnings) has even declined in the past ten years. In the Netherlands, as in Sweden, the table shows a slight rise in both the D9/D5 and the D5/D1 ratios. In the USA the widening in the earnings distribution was accompanied by a fall in the real wages of the low paid workers (i.e. the bottom decile). This has not been the case in the UK. The real wages of the bottom decile have risen despite a more uneven earnings distribution (OECD 1996c, p. 67).

The incidence of low paid employment is inversely related to the occurrence of collective wage-setting practices and the extent of social security arrangements (OECD 1996c, pp. 71-76). The figures in Table 4.16 for a smaller sample of countries confirm this: in Germany, the Netherlands and Sweden, the earnings distribution has remained fairly stable in the past decade. The existence of a central and/or a sectoral structure for consultation and negotiation in industrial relations and other institutions, such as legal minimum wages and relative generous welfare benefits, appear to set a binding wage floor and prevent a widening of the earnings distribution to occur (OECD 1996c, p. 60).

Having established a link between the welfare state and the earnings distribution, the question remains as *to what extent welfare state institutions* (including wage formation in industrial relations) *inhibit the performance of the labour market*? A first observation (from Table 4.4 above) is that unemployment in Germany, the Netherlands and Sweden is not more concentrated among low skilled than is the case in the USA and the UK. The OECD supports this by concluding that "there is little solid evidence to suggest that countries where low paid work is less prevalent have achieved this at the cost of higher unemployment rates and lower employment rates for the more vulnerable groups in the labour market, ..." (OECD 1996c, p. 76). A second observation (see Table 4.3 above) is that long-term unemployment is high in Germany and the Netherlands but in the UK as well. In the UK, since the early 1990s the proportion of long-term unemployed has risen more than the overall rate of unemployment (OECD 1996f, Figure 15 panel C, p. 84). All this would suggest "that factors other than relative wages, such as the overall level of aggregate demand or the amount of training received, may be more important for determining labour market outcomes of [vulnerable] groups." (OECD 1996c, p. 94). Indeed Germany, the Netherlands and Sweden on educational attainment perform rather well as compared with the UK and have established sophisticated vocational training systems that do not exist (or at least to a far lesser extent exist) in both Anglo-Saxon countries (see Subsection 4.2.1). On the other hand, this does not rule out the possibility that a widening of the wage spread may well be effective in Germany, the Netherlands and Sweden as a policy measure to lower the share of unemployed in the low-skilled segment. Franzmeyer et al. (1996, p. 24) point at this: "As the growing dispersion of wages does not result in a decline of overall unemployment in the UK and US, because the overall quality of their labour supply is too low, the strategy of fighting unemployment among low-skilled workers by reducing their [labour costs] might, in fact, work in countries with well-functioning systems of vocational and company training." This would provide some support for policies (as currently implemented in the Netherlands) that aim at lowering the non-wage labour costs, targeted at the low-skilled end of the labour market.

For an adequate analysis of the performance of the labour market one must further take into account whether a prevailing level of earnings inequality is efficient from a microeconomic point of view. Two topics stand out in this respect: (i) are there *rent seeking* effects due to institutional rigidities or concentration in industrial relations?; and (ii) are individuals in the bottom earnings deciles to a large extent new entrants who will subsequently advance into higher deciles or are they part of a static pool caught in low paid jobs of poor quality, cycling in and out of unemployment? (the OECD 1996f, p. 96, labels this as the key issue in assessing microeconomic efficiency). The remainder of this subsection will discuss both topics.

Rent seeking due to a concentration of power of trade unions is reflected in the *union mark up* on wages. Such a mark up could be expected if the proportion of union members among workers in a firm or a sector is high. American unions appear to realise high wage mark ups (of over 20%) compared with the UK, Germany (both circa 8%) and the Netherlands (approximately 4%). Both in Germany and the Netherlands the extensive coverage of collective agreements (Subsection 4.3.1.2 reported a coverage rate of circa 90%) may provide an explanation for these results. Hartog and Teulings (1994, p. 79) suggest that corporatism reduces non-competitive wage differentials and thus serves both efficiency and equity objectives. For the UK a decrease in unionisation in the 1980s is considered to be offset by an increase of the power of large firms in wage setting. This *size of firm* effect on the level of wages is relatively large in the USA, the UK and Sweden: e.g. in the United Kingdom a 10% increase in the number of workers in a firm results in a 0.47% wage increase; this size of firm effect is more moderate in Germany (0.31%) and it is minor in the Netherlands (0.06%). Roorda and Vogels (1997, pp. 92-101) provide an overview of the literature of non-competitive pay differentials.

Table 4.17 gives some data on *earnings mobility* in Germany, the USA, the UK and Sweden. The data are from Chapter 3 of the OECD *Employment Outlook 1996* and unfortunately the Netherlands was not included in the sample of countries. All countries have a correlation coefficient, measuring the persistence in individual earnings over a five year period, that ranges in between 0.68 (USA) and 0.79 (Germany). This means for example that roughly two-thirds of inequality observed in the USA in a single year is persistent. The table also reveals transition probabilities for moving upward (column 2). These transition probabilities give the likelihood that a worker who for instance was in the bottom quintile in 1986 still was in the bottom quintile five years later. To control for the effect of a wider earnings dispersion in some countries (USA, UK) on the width of the quintiles (thus influencing the transition probabilities of moving up one quintile or more), the table (column 3) gives also transition probabilities in 'equal width earnings bands' (OECD 1996c, pp. 78-79 explains the methodology). In the USA 49% remained in the same quintile; in Germany this is 53%. Measured in earnings bands the difference is a little more pronounced but still small. The largest difference between the two countries is the percentage of workers that moved up two earnings bands: 17% in the USA and 7% in Germany (not in the table). The OECD finds some evidence of a positive relationship between point-in-time earnings inequality and mobility across median-proportions earnings bands (OECD 1996c, Chart 3.6A, p. 84). Individual earnings in fact, tend to be more volatile in the USA than in for example Germany.

Table 4.17 Earnings mobility, 1986-1991

Panel A Five years earnings mobility for full-time wage and salary workers

	Correlation of 1986 and 1991 earnings[1]	Stayed in the same quintile	Stayed in the same earnings band[2]
Germany	0.793	53.0	55.3
Sweden	0.711	52.7	61.6
United Kingdom	0.705	48.1	48.2
United States	0.680	48.8	47.8

Panel B Five years earnings mobility low-paid workers who were employed full-time both in 1986 and 1991

	1991 Earnings status of 1986 low paid workers			
	In bottom quintile	Moved to 2nd-5th qnt.	Below 0.65 median	Moved above 0.65 median
Germany	45.1	54.9	26.0	74.0
Sweden	49.1	50.9	-	-
United Kingdom	41.1	58.9	39.0	61.0
United States	52.2	47.8	55.8	44.2

[1] Pearson correlation coefficient.
[2] The five earnings bands relative to the median are: Less than 0.65, 0.65 to 0.95, 0.95 to 1.25, 1.25 to 1.55, and greater than 1.55.
Source: OECD 1996c, p. 81, p. 95.

The key issue, however, is whether this is also the case for low-paid workers. Is there evidence of a trade-off between point-in-time inequality and life-time inequality? Panel B in Table 4.17 gives the results.[6] The probability for Ameri-

[6] For the Netherlands De Beer has examined the upward earnings mobility of Dutch workers who were in the bottom quarter both in 1985 and in 1991. After six (four) years 27.6% (36%) were still in the bottom quarter and 72.4% (64%) moved upward. Compare this with Germany and the USA in Table 4.17: after five years 54.9% of German workers has moved upward and 47.8% of American workers. Of Dutch workers who were in the bottom quarter in 1985, 25% had left employment after four years and 31% after six years. This suggests that the upward mobility of Dutch low-paid workers is comparable with or perhaps even better than the German figures (source: De Beer 1996. The calculations are mine).

can workers to remain in the bottom quintile is larger than for German workers. Moreover, the probability for moving up in terms of median-proportion earnings bands is much higher in Germany than in the USA: only 26% of German workers who were in 1986 below 0.65 of median earnings still were in this range in 1991; in the USA this is 56%. More generally the OECD concludes that low-paid workers have greater difficulty moving up in labour markets in which cross-sectional inequality is higher (OECD 1996c, p. 91; Chart 3.6B, p. 84 is instructive).

It may be concluded that in Germany and the Netherlands real wages have responded to fluctuations in the unemployment rate and have adjusted to the reduced level of inflation in the past 1½ decade. Both countries, characterised by trade unions operating at the sectoral level, perform well on macroeconomic wage flexibility. Moreover, the Dutch trade unions have shown a considerable restraint in the 1980s and in recent years in their wage claims. This has been ascribed to the Dutch system of wage formation and the position of the government towards the social partners. Structural unemployment however, does not exert sufficient downward pressure on German and Dutch wages. This has resulted in high proportions of long-term unemployed in both countries.

Both with respect to non-competitive earnings differentials as to earnings mobility for low-paid workers, the liberalised labour markets of the USA and UK do not perform better than the German and Dutch labour markets. The volatility of individual earnings is higher in the Anglo-Saxon countries as is the overall earnings mobility. But the key issue in assessing microeconomic efficiency is the extent to which low-paid workers benefit from this and this appears less the case for the liberalised labour markets of the USA and UK than for Germany and the Netherlands.

4.4.3 Equity and Efficiency of the Welfare State

Turning from earnings inequality to *household income* inequality two aspects are relevant. The first is the employment effect on the distribution of earnings. As the net labour participation rate is relatively low in the Netherlands and to a lesser extent in Germany as well, the difference between for example the USA and both the Netherlands and Germany in the distribution of household income from employment will reflect a wage effect and an employment effect. In thinking about the impact of labour market reforms on labour income inequality – and if certain income distribution targets are to be met, on redistributional policies – the relative importance of the two effects should be assessed. Taking the employment record of the USA as an example the OECD has concluded that the employment effect may be large. The distribution of earnings of working age households is less equal in the Netherlands than in the USA (OECD 1996d, pp. 40-41). Economists are ill-equiped to judge whether an occurring earnings distribution is equitable: an efficient distribution of earnings is equitable from an economists point of view. However, the previous subsection suggests that the American earnings distribution is not efficient from the point of view of low-paid workers. The share of low skilled out-of-employment is large and there appears to be a substantial cycling in and out of low labour income (OECD 1996d, p. 41).[7] On top of this, upward labour mobility for US low-paid workers is small. In an effort to combine equity and efficiency targets the United States and the United Kingdom have implemented *in-work benefits* (Earned income tax-credit in the USA and Family credit in Brittain). These benefits are phased out as earnings rise and are thus designed to benefit low-paid workers. This has resulted in a high marginal wedge for instance in Brittain in the range of earnings up to 77% APW level. Removing the unemployment trap has thus been effected at the expense of increasing the incidence of the poverty trap: there is less incentive to increase effort once in work (OECD 1996f, p. 94). Still, a reduction of the average wedge on low-skilled labour, even at the expense of increasing the marginal wedge at a relatively short earnings interval, may prove to be a way out of the equity-efficiency dilemma. An alternative is the lowering of non-wage labour costs as is currently undertaken by several continental European countries.

The second aspect to be taken up are the *welfare state income redistribution programmes*. In the objectives of these programmes a distinction can be made in i) equity objectives such as poverty relief and inequality reduction and ii) efficiency objectives: such as insurance that for technical reasons is not or cannot be provided by the private market. The remainder of this section examines first whether the German, Dutch and Swedish *universal* welfare states are more effective in poverty relief and income redistribution than the *residual* Anglo-Saxon welfare states. The aim is to assess whether welfare state programmes of a different signature are equally effective in serving equity objectives. The second issue that is addressed is the efficiency of welfare state institutions. What are the arguments for public insurance? Moreover, is the case for the welfare state supported from the evidence from the previous sections? An effort is made to provide some tentative answers.

Table 4.18 panel A gives some figures concerning the contribution of social security to the decline in *poverty* (i.e. a household income below 50% of average income; the data refer to the mid 1980s). The number of pre-transfer poor households is least reduced in the United States. The poverty gap (the number of poor households multiplied by the income gap) in the USA is reduced after income transfers but remains high. The UK resembles the two continental European countries although the difference is more pronounced when household income with respect to *median* income is taken (SZW 1996, Table 7.7, p. 223). Both the number of poor households and the poverty gap is reduced most in the Netherlands. Panel B of Table 4.18 gives the distribution of transfers. Not surprising is that social security benefits in the USA are low as a percentage of

[7] Stiglitz (1996) reports a marked improvement in the 1993-1996 period, both in the growth of high skilled full-time employment and in median income. Still, the data from the 1981-1993 period indicate that job losers were more likely to be permanently dismissed (rather than temporarily laid-off), that older workers were subject to greater risk of job displacement and that the average real wage loss due to displacement was significant and persistent.

Table 4.18 The contribution of social security to the decline of poverty[1]

Panel A Reduction in percentage households with less than half of average income

	Perc. poor households before benefits	Perc. poor households after benefits	Poverty gap before benefits	Poverty gap after benefits
Germany	40.5	10.3	50.8	4.6
Netherlands	43.6	9.9	57.8	3.8
United Kingdom	45.1	12.4	55.5	7.0
United States	35.8	23.2	79.9	34.4

Panel B Average transfers as percentage of median income[2]

	Quintiles bottom 1	2	3	4	top 5	Overall average
Germany	21.6	21.9	16.5	20.8	18.2	19.8
Netherlands	35.2	30.2	23.9	25.1	27.2	28.3
Sweden	27.0	45.7	38.5	35.4	30.9	35.5
United Kingdom	32.4	31.4	23.5	19.6	14.5	24.3
United States	13.7	9.9	8.0	8.2	7.1	9.4

Panel C Duration of poverty

	Perc. of households with an income below 0.5 median in one year	three years long	reduction[3]
Germany	7.8	1.5	81
Netherlands	2.7	0.4	85
United States	20.3	14.4	29

[1] Data refer to the mid 1980s.
[2] Equivalent household income (see Atkinson et al. 1995, p. 18).
[3] Percentage of households that has escaped poverty within three years.
Source: SZW 1996, p. 216, p. 223; Atkinson et al. 1995, p. 107.

median income and are more targeted to the bottom quintile than in the European countries (note that the data for the UK concern the 1986 situation). Last but not least the persistence of poverty is relevant for an assessment of the efficacy of social security schemes. Panel C of Table 4.18 reveals the number of households remaining in poverty for three years or more. The difference between the USA and both Germany and the Netherlands is striking: only 29% of American poor households have escaped poverty after three years vis-à-vis over 80% in Germany and the Netherlands.

In the discussion on the *efficiency of the welfare state* income transfers are generally assumed to cause disincentive effects. Empirical evidence however, is ambiguous (Aaron 1982, pp. 82-83). Barr concludes even that: "the issue is not only unresolved, but may remain so" (Barr 1992, p. 773). Several theoretical arguments have been forwarded in favour of the welfare state. First the enhancement of risk taking: insurance against the loss of income induces risk-taking. Viewed in this perspective there may not be a trade-off between equity and efficiency at all.[8] Equity may in fact be an aspect of efficiency, as argued by Sinn, although income redistribution programmes have to be well-designed in order not to overshoot the optimal level of risk taking, known as moral hazard (Sinn 1995, p. 2). Sinn further concludes: "Given that the government offers public insurance, the need for self-insurance is reduced. Redistributive taxation with individually tailored transfers increases the marginal post-tax return to risk taking and lowers the marginal compensation for risk taking that economic agents require. This makes it socially optimal to tolerate more risk and inequality in exchange for a higher level of average income. Under the protection of the welfare state more can be dared." (Sinn 1995, p. 12).

In line with this is a set of arguments that emphasise the *efficiency of public insurance*. Due to adverse selection and moral hazard, the insurer does not obtain all the information he requires to calculate a fair (actuarial) premium. Adverse selection (the opting-out of the lowest risks pushing up the average insurance premium and thus enhancing the incentive for second-lowest risks to opt out, et cetera) points to a diversion in efficiency from the point of view of the individual or group of individuals with a common risk-profile on the one hand, and the aggregate community on the other hand. This cannot be solved adequately through the market. On top of this for some events the probability may be unpredictable (future inflation in pensions schemes) or interdependent (unemployment in the business cycle) or close to unity (the case of the chronically ill). Pure private insurance in these cases is infeasible. There is consensus among economists that these issues call for "*social insurance*: pooling arrangements that are not actuarially sound, and hence require support from compulsory taxation" (Robert Lucas as quoted by Barr 1992, p. 754). As Barr further points out: "if preferences are sufficiently similar, the welfare loss from compulsion may be minimal" (Barr 1992, p. 752). Indeed, a comparison of aggregate shares of net social expenditure (both public and private; see Section 4.2) suggests that this is the case. The preferences for social protection, whether provided publicly or privately, are found to be very homogenous in Germany, the Netherlands, Sweden, the United Kingdom and the United States: the share of net total expenditure in these five countries is in a range of 25 to 33% of GDP. This entails that a reduction in *public* social expenditure, as has been proposed as a part of welfare state reform throughout the advanced industrial world, will not to the same extent reduce *total* social expenditure: substitution effects may be expected.

[8] The concept of a trade-off between equity (equality) and efficiency has been coined by Arthur M. Okun in 1975 in an essay *Equality and Efficiency: The Big Trade-off.*

At a less aggregate level, the poor efficiency of the American private health care insurance and private occupational health and safety insurance is a case in point. Competition among insurers generates extra expenses in the sale, purchase and administration of insurance (White 1995, p. 59, p. 153). Initially, when it took office, the Thatcher-government advocated a reform of the British National Health Service that aimed to substitute private health insurance for public provision. The plans were rejected soon, in 1982, when it turned out that private insurance was not a means to contain costs (Pierson 1995, p. 133, remarks: "However unattractive to conservative ideology, the concentration of control over health-care provision had proven to be a powerful cost-containment technique."). For occupational health and safety insurance the difference in administration costs between the USA and Germany, the UK and Sweden has been estimated (SZW 1996, p. 141). The latter three all have public insurance schemes with administration costs that are approximately 10% of total outlays; in the USA on the other hand, administration costs in private insurance are about 40%. The conclusion therefore in line with Pierson would be "that the efficiency argument for many aspects of social insurance remains persuasive, as does the case for many public-sector programmes that the private sector is inclined to treat as externalities" (Pierson 1995, p. 181).

The previous Subsection 4.4.2 discussed the prevailing level of earnings inequality. In the present subsection differences in net labour participation were taken into account. The OECD finds that this *employment effect* on the distribution of income from employment is particularly large and claims that the pre-tax income distribution in for example the Netherlands resembles that of the USA. However, the pre-tax household income distribution leaves many households on both sides of the Atlantic Ocean below the poverty threshold. Income redistribution is designed to cope with this. The evidence points out that *extensive* welfare states are better equiped than *residual* ones to deal with poverty. The evidence is less outspoken when it comes to the *efficiency* of welfare state institutions. A high marginal wedge will induce certain disincentives, for example a reduced labour supply. But social security on the other hand induces risk-taking and may further investment in human capital and economic growth. Porter (1990, p. 344) in discussing the competitive advantages of Sweden conceives of social security as a 'selective factor disadvantage', meaning that it has contributed to the competitiveness of Swedish industries because it has compelled the Swedes to upgrade the skills of their working force. Streeck has commented on the "German model [that its success] derived from the way in which it utilised social pressures for an egalitarian distribution of economic resources to generate an egalitarian distribution of productive capabilities, *with the latter in turn enabling the economy to underwrite the former*" (Streeck 1995, pp. 14-15, his italics). The net effect of social security is not determined nor is it determinable. Much will depend on the exact distribution of taxes and revenues, eligibility-criteria and so forth. On top of this, preferences for social security (be it public or private) are similar across the board. Residual welfare states *on aggregate*[9] do not spend less on social security than universal welfare states.

4.5 Conclusions

To conclude, I will discuss in brief three topics. First, I will readdress the question: are there differences in economic performances between welfare states and liberal market economies (or, for that matter, *universal* and *residual* welfare states)? Second, I will recollect from Section 4.3 the main characteristics of the institutional infrastructure and undertake an effort to combine this with what has been described in Section 4.4 on mechanisms of conduct. Third, I shall return to the two countries that were central in the outset: the Federal Republic of Germany and the Netherlands: what marks the difference between the two?

The labour market record of the USA is often taken as an example to European welfare states to point out that *institutional rigidities* in the wage formation process and social security schemes generate distortions in the market mechanism. However, the US labour market contains some imperfections as well. The employment perspectives for the low-skilled are not favourable. This applies both to the low-skilled out-of-work and to the long-term perspectives of those holding low-paid jobs to move upward. From their part, the German and Dutch labour markets have a problem of persistent unemployment. This has been attributed to institutional rigidities. Yet, long-term unemployment is particularly severe in the UK and this suggests that the supply of low-skilled labour is important as well. On top of this, the latter three countries have a low net labour participation, compared with the USA and Sweden. This would suggest that there is substantial scope for policies that aim at lowering inactivity-rates and upgrading the skills of the working age population (the latter applies most to the UK but to the Netherlands as well).

The *institutional infrastructure* determines the opportunities and constraints that economic agents face and hence influences their conduct. Germany and the Netherlands are neo-corporatist economies, characterised by an elaborate and institutionalised network of intermediary organisations. These organisations (for example trade unions) take part in economic governance and are *public regarding*; they are less inclined to advocate insiders' interests and they support long-term commitments (e.g. in skill enhancement). In Section 4.3 however, it has been argued that for tripartite concertation to be successful there are certain preconditions to be met. Corporatism can be conducive at some points in time

---

[9] Note the italics: there are differences in expenditure on separate schemes. The question then becomes relevant as to what elements in the structure of insurance schemes are conducive and what elements are adversarial. This however, would require a more detailed discussion of the design, the incentive structure, of social security schemes than is undertaken here.

and adversarial in other periods. Immobile Dutch corporatism in the 1970s is a case in point. The institutional order also determines the adjustment potential or competitiveness of an economy. Section 4.4 advanced some evidence pointing out that *universal* welfare states respond differently than *residual* ones to economic trends, such as internationalisation and technological change. There is however, no evidence that macroeconomic performances of extensive welfare states, such as Germany and the Netherlands, are less than those of the United States and the United Kingdom, both liberal market economies. Nor is there evidence that the German and Dutch public social security schemes purchase something that meets no demand: preferences for social insurance in the United States and United Kingdom testify to this.

What marks the difference between Germany and the Netherlands? This chapter has compared the German and Dutch welfare states and confirmed that these have a number of institutional features in common. This is an important condition for a comparison to be meaningful in the first place (Blank 1994). Learning on the impact of welfare state institutions on economic performances requires cases that differ in some but not in all respects. There is *not a single Rhineland model* just as one cannot speak of *the* Anglo-Saxon model. In the latter case, the differences between the British and US enforcement of labour market and OHS-legislation, are but one example. The overruling distinction between Germany and the Netherlands has been the difference in involvement of the government in industrial relations during the post Second World War decades. Despite the fact that there were no overt interventions in the past 15 years, the Dutch government's policies are designed to meet the conditions that are favourable to wage moderation. Wage restraint is furthered through parallel public expenditure policies. On top of this, Dutch industrial relations are characterised by a large extent of bargaining coordination. From the early 1980s onwards the corporatist climate in the Netherlands has changed towards a more pragmatist inclination. The most recent example is found in the reforms of several social insurance schemes; especially the separation of executional responsibilities in order to suppress rent-seeking attitudes. This pragmatism has contributed a great deal to the current adjustment potential of the Dutch economy.

In the case of German industrial relations it appears that several important institutional preconditions currently are not met. The federal government finds itself in a complicated relational framework. Apart from powerful corporatist agents (trade unions and employers associations), the Länder come in as well. This renders German industrial relations rather intransparant as compared to the Dutch case. The federal government finds more difficulties in exerting political power than the Dutch, and it may be more difficult for the German government to commit the corporatist parties into a comprehensive policy framework. On top of this, Section 4.4 has observed a weakening power base of the peak associations of German employers and organised labour. This facing of *difficulties to deliver*, makes it even harder to reach a social contract. The institutional structure of the German economy in the post war decades was geared to support a manufacturing stronghold aiming at high surplus value. Internationalisation from the

1980s onwards has challenged this stronghold position. The current crisis in the aftermath of the unification reflects both internal and external causes. Pointing at internationalisation reflects a wide concern that there is no longer scope for a social market model of the German brand, shielding itself from distorting outside mechanisms. This concern holds that adapting the institutional framework sets in motion a "spiral of institutional erosion and structural downgrading" (Streeck 1995, p. 16) and that in the end it is inevitable that the German model will give way to a liberal market model. Internationalisation however, is not sufficient in explaining the erosion of the German corporatist framework. At least, this makes no sense from the Dutch point of view. In fact Dutch corporatism in the 1970s became immobile due to endemic causes, severed when the international economic environment shifted and put strain on the model. The capacity of the government to act has turned out to be crucial. Lehmbruch (1996) has argued that *Tarifautonomie* without the stabilising role of the state is much more prone to crises of cooperation from the associations. He adds that in the corporatist system of German public health insurance compliance is assured by the authority of the state. The Dutch case learns that corporatism can be altered, that it is possible to *mobilise* it rather than doing it away, and that welfare state institutions can be reformed so as to contribute to the adjustment potential of the economy.

References

Aaron, H.J. (1982), *Economic Effects of Social Security*, The Brookings Institution, Washington D.C.

Adema, W., M. Einerhand, B. Eklind, J. Lotz, M. Pearson (1996), Net public social expenditure, *OECD Labour Market and Social Policy Occasional Papers*, no. 19, Organisation for Economic Co-operation and Development, Paris.

Albert, M. (1992), *Kapitalisme contra Kapitalisme*, Contact, Amsterdam/Antwerpen (in Dutch).

Atkinson. A.B., L. Rainwater, T.M. Smeeding (1995), Income Distribution in OECD Countries: Evidence from the Luxembourg Income Study, *OECD Social Policy Studies*, no. 18, Organisation for Economic Co-operation and Development, Paris.

Barr, N. (1992), Economic theory and the welfare state: A survey and interpretation, *Journal of Economic Literature*, pp. 741-803.

Beer, P. de (1996), *Het onderste kwart: Werk en werkloosheid aan de onderkant van de arbeidsmarkt*, Sociaal en Cultureel Planbureau, Rijswijk (in Dutch).

Blanchflower, D.G. and A.J. Oswald (1995), *The Wage Curve*, Massachusetts Institute of Technology Press, Cambridge (USA)/London.

Blank, R.M. (1994), Introduction, in: R.M. Blank (ed.) *Social Protection versus Economic Flexibility: Is there a Trade-off?*, The University of Chicago Press, Chicago/London.

Broeder, C. den (1996), Institutions at work: Commitment and flexibility on the German and Dutch labour markets, *Research Memorandum no. 123*, CPB Netherlands Bureau of Economic Policy Analysis, The Hague.

Calmfors, L. (1993), Centralisation of wage bargaining and macroeconomic performance; A survey, *OECD Economic Studies*, no. 21, pp. 161-191.

Calmfors, L. and Driffill, J. (1988), Bargaining structure, corporatism and macroeconomic performance, *Economic Policy*, 6, pp. 13-61.

CPB (1996), *Centraal Economisch Plan 1996*, CPB Netherlands Bureau of Economic Policy Analysis, Sdu Uitgeverij, The Hague (in Dutch).

Eichengreen, B. (1994), Institutions and economic growth: Europe after World War II, *CEPR Discussion Paper 973*, Centre for Economic Policy Research, London.

Esping-Andersen, G. (1990), *The Three Worlds of Welfare Capitalism*, Polity Press, Cambridge (UK).

Franzmeyer, F., L. Lindlar, H. Trabold (1996) *Employment and Social Policies under International Constraints*, Deutsches Institut für Wirtschaftsforschung Berlin, Vuga, The Hague.

Geelhoed, A. (1996), Markt, ordening en sturing: Schuivende posities, in: A. Nentjes (ed.) *Marktwerking versus Coördinatie*, Lemma, Utrecht (in Dutch).

Hartog, J, and C.N. Teulings (1994), Markets, institutions and wages, *Research Memorandum no. 8*, Ministry of Social Affairs and Employment, The Hague.

Hemerijck, A.C. (1992), *The Historical Contingencies of Dutch Corporatism*, University of Oxford, doctoral thesis, Oxford.

Hu, F. and J.D. Sachs (1996), Executive summary, *The Global Competitiveness Report 1996*, World Economic Forum, Geneva.

ILO (1996), *World Employment 1996/97: National Policies in a Global Context*, International Labour Office, Geneva.

Israel, J. (1995), *The Dutch Republic; Its Rise, Greatness and Fall 1477-1806*, Clarendon Press, Oxford.

Layard, R., S. Nickell and R. Jackman (1990), *Unemployment: Macroeconomic Performance and the Labour Market*, Oxford University Press, Oxford.

Lehmbruch, G. (1995), From state of authority to network state: The German state in developmental perspective, in: F. Naschold and M. Maramatsu (eds.), *State and Administration in Japan and Germany*, Berlin.

Lehmbruch, G. (1996), *Crisis and Institutional Resilience in German Corporatism*, Paper prepared for the 8th International Conference on Socio-Economics, Geneva.

Lindbeck A., P. Molander, T. Persson, O. Pettersson, A. Sandmo, B. Swedenborg, N. Thygesen (1994), *Turning Sweden around*, MIT Press, Cambridge Massachusetts.

OECD (1993), *Employment Outlook, July 1993*, Organisation for Economic Co-operation and Development, Paris.

OECD (1994), *The OECD Jobs Study, Evidence and Explanations, Part II: The Adjustment Potential of the Labour Market*, Organisation for Economic Co-operation and Development, Paris.

OECD (1996a), *Economic Surveys: Germany 1996*, Organisation for Economic Co-operation and Development, Paris.

OECD (1996b), *Economic Surveys: Netherlands 1996*, Organisation for Economic Co-operation and Development, Paris.

OECD (1996c), *Employment Outlook, July 1996*, Organisation for Economic Co-operation and Development, Paris.

OECD (1996d), *Economic Outlook 60*, December, Organisation for Economic Co-operation and Development, Paris.

OECD (1996e), *Economic Surveys: United States 1996*, Organisation for Economic Co-operation and Development, Paris.

OECD (1996f), *Economic Surveys: United Kingdom 1996*, Organisation for Economic Co-operation and Development, Paris.

OECD (1997), *Economic Surveys: Sweden 1997*, Organisation for Economic Co-operation and Development, Paris.

Okun, A.M. (1975), *Equality and Efficiency: The Big Trade off*, The Brookings Institution, Washington D.C.

Pierson, P. (1994), *Dismantling the Welfare State? Reagan, Thatcher and the Politics of Retrenchment*, Cambridge University Press, Cambridge.

Porter, M.E. (1990), *The Competitive Advantage of Nations*, Free Press, New York.

Roorda, W.B. and E.H.W.M. Vogels (1997), Concurrerende arbeidsverhoudingen, *Research Memorandum no. 33*, Ministry of Social Affairs and Employment, The Hague (in Dutch).

Sachs, J. and A. Warner (1996), The social welfare state and competitiveness, in: *The Global Competitiveness Report 1996*, World Economic Forum, Geneva.

Schröder, J. and U. van Suntum (1996), *International Employment Ranking 1996*, Bertelsmann Foundation Publishers, Gütersloh.

Schut, F.T. (1995), *Competition in the Dutch Health Care Sector*, doctoral thesis, Rotterdam.

Sinn, H.W. (1995), A theory of the welfare state, *CEPR Discussion Paper 1278*, Centre for Economic Policy Research, London.

Stiglitz, J. (1996), *Job Creation and Employment Opportunities: The United States Labour Market 1993-1996*, Report by the Counsel of Economic Advisors with the US Department of Labour, Washington D.C.

Streeck, W. (1995), German capitalism: Does it exist? Can it survive?, *Discussion Paper 95/5*, Max-Planck-Institut für Gesellschaftsforschung, Köln.

Swaan, A. de (1989), *Zorg en de Staat*, Bakker, Amsterdam (in Dutch).

SZW (1996), *The Dutch Welfare State from an International and Economic Perspective*, Ministry of Social Affairs and Employment of the Netherlands, The Hague.

Teulings, C.N. (1995), *Corporatist Wage Setting in Models of Surplus Sharing*, Discussion paper Tinbergen Institute, University of Amsterdam.

UNICE (1995), *Releasing Europe's Potential Through Targeted Regulatory Reform*, The UNICE Regulatory Report, Brussels.

VWS (1996), *Jaaroverzicht Zorg 1997*, Ministry of Health Care of the Netherlands, Sdu Uitgeverij, The Hague (in Dutch).

Voogd, J. de, N.B.J.G. 't Hoen, M. Arents, J.T. de Booij (1996), *Inactivity/Activity ratios: A descriptive analysis for six European countries*, Netherlands Economic Institute Rotterdam, Vuga, The Hague.

Waarden, F. van (1997), *Institutions of Socio-Economic Coordination: A European Style?* Paper prepared for the EU-Conference Social Policy and Economic Performance, Ministry of Social Affairs and Employment, The Hague.

White, J. (1995), *Competing Solutions: American Health Care Proposals and International Experience*, The Brookings Institution, Washington D.C.

Part III

Financial and Competition Policies

5 The Financial Structure in the Netherlands and Germany: Different, Harmonious, and on the Move?

Lex Hoogduin and Henk Huisman[1]
European Monetary Institute, Frankfurt, Germany
De Nederlandsche Bank, Amsterdam, the Netherlands

5.1 Introduction

The current favourable economic performance of the Netherlands compared to Germany is often attributed to moderate wage developments as well as to the fact that structural measures have been taken at a relatively early stage. These structural measures have mainly served to improve the functioning of labour and goods markets. Apart from differences in the structure of labour and goods markets, many differences also exist between German and Dutch capital markets. Apparently, these differences in the structure of financial markets have not harmed the close monetary relations between the two countries. For almost 15 years now, the guilder has been linked very tightly to the Deutschmark, and the credibility of this link is not a heavily debated issue in financial markets, to say the least.

Here, we will discuss whether the financial structures of the Federal Republic of Germany and the Netherlands actually differ to a great extent, and whether one could also identify some common features. In addition, we will ponder some likely future developments. Before doing so, however, we would briefly like to take a step back and address the more general issue of the factors by which a country's financial structure is determined (Sections 5.2 and 5.3). In Section 5.4 the German and Dutch financial structures are compared. Future developments are discussed in Section 5.5. Conclusions are drawn in Section 5.6.

[1] The authors wish to thank Job Swank for his useful comments. Responsibility for the final text lies with the authors. When writing this article Lex Hoogduin was working at De Nederlandsche Bank.

5.2 What is the Financial Structure, and how Important is it?

In a world of perfectly competitive markets and perfect information, the financial structure would play no role. As shown by Modigliani and Miller (1958), such a world could do without shares and bonds, and even if there would be a place for them, it would not matter whether a company would acquire funds through issuing new shares or through debt instruments. Evidently, even as an exercise in fantasy, it is difficult to imagine such a world. In reality, the *structure of financial markets* is determined not only by economic factors, but also, and probably to an even greater extent, by non-economic factors. The latter concern a broad array of factors and preferences of a geographical, philosophical, cultural and social nature (see Gardener and Molyneux 1990, p. 29). They form the basis for the way in which societies formulate and create rules, regulations and institutions. Thus, every country has its own unique financial system with often complex institutional arrangements and legal frameworks (see Hoogduin 1996, p. 11).

Throughout the major economies, one can observe different types of financial systems. Financial systems vary from the Anglo-Saxon *'market-based' model* to the *'bank-based' system* as it exists in, for instance, Germany and other continental European countries. Roughly speaking and somewhat generalised, these differences can be characterised by the following antonyms: risk-taking versus risk-avoiding, competition versus co-operation, and short-term versus long-term relationships between those who demand and those who supply capital (see also Gelauff and Den Broeder 1996, p. 29). A striking feature of the *Anglo-Saxon model* is the separation between commercial and investment financing: in the United States, the Glass-Steagall Act prohibits banks from holding shares for their own account. Accordingly, commercial banks are mostly involved in the financing of trade and not in the financing of firms. In the so-called *'German model'*, banks are of a universal nature and they have often a long-standing tradition of strong links with the corporate sector: there are no legal restrictions prohibiting banks from holding equity capital. Bank involvement in the financing of firms is therefore much greater in Germany, either through bank loans or through equity financing. These differences in financial structure have an important bearing on the relationship between investors and companies – or, in more trendy terms, on 'corporate governance'. One might say that in the Anglo-Saxon world it is the shareholder, and in the German model the stakeholder who exercises control over the management of enterprises.

Each of the systems has its own pros and cons, making it difficult to define the *optimal financial system.* A strong feature of the Anglo-Saxon model is the relatively speedy transfer of capital from sectors/companies with unfavourable prospects into promising new sectors, something that is lacking in the German system (see also Gelauff and Den Broeder 1996, p. 34). A major drawback of the Anglo-Saxon system is the inherent focus on short-termism: for shareholders often the only viable way of exercising control over the management of firms, is to sell shares, to threaten to do so, or to engage in hostile take-overs. On the contrary, in the German model, the relatively stable relationship between investors and companies allows the management to focus more on longer-term perspectives.

5.3 Financial Structure and Monetary Policy

The financial structure is also important to central banks, as it is a major determinant of the *monetary transmission mechanism.* Changes in official interest rates and intervention rates affect economic activity through different channels, namely (1) through short-term and long-term market interest rates on new financing; (2) through changes in adjustable rates on outstanding contracts; (3) through the implied revaluation of assets; and (4) through the effects on exchange rates. The financial structure has a decisive influence on these transmission channels, since it determines the speed at which and the extent to which monetary policy affects market interest rates. Moreover, the level and composition of wealth and indebtedness are of importance. Evidently, these are significant issues with regard to exchange rate policies: the transmission channels in countries that peg their currencies should not differ too much from those in the anchor country. Otherwise, the economic and political costs of 'common' interest rate policies might become too high.

A recent study by the Bank for International Settlements (BIS) (1995) deals with these issues. The study shows that the impact of an increase in official rates on economic activity tends to be comparatively strong in English-speaking countries and much weaker in continental European countries, whereas the position of Italy is somewhere in the middle. This is attributed to the following key elements in the financial structure of English-speaking countries. First, households are more heavily indebted and hold a larger part of their wealth in the form of assets (such as equity and real estate) whose price is highly interest rate sensitive. Second, the share of securities in total credit is comparatively high. Third, the share of adjustable rate credit and mortgages is relatively high. Fourth, the share of loans backed by real estate collateral is relatively high.

5.4 The Financial Structure in the Netherlands and Germany Compared

Where does the financial structure in the Netherlands stand? At first sight, the *Dutch financial structure* does not seem to fit into one of the extremes that we mentioned earlier: it is neither a bank-based nor a market-based system. Three major differences can be identified compared to the situation in the Federal Republic of Germany. To start with, there is the very special system of compulsory savings and, as a result, the important role *institutional investors* play in the economy. Indeed, the first thing that strikes when considering the Dutch financial structure, is the way in which savings find their way to the capital market: the Dutch save through pension funds and insurance companies, rather than through banks as in Germany. The pension fund framework is uniquely institutionalised: participation is compulsory and the financing is in the form of a (long-term) funding system compared to a pay-as-you-go system as in most other countries, including Germany[2] (see also Jochimsen, Chapter 6 in this volume). These features have resulted in colossal portfolios held by institutional investors: total assets amount to substantially over 100% of Gross Domestic Product (GDP), whereas in Germany the corresponding ratio is nearly 35%.

A second difference is that in the Netherlands some very *large financial conglomerates*, established through either bank-bank or bank-insurance mergers, dominate the financial scene at present. In Germany, the bank loans market is not dominated by a small number of banks: the market share of the three largest banks is less than 15%, compared to well over 75% in the Netherlands. Apart from these differences in market shares, banks also play different roles in the financing of companies. In Germany, banks are typically *universal banks* that provide both debt and equity financing to firms. In the Netherlands, banks have always been faced with restrictions as regards equity investments and they therefore mainly concentrate on providing credit.[3] German banks' shareholdings are quite large compared to those in other countries: they amount to approximately 15% of total equity capital, whereas for the Netherlands the figure is less than 1%. This has led to close house-bank relationships in Germany between firms and banks and to widespread bank representation on the supervisory boards of firms.

A third difference between the Dutch and German financial structures is that the Netherlands have always had a fairly open and relatively large *stock market* compared to Germany. At the end of 1995, market capitalisation (in terms of gross domestic product) in the Netherlands amounted to almost 75% compared to nearly 25% in Germany. It should be noted, though, that specific anti-takeover defences have significantly restricted shareholders' power in the Netherlands.

Despite these differences in financial structure, however, it seems fair to say that, in its underlying characteristics, the Dutch system more closely resembles

---

[2] In Germany, pension benefits based on the pay-as-you-go system are quite generous compared to those in the Netherlands (AOW), which reduces the need for supplementary savings (although some company-related pension funding systems do exist). It should be noted that the pension system is currently reviewed by a committee chaired by Minister Blüm, since it is unsustainable in the longer term as the German population ages. In light of the traumatic hyper-inflation experiences of the 1920s, however, there is widespread resistance in Germany to a long-term funding system.

[3] Regulations were liberalised in 1992. Banks have to obtain permission from the Ministry of Finance and the central bank, De Nederlandsche Bank, if they want to acquire more than 10% of total equity of a non-financial company. Before 1992, this threshold was 5%.

the German system than the Anglo-Saxon system. This is apparent from the following facts. We will start by referring again to the 1995 BIS-study on monetary transmission mechanisms. The study shows that various aspects of the *structure of credit* to the non-governmental sector are quite similar in the Netherlands and Germany, as is shown in Table 5.1 (for comparison, figures for the United States of America and the United Kingdom are also included in the table).

Table 5.1 The structure of credit, 1993

	Germany	Netherlands	United States	United Kingdom
Loans (% of total credit)	98	96	80	81
Banks loans (% of total loans)	89	73	50	56
Medium/long-term loans (% of total loans)	84	83	85	69
Fixed rate loans (% of total loans)	65	75	66	27

Source: Bank for International Settlements 1995, pp. 59-105.

From Table 5.1 it follows that in the Federal Republic of Germany and the Netherlands overall credit is overwhelmingly in the form of *loans*; this implies that the significance of securities is limited. A second feature is that banks account for the bulk of lending in both countries, although, not surprisingly, in the Netherlands other financial institutions, such as institutional investors, also provide a significant part of total credit (for instance in the form of mortgage loans). In the United States and the United Kingdom, the role of banks is much more limited. Third, the bulk of German and Dutch (and United States) loans is in the form of medium-term and long-term loans. In this regard, it is interesting to point to the fact that (bond) loans in countries with a low inflation rate generally tend to have longer maturities than loans in high-inflation countries. Finally, medium and long-term loans in Germany and the Netherlands are predominantly at fixed rather than adjustable rates, which goes for the United States as well. The exception is the United Kingdom where loans at adjustable rates play a much more important role.

The fact that the *structure of credit* in the Netherlands is quite similar to that in Germany, implies that the monetary transmission channels in both countries show a great deal of correspondence. This is an important finding from the viewpoint of the sustainability of the guilder-Deutschmark peg.

In addition, it seems useful to take a closer look at the behaviour of the major *capital market participants* in the Netherlands and Germany, namely the banks, institutional investors, and companies. As regards banks, shareholder power of German banks should not be exaggerated. The larger part of equity participations of German banks is in other financial institutions, such as insurance companies, and, conversely, financial institutions substantially participate in the equity capital of banks. Thus, the relevance of shareholdership of German banks in non-financial institutions is less significant, namely of the order of about 4% of equity capital of listed companies (Gelauff and Den Broeder 1996, p. 66). In practice, it appears that the vast bulk of the finance supplied by German banks to companies takes the form of debt (Edwards and Fischer 1994, p. 230). Moreover, empirical evidence shows that the German bank-based system does not lead to a situation where external financing is more readily available at lower costs than in other countries (Edwards and Fischer 1994, p. 231). Also, supervisory functions and equity underwriting are often performed chiefly by the three main banks, so that a large part of bank lending to firms is undertaken by banks that are not in a position to influence *corporate governance*. Furthermore, Dutch banks frequently have a seat on companies' supervisory boards because of their creditor relationships with the companies concerned. In fact, the relative position of German and Dutch banks on the supervisory board (percentage of seats occupied by banks) is almost equal (Gelauff and Den Broeder 1996, p. 73). Thus, without participating in the equity capital of companies, the supervisory role provides Dutch banks with an opportunity to exercise control over the management of companies.

As regards Dutch *institutional investors*, it should be noted that until a few years ago, pension funds were bound by rather strict rules and principles. For instance, equity investments were not allowed above certain specified limits, so that institutional investors were no major providers of risk capital. A few years ago, however, such rules were liberalised considerably and institutional investors have significantly increased their equity participations since, to about 25% of total portfolios (compared to less than 15% in 1990). This could be an important development with regard to *corporate governance* in the future. Some observers argue that, contrary to Dutch banks, institutional investors might be more focused on actively seeking influence in the strategic decisions of a company (Gelauff and Den Broeder 1996, p. 77). On the other hand, it should be stressed that, because of their long-term contractual obligations vis-à-vis their customers, institutional investors will continue to consider their shareholdings predominantly from a longer-term investment perspective. Unlike Anglo-Saxon mutual funds, they will be less inclined to sell shares of a company that occasionally presents disappointing profits.

Finally, an important similarity between the Netherlands and Germany is that companies finance their investments to a great extent from *internally generated* funds. There are several reasons for this behaviour that have to do with all kinds of regulations, including fiscal ones. In any case, it is clear that stock markets play a relatively unimportant role with regard to corporate governance. In the Federal Republic of Germany, shareholding is concentrated: huge blocks of the shares of large companies are often owned by founders (families) and by banks and other companies. As noted above, the stock market in the Netherlands has traditionally been very open and is quite large in terms of market capitalisation. Consequently, shareholdership is much more dispersed, as may be illustrated by the fact that over 50% of the shares of listed companies is owned by foreigners.[4] However, until recently shareholders' voting power was fairly restricted by all kinds of anti-takeover defences.

5.5 On the Move, but Where are we Going to?

Having described the main differences and similarities between the financial systems in Germany and the Netherlands, we would like to add instantly that financial systems are not, of course, static entities. They are in a constant state of flux, prompted by changes in regulation and by forces such as liberalisation, internationalisation, and securitisation. The authorities in both countries have been implementing policy measures aimed at aligning their financial systems with 'the European Union 1992' regulations so as to provide for the free movement of capital and financial services. As a result, financial markets in Germany and the Netherlands are changing rapidly. These changes go some way in the direction of the Anglo-Saxon system, as may be illustrated by the following developments.

We have already mentioned the considerable changes in the Dutch financial landscape. In Germany, too, there is a growing tendency for financial institutions to *take stakes in each other*, as illustrated by the recent announcement by the German central bank, the Deutsche Bundesbank, that it owns a substantial part of the fourth largest German bank, the Bayerische Vereinsbank.[5] These developments are induced by increased competition from foreign financial institutions. German banks have been very busy revising their banking strategies, and increasing their international ties. This goes particularly for the largest banks, which recently expanded their investment banking activities by taking over London-based banks. But also the traditionally more specialised banks, such as the savings banks, are involved in mergers and acquisitions with the aim to expand their banking activities beyond the retail markets.

The focus in Germany and the Netherlands is furthermore on expanding (international) access to *securities markets*, and on increasing the attractiveness of the respective *financial centres*. In the Netherlands, the Amsterdam Stock Exchange (ASE) and the European Options Exchange (EOE) agreed on a merger, which has become effective as of January 1, 1997. In recent years the ASE has, among other things, adjusted its trading system, thus increasing the possibilities

---

[4] It should be noted that this figure is distorted due to the fact that the largest listed companies on the Amsterdam Stock Exchange are half Dutch – half British.

[5] Cat set among the pigeons, *Financial Times*, September 6, 1996.

for wholesale trade. Moreover, legislation has been adopted to outlaw insider trading, and to remove barriers in the area of anti-takeover codes. These developments should enhance the appeal of holding shares in the Netherlands. In Germany, too, several important steps have been taken in order to improve the international position of Germany's financial markets. A relevant development is the centralisation of German stock exchanges that was agreed last year. Moreover, the Deutschmark bond market has been opened to foreign issuers and intermediaries, and the supervision of security markets has been streamlined. Noteworthy have been the decisions by the Bundesbank to gradually lower reserve requirements on savings and deposits in view of increased competition from other European financial centres. This latter consideration has also been an underlying factor in the recent announcement by the German government to issue short-term treasury paper. The Dutch government, too, covers a small part of its finance requirements with short-term paper. These financing policies should not be seen as a major shift in financing behaviour, but inter alia as a means to better serve the interests of investors.

This brings us to a discussion of some future developments, in particular the likely consequences of the creation of the *Economic and Monetary Union* (EMU) and the introduction of the *euro* on January 1, 1999.[6] In general, one could say that EMU and the euro will strengthen current trends of internationalisation, securitisation and increased competition on financial markets. The elimination of currency risks within the euro area implies that euro financial markets, and particularly bond markets, will gain in depth and liquidity. Moreover, differences in long-term interest rates based on exchange rate risks will disappear. There will thus be a tendency for institutional investors to further diversify portfolios, and to pursue more active investment policies. They will concentrate on default risks and liquidity differences. This makes it, by the way, even more necessary for the political authorities to prudently steer their macroeconomic policies in an environment where financial market volatility has potentially increased. The consequences of the euro introduction on equity markets might initially be a little more limited, due to differences in both legal and fiscal treatment of shares and in corporate governance cultures. But, definitely, pressure will increase to harmonise rules and fiscal treatment of equity capital, thereby increasing the transparency and liquidity of equity markets in the longer term.

Having described some spectacular developments in financial markets, we would like to note at the same time that, although financial structures change over time, they do not, of course, do so overnight. Institutional changes are gradual processes almost by definition. One compelling example in this respect concerns the developments in *retail banking* within the European Union. Although there are no legal restrictions on undertaking retail banking activities throughout the European Union, national markets are still overwhelmingly dominated by national banks: for 'Joe six-pack' or for 'Otto Normalverbraucher'

---

[6] See for an extensive discussion of this issue Bakker (1996).

the common market in retail financial services is still virtually non-existent. Competition in retail banking is influenced by some very simple practical mechanisms. Cliënts prefer the convenience of a nearby branch. Retail markets are difficult to penetrate, considering the need for branch networks and knowledge about preferences and habits of customers. Those financial institutions that seek to penetrate into foreign markets have to acquire foreign banks with branch networks. Obviously, this is a time-consuming process.

5.6 Conclusion

To summarise, we have tried to make clear that the financial structures in the Netherlands and the Federale Republic of Germany differ to some degree, in particular as regards the role of the banks and institutional investors. Nevertheless, it is fair to say that, in its underlying characteristic, the Dutch financial system resembles the German system to a great extent, given the fact that the behaviour of the major participants in financial markets is largely aimed at cooperation and long-term relationships between stakeholders and companies. As a result, the structure of credit and the monetary transmission channels in the Netherlands and Germany are quite similar, thus providing a sound basis for the close monetary links between the two countries. Finally, we have noted that the German and Dutch financial systems are changing, to some degree, in the direction of the Anglo-Saxon system. This should not be a major impediment to the close monetary relationship, since the changes in both countries go in the same direction.

References

Bakker, A.F.P. (1996), De euro: gevolgen voor de financiële markten, *Bank- en Effectenbedrijf*, September, pp. 13-18 (in Dutch).

Bank for International Settlements (1995), *Financial Structure and the Monetary Policy Transmission Mechanism*, C.B. 394, Basle.

Bergeijk, P.A.G. van, C. van Gent, R.C.G. Haffner and A.J.M. Kleijweg (1995), Mobiliteit en concurrentie op de kapitaalmarkt, *Economisch Statistische Berichten*, pp. 780-784 (in Dutch).

Conti, V. and M. Maccarinelli (1993), Deregulation and Profitability in Different OECD Banking Systems, *IEF Research Papers*, RP 93/18.

Duisenberg, W.F. (1992), *Financiële Sector in Beweging: Kansen en Risico's*, De Nederlandsche Bank, Amsterdam (in Dutch).

Edwards, J. and K. Fischer (1994), *Banks, Finance and Investment in Germany*, Cambridge University Press, Cambridge (UK).

Gardener, P.M. (1995), Banking strategies in the European Union: Financial services after the Cecchini Report, *IEF Research Papers*, RP 95/7.

Gardener, P.M. and P. Molyneux (1990), *Changes in Western European Banking: An International Banker's Guide*, Cambridge University Press, Cambridge (UK).
Gelauff, G.M.M. and C. den Broeder (1996), Governance of stakeholder relationships: The German and Dutch experience, *CPB Research Memorandum No. 127*, CPB Netherlands Bureau of Economic Policy Analysis, The Hague.
Goor, L.H. van and L.J.R. Scholtens (1996), Zijn we beter af met industriebanken?, *Economisch Statistische Berichten*, pp. 704-708 (in Dutch).
Hoogduin, L.H. (1996), *Konijn, Olifant of Konifant?: Op Zoek naar een Vruchtbare Beschouwingswijze van Geld en Financiële Verschijnselen*, State University of Groningen, Groningen (in Dutch).
Klein, D.K.R. (1995), *The Banking Systems of EU Member States*, Gresham Books, Cambridge (UK).
Ministerie van Economische Zaken (1995), *Toets op het Concurrentievermogen*, The Hague (in Dutch).
Modigliani, F. and M. Miller (1958), The cost of capital, corporation finance and the theory of investment, *American Economic Review*, 48, pp. 261-297.

6 A Stable Partnership – German-Dutch Monetary Relations in the Run-up to EMU[1]

Reimut Jochimsen
Landeszentralbank in North Rhine-Westphalia, Düsseldorf, Germany

6.1 Introduction

For a long time now German-Dutch monetary relations have been just as they ought to be between all future partners in the monetary union: trouble-free, steady and very close. The exchange rate of the Dutch guilder against the Deutschmark has been stable for years, and long-term interest rates are virtually identical.

This high degree of convergence is epitomised not least by the fact that, following the crisis in the European Monetary System in summer 1993 – when the permissible margins for exchange rate fluctuations were generally widened to ±15% – the Netherlands and the Federal Republic of Germany were the only countries to retain their existing narrow exchange rate band of ±2.25%.

If domestic and external monetary policy is construed somewhat more broadly, i.e. if the fiscal policy, social policy and wage policy settings are also taken into consideration, it certainly cannot be said that there is any clear leader-follower relationship between the Netherlands and Germany. And it is definitely not the case that the Netherlands always follows in the wake of the much larger Federal Republic of Germany – which some people might assume, given the two countries' respective size. I think rather that the two countries have been marching side by side in stability-policy harmony for many years, with sometimes the smaller marcher and sometimes– especially in recent years – the larger marcher finding it hard to keep in step. This shoulder-to-shoulder pace of advance dates right back to the Bretton Woods system and has continued ever since in an unbroken line via the European exchange rate cooperation and the European Monetary System (EMS) right up to the preparation for the European Economic and Monetary Union (EMU).

This chapter analyses the monetary relationship between Germany and the Netherlands and tries to answer what role both countries can and should play in

[1] This paper is based on information available on October 25, 1996.

establishing a stable and sustainable Economic and Monetary Union. Section 6.2 links central bank autonomy and German and Dutch monetary stability. Section 6.3 deals with the role of other policy areas in achieving monetary stability and discusses the differences in the stability record between Germany and the Netherlands. Section 6.4 goes into the role Germany and the Netherlands can play in creating stable foundations for EMU. The final Section 6.5 briefly discusses the temporary postponement of EMU.

6.2 Stable Monetary Performance

Germany and the Netherlands have a correspondingly positive track record in terms of monetary stability. That is especially true of the period since the establishment of the European Monetary System in 1979:

- on average since 1979 the Netherlands have had a lower *inflation rate*, at 2.6%, than any other European partner, including the Federal Republic of Germany, at 2.7%. At the moment Germany, at 1.4%, is slightly in the lead. However, Dutch inflation, at 2.0%, is only a fraction away from having a one before the decimal point (position as of September 1996);
- the *exchange rate* between the guilder and the Deutschmark has been more or less stable since April 1983. The sole deviation occurred in the initial years of the EMS between 1979 and the beginning of 1983 when the Dutch currency either did not follow certain appreciations of the Deutschmark at all (September and November 1979, March 1981) or matched them only to a limited extent (as in March 1983). For years afterwards this deviation could still be seen in slightly higher interest rates at the long end of the market. Since then the two currencies have advanced very much in parallel; the deviations from the bilateral central rate are well below 1%-point. Incidentally, for about the past four years the guilder has been slightly above the Deutschmark parity, which impressively attests the Dutch currency's innate strength. The OECD came to the same conclusion in its latest report on the Netherlands (see OECD 1996a);
- the *interest rate* difference for ten-year paper has contracted continuously since the start of the 1980s (see Figure 6.1). In the last few months and years the guilder yield has not infrequently been even lower than the German yield, as it is, for example, at the moment on October 24, 1996 (5.89%, against 6.00%);
- in the institutional setting for monetary policy the parallels between the two countries are likewise clear: Germany and the Netherlands both placed responsibility for ensuring stable money in the hands of their central banks much earlier than most other European partner countries and also granted their central banks an extremely high degree of *independence* in performing this task. While it is true that the Dutch Minister of Finance has the right to issue instructions to the Dutch central bank, De Nederlandsche Bank, he has

never exercised that right, so that *de facto* the Dutch central bank is just as independent as the German central bank, the Deutsche Bundesbank. The stability policy results speak for themselves; they prove once again that there is a close link between a high degree of central bank autonomy and success in ensuring monetary stability.

Figure 6.1 Long-term interest rates in Germany and the Netherlands, 1970-1996 (yearly averages)

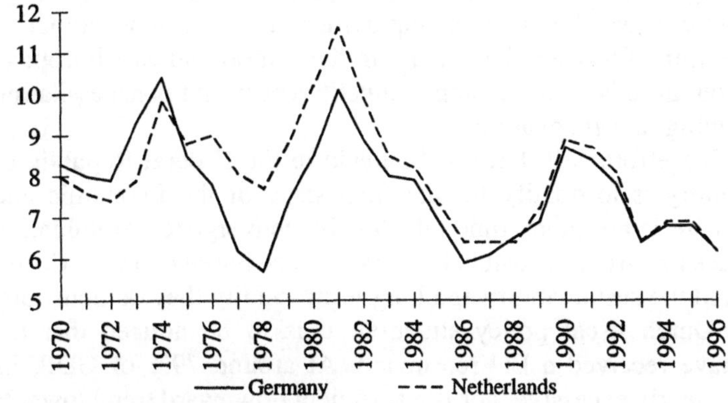

Source: De Nederlandsche Bank.

6.3 The Role of the Other Policy Instruments

There can be no doubt that the outstanding stability performance, measured by the European average, is not due exclusively to the long-term pursuit of a sound monetary policy. It is rather a product of the *interplay* of all economic policy agents and, in particular, of the support given to monetary policy by healthy public finance and a wage policy which takes due account of stability requirements. On the whole, this has functioned fairly well over the years both in the Netherlands and in the Federal Republic of Germany (see Soskice et al., Chapter 2 and Van de Meerendonk, Chapter 4 in this volume).

However, 'fairly well' does not necessarily mean well enough. In both countries substantial misalignments have occurred during the past few years which are posing major locational problems both in the Netherlands and in Germany. In the field of *fiscal policy*, in particular, it is the Federal Republic which is currently lagging behind the Netherlands. With a budget deficit of around 4% of Gross Domestic Product (GDP) and an aggregate debt of a slightly over 60% of GDP, Germany is clearly breaching the Maastricht ceilings, at least in 1996 on both counts. Even in 1995 Germany had problems with its current deficit, which reached approximately 3.5% of GDP. As a result, Germany received a reprimand from the European Union (EU) this year, as it did in 1994, as part of its Excessive Deficit Procedure.

In the wake of the reunification, Germany is still a long way from becoming a normal country again with 'normal' cyclical fluctuations. It is beset by a persistent fiscal crisis stemming from the high *costs of the unification*, the overburdening of labour costs with taxes and social security contributions and the still far too weak industrial base in eastern Germany which will necessitate massive transfer payments for a long time to come. The Federal Government itself is talking for the first time of at least a further 15 years – not to mention the pressing and unresolved problems of financing the pension insurance scheme, the health and nursing insurance funds and the hospital system. Given the high cost burdens on enterprises, the high unemployment and the new attractive locations elsewhere in the European Union and in the central and east European countries in transition, all this is depressing competitiveness and is necessitating higher levels of training and innovation.

Hence considerable efforts still have to be made in the Federal Republic of Germany if the country is to qualify for the final stage of the Economic and Monetary Union. There is not much time left, for the convergence examination (which is to take place as early as possible in 1998) is to be based on the performance data of 1997 and the sustainability and long-term solidity they demonstrate.

Looking at the Dutch fiscal policy situation, it is to be noticed that the Netherlands, too, have received a EU reprimand. At around 79% of GDP, its overall debt level is clearly excessive, nor is a sufficient downward trend towards the reference value apparent in the actual data available so far, in contrast to the situation of the Irish and the Danes.

This high level of *government debt* is the sole blot on the otherwise spotless stability record of the Netherlands. It should be noted, though, that – particularly in comparison with the Federal Republic of Germany – the Netherlands are much better prepared than, say, Germany for the *pension funding problems* with which it, too, will have to cope. The total assets of the pension funds in the Netherlands amount to more than 80% of GDP, with the capital accumulated by the civil servants' pension fund alone coming to around 30% of Dutch GDP. In Germany, where the pension insurance system is largely financed on a pay-as-you-go basis, the total assets of the pension funds account for a paltry 6% of GDP, while dedicated funding for civil servants' pensions is virtually non-existent (see also Hoogduin and Huisman, Chapter 5 in this volume).

But this structural advantage is not the only positive point in assessing the Dutch situation. The Netherlands have also gone a long way towards tackling their economic policy problems. They are quite some way ahead of Germany in terms of undertaking rigorous *consolidation* efforts. The Dutch budgetary situation is well on course for Maastricht. New borrowing will be cut from just under 3% in 1996 to 2.25% in 1997.

This target seems plausible and attainable both regarding the country's ability to continue the resolute retrenchment policy of the past few years – which, of course, determines how the deficit develops – and regarding the *growth prospects* which determine the other reference variable, namely GDP. Thus a real GDP growth of a solid 2.4% is forecast for 1997. That growth is not only to be fuelled by exports but is also to be boosted, in particular, by private consumption stemming from rising consumer confidence.

The cyclical outlook for Germany, by contrast, is far less convincing. The economy is starting to pick up only gradually and the upturn is not yet firmly established. Nevertheless, for 1997 a growth rate of 1.1% is expected (OECD 1996b). As long as the improvement in export business fails to galvanise domestic demand and as long as government consumption remains the engine of growth, the propensity to invest in Germany will likewise remain sluggish.

These different trends in the two countries are reflected in their respective employment figures. Thus whereas the Federal Republic of Germany continues to face the problem of excessively high *unemployment* – with an unemployment rate of 8.9% (the seasonally adjusted figure for Germany as a whole according to the recent *OECD Economic Outlook*[2] (OECD 1996c) – an extremely positive development has occurred on the labour market in the Netherlands during the past few months. According to the latest reports, the first shortages have already begun to appear in filling the existing vacancies. The Dutch unemployment rate came to 6.0% in the second quarter of 1996, compared with 6.6% in the first quarter of 1994.

It is quite obvious that these striking differences have material causes. One of the secrets of the Netherlands' success is that the government sector and the two sides of industry in this country, in contrast to the situation in Germany, not only acknowledged the economic necessities earlier but were also prepared to undertake a radical change of course, even if that called for sacrifices.

A very important role is being played by the *reform of the social security system*, which has laid a solid base for fiscal policy consolidation (see also Van de Meerendonk, Chapter 4 in this volume). The reformed Dutch pension insurance system ('*capuccino model*'), with its three ingredients – state retirement pension (= 'coffee'), voluntary company pension schemes (= 'cream') and supplementary private provision by citizens themselves (= 'cocoa on the cream') – is considered exemplary by many people. The sickness benefit scheme was privatised in March of 1996 and is now exclusively a matter for management and labour. That will save the state billions. Equally important was the revision of the occupational disability insurance scheme, which had been wide open to abuse.

Assuming that the *tax reforms* which are now being set in train will be as successful as the social security reforms, the further outlook for the Dutch economy appears positive.

That is all the more likely as important *deregulation measures* are aiding the recovery process. These include the lifting of restrictions on shopping hours (see also Gradus, Chapter 7 in this volume) and, above all, the far more flexible

---

[2] OECD figures are used for the sake of better comparability. According to the Deutsche Bundesbank, the seasonally adjusted unemployment rate in September 1996 for Germany as a whole was 10.4% (9.3% in western Germany, 15.3% in eastern Germany).

labour market compared with the Federal Republic of Germany (see also Schmid and Helmer, Chapter 3 and Van de Meerendonk, Chapter 4 in this volume). These two factors, together with the wage moderation over the past few years, have contributed significantly to creating new jobs.

6.4 Germany and the Netherlands: Natural Allies

The conclusion to be drawn from all this is quite clear to me: it is that the Germans can learn lessons from the Dutch. That applies to politicians, entrepreneurs, trade unionists and employees alike. It is not sufficient to identify locational weaknesses and to discuss and endlessly bemoan supposed or real excesses of the social security system. The interminable debates in Germany and the small progress achieved provide ample evidence of that. Only the resolute implementation of far-reaching but fair reforms can take us further – certainly based on a *consensus* and maintaining a social equilibrium but not in such a way that, following the 'careful' balancing of interests, hardly anything is left of the original good intention. The transition to flexible regional wage agreements belongs to it, not its removal. The monetary policy makers must not remain aloof from this debate, they must argue insistently for this change. For stable and sustainable underlying conditions in the other policy fields are likewise – as I indicated at the beginning of this chapter – a major prerequisite for safeguarding the purchasing power stability of money.

Around 1.5 years before the decision is due on which countries will form the vanguard of Economic and Monetary Union, the European countries cannot confine their efforts to putting their own houses in order. It is no less important to lay the foundations for the period after 1999, i.e. to insist that EMU is placed on a sound footing. In this context, the Netherlands and the Federal Republic of Germany are natural allies and partners.

- That applies, firstly, to the mutual interest in ensuring that the *terms of trade* are as stable as possible. The Federal Republic of Germany generates 12% of its GDP through exports to countries within the European Union (exports to the EU make up 57% of total German exports). The Dutch figures are far higher still, with over 32% of GDP resulting from intra-EU exports (which account for 80% of all Dutch exports).
- Secondly, it goes without saying that Germany and the Netherlands have the same interest in a *stable euro* which enjoys public confidence. Citizens who today use money with a stable purchasing power have no wish to exchange it for a currency which is less solid – even if they can use it anywhere in the European Union. The mere suspicion that the inflation rate in the monetary union could be a few percentage or decimal points higher than the level the Netherlands and Germany are accustomed to, would promptly transform the expected benefits of monetary union into tangible drawbacks by way of higher market interest rates.

It is therefore equally imperative for both partners to seek to build a solid and lasting stability policy foundation for the European Economic and Monetary Union which not only ensures a convincing start for EMU but also facilitates ongoing stability, investment, growth, and employment – in other words the sustainability which the Maastricht Treaty demands. And on that point the Dutch and German central banks have a virtually identical position. The articles, interviews and other publications emanating from the Dutch central bank on the subject of EMU always give me particular pleasure. It is not just a question of the matching basic philosophies, what impresses me again and again is the steadfastness with which the Dutch central bank invariably champions these positions. It is no coincidence that Wim Duisenberg, for many years the Governor of the Dutch central bank (and the current President of the Bank for International Settlements), has been chosen to succeed Baron Lamfalussy as President of the European Monetary Institute when he steps down in the middle of 1997.

In this connection it is worth taking a look back at the Maastricht preparations. Professor André Szász, at the time a member of the Board of the Dutch central bank, was one of those who could always be relied upon to put his finger with utmost clarity on the key points. At a public hearing of the Finance Committee of the German Bundestag on September 18, 1991 he remarked:

> "To ensure that within the European and economic monetary union top priority is given to price stability, we need a firm rule on two points:
> (a) a statutory clause spelling out the independence of the European Central Bank (ECB), which is committed to price stability;
> (b) effective rules for ensuring sufficient budgetary discipline which prevent or correct excessive budget deficits in the member countries."

Even if improvements are still needed in the Statute of the European Central Bank and of the European System of Central Banks, this section of the Maastricht Treaty appears to me on the whole to be quite acceptable. However, a good central bank statute is merely a necessary but certainly not a sufficient condition for lasting monetary stability. It must be buttressed by a *stability philosophy* which is shared by all economic policy agents in the currency area and whose actions must accord with that philosophy both persistently and rigorously. This requirement is addressed above all to the government sector. The Maastricht Treaty does not contain effective rules for ensuring adequate budgetary discipline after the final stage of EMU has been launched.

The German Government's proposal of a stability pact, with the automatic penalising of budgetary delinquents, could plug the gap. At the informal Economic and Financial (ECOFIN) Council meeting in Dublin on September 20-21, 1996 the economic and finance ministers of the EU countries basically approved this plan for imposing the requisite financial discipline. Unfortunately, however, it seems that the stability pact will be diluted before it reaches the statute book. According to the latest EU-Commission proposals, the pact shall contain both preventive measures in such a way that undesirable developments in public finances are identified and corrected at an early stage as well as more specific, tighter and, at ten months, shorter budget monitoring procedures. Within four months after the European Commission (EC) has found that a member state has an excessive deficit, the member has to implement effective measures to reduce this deficit within the next year. In case the member state refuses to take measures, the EC can implement sanctions, such as the obligation to put a deposit (which does not bear interest) at the EC. This deposit will become a fine if after two years the deficit still is excessive. Thus, the treaty provisions are clarified and strenghened to a certain extent, and the arrangement might foster stability policy confidence in the collective action of the member states. However, all our hopes are pinned on its deterrent effect as the automatic sanction mechanism, which makes the "Waigel plan" so interesting, has not (yet) found a consensus. How binding is a sanction which would at least be imposed "as a rule"? Consequently, further negotiations are absolutely necessary in the run-up to the EU summit in Dublin in December.

6.5 Stick to the Deadline

Both regarding the further institutional support of the EMU project through a hopefully effective stability pact and a reformed EMS between the euro area and those EU currencies which initially remain outside, and regarding a narrow and restrictive interpretation of the convergence criteria in line with a rigorous stability policy, the Dutch and the Germans are in the same boat. Both economies are tightly enmeshed with the rest of Europe. And so both have much to gain if the Economic and Monetary Union is realised as a *community of stability*. But both also have much to lose if the standard of stability to which they are accustomed cannot be maintained in the future EMU. I think that the Dutch and German economic policy makers, and especially the two countries' monetary policy makers, will have to shoulder a heavy burden of responsibility for their common future. Otherwise the single currency could collapse under the weight of the necessary ongoing integration efforts, which are the *sine qua non* of a community of stability.

First of all, however, we must await the decision, which is to be made in spring 1998, on which countries will participate in the launching of the monetary union in 1999. That decision is already overshadowed by a double dilemma or, as I call it, a TRILEMMA: keeping to the deadline, meeting the convergence criteria and wanting to have certain countries aboard – conflicting objectives which require the setting of clear priorities. I believe that the strict and rigorously interpreted compliance with all the convergence criteria as well as the other preconditions (two-year participation in the exchange rate mechanism of the EMS and autonomy of each national central bank) must be the top priority: quality must take precedence over the calendar, with no dilution. If, however, sticking to the set deadline is the second priority, the desire to engineer a particular constellation of participating states (a political 'dream team') cannot be accomplished simultaneously;

instead the monetary union will be confined to a group of countries showing parallel paths of economic development and durability of relative convergence. And that is also how the Dutch Prime Minister Wim Kok saw things in spring 1996 when he mooted the possibility of a temporary postponement.

Professor Szász said in 1991:

"If Germany and the Netherlands believe it is necessary that, in a future European economic and monetary union, price stability is given due priority, they ... will have to insist on their point of view."

Enduring price stability requires a well-ordered general framework, particularly in the field of fiscal policy, and on that count there is still a lot to be done. That is as true today as it was five years ago. Let us act accordingly!

References

OECD (1996a), *OECD Economic Surveys. Netherlands*, Organisation for Economic Cooperation and Development, Paris.

OECD (1996b), *OECD Economic Surveys. Germany*, Organisation for Economic Cooperation and Development, Paris.

OECD (1996c), *Economic Outlook June 1996*, Organisation for Economic Cooperation and Development, Paris.

7 Comparing Dutch and German Competition Policies

Raymond Gradus[1]
Ministry of Economic Affairs, The Hague and Research Centre for Economic Policy, Erasmus University Rotterdam, the Netherlands

7.1 Introduction

The issue of comparing the Dutch and German economies has received considerable attention, in particular on the Dutch side of the border. The general view is that both economies are very closely related and that Germany acts as a leader. This leads some economists to think, that Dutch growth figures can be forecasted merely by looking to Germany to see what the Dutch economic growth figures are (cf. Fase and De Bondt 1994). Recently, however, this view has been criticised. Dutch employment and growth forecasts for 1996 and 1997 are substantially higher than German forecasts. It is the combination of Dutch structural policy, wage moderation and sound public finance, which is responsible for our better economic performance.

However, the Dutch leadership should not be exaggerated. I would like to say that with respect to most fields of competition policy the Federale Republic of Germany acts as the leader and the Netherlands as the follower. It is interesting to observe that after implementing deregulation policy the Netherlands have followed this policy more consistently than Germany.

In this chapter I would like to differentiate three fields of competition policy. The first field is competition law, or what the Americans call antitrust policy. The second field is deregulation. In this field measures for special sectors are studied. The third field is privatisation. The importance of studying these three fields lies in the particular merits for each one.

In Section 7.2 I compare Dutch and German competition law, in Section 7.3 the deregulation practice of both countries is described and in Section 7.4 their respective privatisation policies are reported. In Section 7.5 the literature on the effects of competition policy is reviewed, and Section 7.6 contains a conclusion.

---

[1] The views in this chapter are the author's own.

7.2 Comparing German and Dutch Competition Law

Dutch and German competition law can be compared in several ways. One very important way is whether they are based on an abuse system or a prohibition system. Dutch competition policy has been based on the *abuse system* since World War II (see Table 7.1).

Table 7.1 Comparing German and Dutch competition law

Netherlands		Germany
Old law (1956)	New law (1998)	(1957)
Abuse	Prohibition	Prohibition (some abuse elements)
No merger control	Merger control	Merger control
Executed by Ministry of Economic Affairs	Executed by Agency at arms length of Ministry of Economic Affairs	Autonomous federal office
Criminal	Administrative	Administrative

Under the law of 1956 it is possible for the Minister of Economic Affairs to prohibit an agreement which regulates competition. However, the onus of proof lies with the Minister of Economic Affairs. Because of this, in practice, over the years there have been amazingly few cases of prohibitions. The first prohibition of a restrictive agreement was issued in 1959 and the second in 1986 (see Van Gent 1996). Together with the United Kingdom and Denmark there are only three countries in the European Union which have such a system (see Gradus 1994). Moreover, the system in the European Union (EU) itself is based on prohibition. However, the situation in the Netherlands has changed considerably during recent years. In 1993 and 1994 a general prohibition on price-fixing, market sharing and collusive tendering was announced. Furthermore, the Parliament has just discussed a new law on competition policy, which is based on the prohibition system and which will be in power from January 1998.

The aim of German competition policy is to safeguard competition, which is the reason why since 1958 the German competition policy has been based on the *prohibition principle* (see Table 7.1). Nevertheless, there are some exceptions in German competition law. These apply to agreements on uniform business conditions, standardisation arrangements and cartels established for export purposes. Moreover, non-binding uniform retail prices may be recommended to partners in small and medium-sized enterprises. In the new Dutch law such retail pricing is forbidden. Some criticism of this special part of this law has been voiced (see Van der Ploeg 1996).

Another aspect is *merger control.* Mergers may be even more effective in restraining competition than cartels. In the current Dutch law, there are no legal restrictions on mergers with the exception of financial markets. Since 1973 mergers in Germany have been forbidden if they give rise to market dominance or if they strengthen a dominant market position. In the new Dutch act a *preventive system* of merger control will be in place. The procedure in the new act bears many similarities with German practice.

Similar to Germany, there will be a two-stage decision making process. Once a negative decision has been taken by the competition authority, the Minister of Economic Affairs may still grant permission to merge on non-competitive grounds, such as social or environmental considerations. Information concerning the nature of these grounds should be made available to the public.

In Germany this ministerial consent clause has been used in allowing the takeover of the Messerschmitt-Bolkow-Blohm (MBB) aerospace company by the Daimler-Benz group in 1989, which had been prohibited by the Bundeskartellamt because the merger would have led to a dominant market position.

Table 7.2 Subject to merger control in Germany, the Netherlands and the European Union

Country	Turnover threshold
Germany	Σ_i $TU_i \geq$ 500 million DM
Netherlands	Σ_i $TU_i \geq f$ 250 million (or 220 million DM)
European Union	Σ_i $TU_i \geq$ 5 billion ECU (or 10 billion DM)

TU_i refers to the turnover of firm i.

In both regimes *thresholds* will be in place to avoid regulation of non-dominant mergers. In the Netherlands, only mergers with an overall turnover of 250 million Dutch guilders are subject to this new Act (see Table 7.2). In Germany the threshold is higher. The ceiling below which enterprises are free from merger control stands at 500 million German marks, while according to European Union legislation, the limit lies at 5 billion ECU (or about 10 billion German marks).

Another important aspect of competition law is *enforcement* (cf. Gradus 1994). In the Federal Republic of Germany the competition act is enforced by the Bundeskartellamt in Berlin, a highly independent authority with wide-ranging powers. In the Netherlands the competition act is enforced by the Ministry of Economic Affairs. Under the new act a competition authority will enforce this law at arm's length from the Ministry. The director-general of the authority will have ample powers by applying the law.

However, unlike the Bundeskartellamt it will not be a wholly independent body, as the Minister of Economic Affairs shall retain full responsibility. According to the economist and member of Parliament, Rick van der Ploeg, the way in which the competition authority is set up is crucial for the implementation of stronger competition policy (Van der Ploeg 1996). Therefore, recently, the

Minister of Economic Affairs announced that after a start-up of three years there will be a *separation* between the competition authority and the Ministry of Economic Affairs.

The last point I would like to address is the legal system. Two approaches are possible (see Table 7.1). Germany makes use of *administrative law*, which is the easier route from the point of view of the competition agency. On the other hand, in the Netherlands *criminal law* is applied. Thus, the prosecution of cartels and dominant market positions seems more difficult to carry out in the Netherlands than in Germany. However, this will also change within the near future.

7.3 Comparing German and Dutch Deregulation Policies

Deregulation became an issue in Germany after an independent Deregulation Commission (German Deregulation Commission 1991) examined regulation in the insurance, transport, electricity and service sectors as well as in the labour market (see for instance Kremers 1992; Bolhuis and Gradus 1994). The commission comprised of academic experts and (independent) representatives from employers' associations and trade unions.

The report contained concrete proposals to forego unnecessary rules and to promote competition. After the report was presented in March 1992, a steering group was founded consisting of members of Parliament of the coalition parties. This group adopted most proposals put forward in the report. The exceptions concerned proposals for notary public, transport, taxi and most labour market measures. After this, Cabinet ministers were made responsible for implementing a specific set of proposals, albeit in consultation with interest groups. However, this is the limit of the ample scope for deregulation in the Federal Republic of Germany. In an article for *Wissenschaft für die Praxis* in 1993 Agnus Held argued that too many interest groups or 'Konservierende Gruppen' are involved in the decision process.

One exception is *shop-opening legislation.* Following the discussion in other European countries, Germany recently implemented less stringent legislation. In June 1996, after a difficult discussion in Parliament, liberalisation measures were announced, due to take effect from November 1996. Shops are now permitted to remain open until 8 p.m. on weekdays and 4 p.m. on Saturdays.

With the exception of some earlier initiatives, such as in 1992 with respect to alleviating the business establishment act, the main Dutch initiatives for deregulation are of recent date. In 1994 the new Dutch government presented a plan to promote efficient markets, deregulation and the quality of law. Every year a number of specific issues are dealt with. The trade unions and employers' organisations are requested to submit suggestions. A ministerial committee then decides on the proposals and the minister involved is responsible for all further actions taken. In Table 7.3 the specific areas for deregulation in the years 1995, 1996 and 1997 are given.

Table 7.3 Deregulation-projects in the Netherlands

Year	Project
1995[1]:	The Shop Opening Hours Act; Taxi services; The Enviromental Management Institutes and Licensing Decree; The Driving Hours Decree; The Work Environment Act; The lawyers monopoly.
1996[2]:	Legislation on food; Obstacles to the market-oriented operation of educational institutes; Hospitals; Planning and information requirements: specific funding; Preventive company supervision; Passing on enforcement costs; The Insurance Agents' Act; Noise Abatement Act; Occupational pension funds.
1997[3]:	Competition clause; Accountancy; Competition and price-making forces in health care; Permit issue with respect to the Surface Water Pollution Act; Product legislation; Baliffs; Construction Regulations.

[1] These working groups started in December 1994.
[2] These working groups started in September 1995.
[3] These working groups started in September 1996.

The committee on efficient markets, deregulation and the quality of law bears some interesting similarities with the German Deregulation Commission. Each working group has an independent chairman and tries to evaluate existing regulation in terms of non-competition costs.

In the Netherlands the process of reducing obstructive legislation is clearly under way, and recently measures have been taken regarding shop-opening hours, environmental and labour market legislation. In June 1996 a new law, where shops may be open from 6 a.m. to 10 p.m. from Monday to Saturday, was passed by Parliament in the Netherlands. Furthermore, the Dutch cabinet published a white paper entitled *Towards Lower Administrative Costs* with the aim of cutting the red tape. As a consequence several measures have been taken to lower the administrative side-effects of *this* legislation.

In some respects, the Netherlands go further than Germany (taxis, shop-opening hours). At the moment it seems that Germany is more reluctant to avoid obstructive regulation than the Netherlands.

7.4 Comparing Dutch and German Privatisation Policies

Compared with economies such as the United Kingdom and reforming socialist economies, the scope of state-owned enterprises in West Germany and the Netherlands has been rather limited. From 1984 until 1990, accumulated privatisation proceeds represent in West Germany 0.5% of Gross Domestic Product (GDP), compared with 1.0% in the Netherlands and 12% in the United Kingdom during approximately the same period (Van Bergeijk and Haffner 1996, p. 28).

The *privatisation of post, telecommunication and railway services* is now under way in both economies. In Germany the Postreform I of 1989 divided the federal post office into three public enterprises (postal services, banking and telecommunications) and opened the market for equipment and business telecommunication services for competition. In 1995, the Postreform II transformed the organisation of the three public enterprises (Telekom, Post and Postbank) into joint stock companies. On November 18, 1996 a first block of Telekom shares totalling 15 billion German marks was floated. This is the greatest float of public owned shares in Europe to date. There are already plans for a new float of shares in 1998.

Moreover, the same procedure for privatisation of *telecommunication* services has been followed in the Netherlands. In 1989 the state runned entity 'Post en Telecommunicatie' was transformed into one public enterprise, KPN. Furthermore, the market for equipment and certain business telecommunication services was opened-up to competition. A first block of KPN shares (30%) was floated in 1994 and a second block of KPN shares (25%) in 1995. At the moment, the government still owns 45% of KPN's shares.

In both countries the national *railway* has already been transformed into a public enterprise and a more market oriented exploitation of the rail network has been initiated. Since January 1, 1996 the Dutch railway company, Nederlandse Spoorwegen, has been split up into separate parts: passengers, freight/cargo, infrastructure, capacity-management, real estate, stations and telecom.[2] However, there are no current plans for floating the shares. Likewise, in Germany the distance between the department for transport and the railway company has increased.

Compared with other European countries, such as France, more progress in privatisation has been made in the Netherlands and in the Federal Republic of Germany. However, in comparison with some Anglo-Saxon countries, many avenues remain to be explored. The government still owns most companies in the electricity, water, refuse and cable-television market.

---

[2] There are serious plans for this part to become a competitor of KPN.

7.5 The Economic Effects of a Stronger Competition Policy

In the previous sections I have described Dutch and German competition policies. Now, I would like to address the economic consequences of such policies and the growing literature on this issue. I will distinguish four branches of literature.

Firstly, there is a huge body of *microeconomic and industrial organisation* (IO) literature aimed at understanding competitive and anti-competitive behaviour. In Europe, Jacquemin, Tirole, Kay and Vickers are important contributors to this field, in which research may be purely theoretical as well as applied (see for instance Jacquimin 1996; Tirole 1987 and Kay and Vickers 1988). In this literature, an intensive use is made of new tools such as game theory and imperfect information. Until recently, this branch of literature was relatively scarce. An interesting observation of Van Gent (1996, p. 12) is that "the fact that IO as a branch of economics has been relatively underdeveloped in the Netherlands ... is a pity, but seems not an insurmountable barrier to the development of a fully-fledged competition policy in the Netherlands".

Secondly, from a policy point of view another branch of literature seems more important. Here, empirical research measuring the *economic costs* of below optimum competitive situations is examined. Despite evidence that a weak competition policy hampers growth and employment, it often turns out to be difficult to deregulate, given that general efficiency considerations must be weighed against the interests of specific groups. Therefore, a clear understanding of the economic costs of below optimum competition is important. Or in the words of Van Gent (1996, p. 13): "This information is absolutely necessary as a counterweight and catalyst in an Olsonian situation of a small, coherent group of beneficiaries versus a much larger and unstructured group of payers". This literature has been dominated mainly by Anglo-Saxon contributions. In a review study, Winston (1993) shows that in the United States GDP would be 7-9% higher if there were stronger deregulations in the rail, road transport, media and brokers sector. Until recent years, this kind of study was rarely published in the Netherlands. This has changed recently due to initiatives of the Research Centre for Economic Policy (OC*f*EB) in Rotterdam. According to Cees van Gent, since 1993 twenty three empirical studies on banking, shop-opening hours, business-licensing law, public notaries and health care have been published (Van Gent 1996, p. 16). Unfortunately, for a broader audience, most of this literature is in Dutch. Two articles are in English. Job Swank (1995) published an article regarding competition in the deposit and saving market. His conclusion was that competition in the deposit market is tight, whereas competition in the savings market is weaker. In an other article the economic impacts of extending shop-opening hours are discussed (Gradus 1996). No general statements can be made for comparing the restricted, the (unrestricted) non-cooperative and the cooperative equilibria.[3] These *ambiguous welfare effects* are similar to those described by Clemenz (1994). In the non-cooperative equilibrium the producers' surplus is lower, but consumers' surplus is higher, while in the cooperative equilibrium the reverse is true. Using empirical evidence it is possible to see that the total of consumers' and producers' surplus ranks the lowest in the restrictive equilibrium, but the highest in the non-cooperative equilibrium. This evidence provides an argument for lifting shop-opening hours restrictions.

The German Deregulation Commission (1991) investigated the *welfare costs* for several sectors of below optimum competition, and the Institut für Wirtschaftsforschung (IFO) in Munich investigated the economic effects of extending shop-opening hours (IFO 1995). A novel element of the Deregulation Commission was that they evaluated existing regulation in terms of costs of non-competition. The IFO institute estimates that turnover in retailing could increase by 2-3% over a three year period as a result of complete liberalisation of shop-opening hours. The benefits would be concentrated on large-scale outlets, which could see their turnover increase by 5-7%. Given the higher productivity levels in large stores, full-time employment will increase by only 1.3%. It is interesting to notice that these effects, based on detailed surveys amongst retailers, employees and consumers are almost the same as those made by Gradus (1996).

Thirdly, another stream of literature focuses on the macroeconomic effects of restrictions in competition policy within the context of a general equilibrium model. Research on the *macroeconomic effects* of a tighter competition policy for the Netherlands has been carried out by Peter van Bergeijk and others (Van Bergeijk et al. 1993 and Van Bergeijk and Haffner 1996). They argued that the annual growth from 1984 until 1990 could have been 0.5% higher if product markets had been more flexible. For Germany, studies have been carried out by the International Monetary Fund (IMF) to estimate the benefits of deregulation and more flexibility (see Lipschitz et al. 1989). With the help of a dynamic macroeconometric model they found that GDP growth would be 0.3% higher and employment would be 0.6% higher, if product markets were more flexible.

Fourthly, another way to show the macroeconomic consequences of deregulation is to *construct an indicator*, directly incorporating information on competition law, deregulation and privatisation, and to investigate whether a link can be established between this indicator and economic performance (see for instance Gradus 1994 and Koedijk and Kremers 1996). Recently, Kees Koedijk and Jeroen Kremers published such an approach in *Economic Policy*. They ranked productivity growth and product regulation of eleven European countries, in which 1 respectively equals the lowest growth and increasing degree of regulation (and laxity of competition law) (see Figure 7.1). Some critism has been voiced to this approach, due to the sensitivity to some observations (see, for example, the discussion in the same issue of *Economic Policy*). Despite the

[3] As non-cooperative equilibrium the symmetric Nash equilibrium is calculated and as cooperative equilibrium the symmetric collusion equilibrium is calculated.

simplicity of this approach, the correlation between total factor productivity and product market regulation remains appealing.

Figure 7.1 Productivity and product market regulation

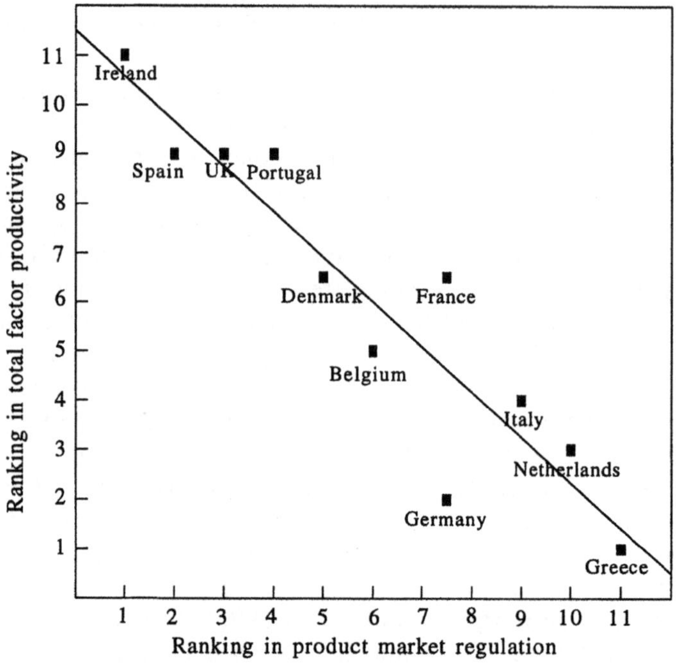

Source: Koedijk and Kremers 1996.

7.6 Conclusion

In the previous sections it was stated that, with respect to competition policy, the Federal Republic of Germany acts as the leader and that the Netherlands act as the follower. Since 1957 Germany's competition policy has been based on the prohibition system and deregulation became an issue at the end of the 1980s. In the Netherlands, competition law was very weak. This has changed considerably during recent years, and deregulation has become an issue since 1994. These changes have been motivated by the growing evidence at the macro level that a weak competition policy hampers growth and employment. At the micro level, however, it often turns out to be difficult to deregulate, due to the fact that general efficiency considerations have to be weighed against the interests of specific groups. Therefore, it is important to have a clear understanding of the economic effects of the different deregulation options. It is interesting to note that after implementing deregulation policy the Netherlands have continued to follow this policy more consistently than in Germany. It seems that the Netherlands are more aware of special interest groups, which according to Held (1993), defend vested interests and are able to slow down or weaken the reform.

References

Bergeijk, P.A.G. van, R.C.G. Haffner and P.M. Waasdorf (1993), Measuring the speed of the invisible hand: The macroeconomic costs of price rigidity, *Kyklos*, 46, pp. 529-544.

Bergeijk, P.A.G. van and R.C.G. Haffner (1996), *Privatization, Deregulation and the Macroeconomy*, Edward Elgar, Cheltenham.

Bolhuis, E.A. and R.H.J.M. Gradus (1994), Deregulering: Ervaringen in het buitenland, *Economisch Statistische Berichten*, 27 April, pp. 384-389 (in Dutch).

Clemenz, G. (1994), Competition via shopping hours: A case for regulation? *Journal of Institutional and Theoretical Economics*, 150, pp. 625-641.

Fase, M.M.G. and G.J. de Bondt (1994), Duitsland als spil van economische activiteit, *Economisch Statistische Berichten*, 28 September, pp. 864-868 (in Dutch).

Gent, C. van (1996), *New Dutch Competition Policy: A Revolution with Revolutionaries*, working paper, Ministry of Economic Affairs, The Hague.

Gradus, R.H.J.M. (1994), Nederlandse economie relatief rigide in Europa, *Economisch Statistische Berichten*, 12 October, pp. 921-924 (in Dutch).

Gradus, R.H.J.M. (1996), The economic effects of extending shop opening hours, *Journal of Economics*, Vol. 64, pp. 247-263.

German Deregulation Commission (Unabhängige Expertkommission zum Abbau marktwidriger Regulieringen) (1991), *Marktöffnung and Wettbewerb*, Poeschel Verlag, Stuttgart (in German).

Held, A. (1993), Dereguliering in Deutschland - Ein Erfolg?, *Wissenschaft für die Praxis*, pp. 215-220 (in German).

IFO Institut für Wirtschaftsforschung [IFO] (IFO Institute for Forecasts) (1995), *Überprüfung des Ladenschlussgesetzes von dem Hintergrund der Erfahrungen im In- und Ausland*, Munich (in German).

Jacquemin, A. (1996), *Industrial Organisation and Competition Policy: Which Links?*, paper presented at the conference 'Economics: art or asset?', organised by the Ministry of Economic Affairs, OCfEB and CentER, 16-17 January, The Hague.

Kay, J. and J. Vickers (1988), Regulatory reform in Britain, *Economic Policy*, 9, pp. 286-352.

Koedijk, K. and J.J.M. Kremers (1996), Market opening, regulation and growth in Europe, *Economic Policy*, 23, pp. 455-467.

Kremers, J.J.M. (1992), Groeidynamiek in Duitsland, *Economisch Statistische Berichten*, 27 May, pp. 512-516 (in Dutch).

Lipschitz, L., J.J.M. Kremers, T. Mayer and M. McDonald (1989), The Federal Republic of Germany: Adjustment in a surplus country, *IMF Occasional Paper* 64, Washington D.C..

Ploeg, F. van der (1996), Vijf kanttekeningen bij nieuwe mededingingswet, *Economisch Statistische Berichten*, 31 July, pp. 652-653 (in Dutch).

Swank, J. (1995), Oligopoly in loan and deposit markets: An econometric analysis to the Netherlands, *De Economist*, 143, pp. 353-366.

Tirole, J. (1987), *The Theory of Industrial Organisation*, MIT Press, Cambridge (Massachusetts).

Winston, C. (1993), Economic deregulation: Days of reckoning for microeconomists, *Journal of Economic Literature*, 31, pp. 1263-1289.

Part IV

Concluding Remarks

8 Germany and the Netherlands: Who Follows Whom?

Lei Delsen and Eelke de Jong
University of Nijmegen, the Netherlands

8.1 Introduction

It is now time to take stock and to see how the arguments presented by the various authors can be used to answer the questions raised in Chapter 1. These questions are:

- what are the advantages and disadvantages of the Rhineland model relative to the Anglo-Saxon model for structuring the economy?
- are the changes in the Netherlands an example for the necessary changes in the Federal Republic of Germany and other Member States of the European Union?
- will the increased internationalisation and the strife for integration in Europe result in a uniform structuring of the European economies?

Section 8.2 contains a comparison of the Rhineland model and the Anglo-Saxon model in order to answer the question whether differences in the institutional settings between these two models of capitalism correlate with economic performance. One of these factors is employability. This is the employees' capability to react to changing conditions. Vocational education enhances the adaptability of employees and the receptiveness to innovation. According to Soskice et al. (Chapter 2 in this volume) wage dispersion and numerical flexibility (temporary contracts) might undercut the attractiveness to young people of investing in lower-level apprenticeships, increasing the pool of low-paid unskilled labour. Hence, there seems to be a trade-off between employability and flexibility. In our view the growing competition created by the internationalisation of economies implies that employability will become an important aspect of the competitiveness of countries. We therefore devote an entire section, Section 8.3, to the trade-off between employability and flexibility. Section 8.4 answers the question raised in the title of this book and deals with the lessons Germany and the Netherlands can learn from each other. Section 8.5 addresses the question whether there is a trend towards a uniform institutional structure of the economies in Europe. The chapter concludes with Section 8.6 on the relevancy of institutions and culture.

8.2 The Rhineland and Anglo-Saxon Model Compared

The economies of the Federal Republic of Germany and the Netherlands are examples of the *Rhineland model.* They are characterised by relatively much government involvement, a general welfare state, tripartism (cooperation) as coordinating device and long-term relationships. These countries may be viewed as consensus economies. The Rhineland model works on the assumption that institutional arrangements exist to overcome various market failures and may therefore be beneficial to national economic performance. The United States of America (USA) and the United Kingdom (UK) are variants of the *Anglo-Saxon model,* characterised by little government involvement, a residual welfare state, coordination by the market (competition) and short-term relationships. The USA and the UK may be viewed as free market economies. The Anglo-Saxon model works on the assumption that the only correction for one market imperfection is yet another market imperfection. Non-market institutions and regulations are considered causes for rigidities (Eurosclerosis). Government intervention should only occur as a last resort.

In Chapter 1 we illustrated that during the 1973-1995 period the two types of models differ with respect to the income distribution and the size of the government sector. In the Rhineland countries income is always more evenly distributed and government expenditures make up a greater part of Gross Domestic Product (GDP) than in the Anglo-Saxon countries. Based on macroeconomic criteria it is concluded that the UK performed worse than the other three countries. Relative to the Rhineland countries, the other Anglo-Saxon economy, the USA, has a slightly higher growth rate of GDP, a significantly higher employment-population ratio and a lower level of long-term unemployment. One of the two Rhineland countries outperforms the other economies under consideration related to the unemployment rate, the inflation rate and growth in unit labour costs. This description of the different aspects of the four economies also illustrates that both *the* Rhineland model and *the* Anglo-Saxon model are inadequate to typify reality. Despite similarities, the countries that are grouped in one of the two models show significant differences in both institutions and performance. Although, the Rhineland model forms the basic structure of the Dutch economy, it contains more elements of the Anglo-Saxon model than the German economy. For example, the Dutch financial system is bank-based but the stock market is much more important than the German stock markets (see Hoogduin and Huisman, Chapter 5 in this volume). The Dutch labour market is also more flexible than the German one (Schmid and Helmer, Chapter 3 in this volume). Moreover, although in both countries wage bargaining takes place at the sectoral level, there are also important differences in this bargaining process (see Chapters 2 and 4).

In this section we use the results of previous chapters to assess the performance of both systems with regard to the following issues: economic growth, the efficiency of social insurance, the trade-off between equality and efficiency. The trade-off between employability and flexibility is dealt with in the next section.

The level and growth of GDP per capita are disaggregated by Schmid and Helmer (Chapter 3). GDP per capita is highest in the USA. However, the level of labour productivity (GDP per hour in 1994) is highest in the Netherlands, whereas the German and American level is of about the same size (the UK was not included in their analysis). The number of hours worked per person is lowest in the two Rhineland countries and, moreover, declined during 1983-1994. During this period the growth in GDP per capita was almost identical in these three countries, but the increase of the number of employed (compared to total population) was higher in the Rhineland countries than in the USA. These results illustrate that in both systems GDP per capita can grow at the same level, while in the USA this is arrived by employing relatively many people and in the Rhineland countries by high productivity rates. The choice between the two depends upon the community's appreciation of leisure and the size of the social safety net. The latter is determined by the willingness of the employed to transfer part of their income to those who are temporary or permanently unable to participate in the working process. The degree of solidarity is in its turn a reflection of the importance of collectivism in the society's values (see Section 8.6).

The share of public social expenditures is higher in the European countries (including the UK) than in the USA. However, in Chapter 4 Van de Meerendonk showed that these differences disappear if account is taken of private social expenditures. Total social expenditures appear to be of the same level in the UK, the USA and the Netherlands, whereas the number is slightly higher in Germany (Table 4.10). In general the social benefit payments in the Rhineland countries are higher than in the UK and the USA (Table 4.11). The same conclusion can be drawn concerning the replacement rates of employment benefits (Table 4.12).

Okun has postulated a trade-off between equality and efficiency. According to Okun (1975, p. 1) inequalities in living standard and material wealth "reflect a system of rewards and penalties that is intended to encourage efficiency and channel it into socially productive activity. To the extent that the system succeeds, it generates an efficient society. But that pursuit of efficiency necessarily creates inequalities. And hence, society faces a trade-off between equality and efficiency". Van de Meerendonk (Chapter 4 in this volume) illustrates that during the last decade in the Anglo-Saxon countries the dispersion in earnings has increased, whereas in the Rhineland countries it has remained at approximately the same level (Table 4.16). Even more important is that for German low-paid workers the probability to move to a higher level of income is greater than for their American counterparts (Table 4.17). Moreover in the European countries (Germany, Netherlands and UK) the social security systems contribute significantly more to the elimination of poverty than that in the USA (Table 4.18). Given the fact that the total amount of expenses on social security (as a percentage of GDP) are of approximately the same size this implies that the European systems are more efficient in reducing poverty. Hence income is most unequally distributed in the Anglo-Saxon countries, but these countries do not systematically outperform Germany and the Netherlands on efficiency criteria such as the GDP per capita and the efficiency of the social security system. These results suggest that for the industrialised countries the trade-off between equality and efficiency is rather flat.

8.3 The Employability-Flexibility Trade-Off

The growing competition created by the internationalisation of economies and the expanding European Union (EU) implies that international differences in the patterns of employment and unemployment increasingly depend on the capacity of national economies to innovate and to absorb new technology. *Human capital* will become more important in explaining international trade (Baily et al. 1993; Porter 1990). Human capital is beyond skills and knowledge. It also refers to people's ability to work together for a common purpose (social capital). The latter depends on trust. Only those societies with a high degree of social trust will be able to create the flexible, large-scale business organisations that are needed to compete in the new global economy (Fukujama 1996, p. 10). Recent research results support Fukujama's 1996 argument that trust facilitates all large-scale activities, not just those of the government (see La Porta et al. 1997).

Accessible education is of importance, certainly for open economies that become more influenced by international competition. There is an increasing awareness that human capital in technology driven economies becomes a decisive factor in contributing to economic performance. In the 1990 report *Labour Market Policies for the 1990s*, the OECD concludes that the emerging 'skill gap' not only results from future demographic developments and technological trends, but also from the maladjustment of the education and training system to the world of work. Forecasting skill needs are unreliable. This puts a premium on flexibility. The key objective must be to impart to all young people a broad base of transferable skills. Both schools and employers are responsible. For adults, the private sector must assume primary responsibility for the provision of training and retraining opportunities (OECD 1990, p. 64). By expanding training opportunities for employed workers, and, hence, making them more employable both elsewhere in their current firm and in other firms, and by easing the consequences of job loss (through training or through the labour market exchange) the stage can be set for more flexible and hence more productive employment systems.

The present flexibilisation and deregulation trends, will be intensified by the European Economic and Monetary Union (EMU), resulting in higher mobility, a growing number of flexible jobs and more *insecurity*. These developments may be detrimental to the necessary investment in human capital by employers and employees. The flexibilisation is accompanied by a decentralisation of industrial relations. Also the latter may be detrimental to investments in human capital for a number of reasons. Despite the fact that individual employers are convinced of the importance of investment in human capital and better industrial relations, actions towards these goals will not be achieved, because they are trapped in a *prisoners dilemma.* Investment in human capital not only has positive internal effects, but also has considerable external effects. In the short-term, however, it puts the individual employer in a cost disadvantage relative to its competitors. The prisoners dilemma and the related *free-rider problem* can only be avoided by agreements at national or sectoral level. Also the administrative extension, that make collective agreements generally binding, like in Germany and the Netherlands, is an answer to this free-rider problem. Moreover, as has been shown in the previous Chapters 2 and 4, the wage determination has an important relationship with the training system. The consensus economies are in a favourable position in this respect. Collective agreements facilitate schooling and other skill-upgrading arrangements. Centralised collective agreements offer the opportunity to the trade unions to make a swap between wages and training or other issues, like employment and working conditions, affirmative action, child care, prevention of sick leave, employment of minorities, etc.. Hence, wage moderation is more easy to achieve at the central level, compared with decentralised bargaining. When trade unions take part in economic governance they will be less inclined to rent-seeking behaviour than trade unions in free market economies. In the latter case insiders' interests will prevail. Decentralised wage negotiations at the establishment level may result in a *hold-up problem.* Players retain their specific investment since they expect that future bargaining on the distribution of the surplus due to specific investments, will deprive them of part of the returns. This hold-up problem may be avoided by sectoral negotiations as is the case in Germany and the Netherlands and provide a type of flexibility that is not available in decentralised economies like the USA and the UK, where the enterprise is the dominant level (see also Teulings 1997).

From this and the previous section we conclude that none of the two models of capitalism always dominates the other. Both system can generate the same growth rates. A more equal income distribution does not lead to less efficiency. The way each of the two models arrive at these results differs and, as will briefly discussed in Section 8.5, depends upon the society's values. There are signs that due to its high degree of flexibility, the Anglo-Saxon model performance better than the Rhineland model during periods of structural changes. As the discussion in this section reveals care should be taken that the flexibility does not harm the employability and in this way prospects of long-term growth.

8.4 Are the Netherlands an Example for Germany?

8.4.1 Introduction

During almost the entire post-World War II period, the economic system of the Federal Republic of Germany was regarded as the role model for many European countries. For example, the low inflation reputation of the Bundesbank has been an argument for the members of the Exchange Rate Mechanism of the European Monetary System to peg their currency to the Deutschmark. The Netherlands can be regarded as the country that in the most strict sense has implemented this strategy of following the German monetary policy (see Chapter 5 by Hoogduin and Huisman and Chapter 6 by Jochimsen). The Dutch competition policy is another field of economic policy in which the Netherlands follows Germany as Gradus showed in Chapter 7.

The recent admiration for the strong employment growth delivered by the Dutch Delta model raises the question whether we have come to a point in time at which the roles will be or should be reversed: Germany follows the Netherlands instead of the opposite. With a view to answer this question we briefly describe the political measures, Section 8.4.2, and external circumstances, Section 8.4.3, which are responsible for this Dutch success. In Section 8.4.5 we put some critical remarks to the main elements of the Dutch employment miracle. Finally, in Section 8.4.6 we answer the question whether Germany should and could follow the Dutch example.

8.4.2 Political Measures

Wage moderation is an important explanation for the strong employment growth in the Netherlands since 1982. In the 1980s, average real wage increases in the Netherlands were below average productivity increases, resulting in additional jobs for over 400,000 persons (CPB 1991). At the same time the Dutch guilder appreciated. As came forward from previous Chapters 2 and 4, in the Netherlands the *profitability* of the manufacturing sector increased significantly, while the German manufacturing firms had to lower their prices in order to maintain their international market share. German profitability rates declined. For the greater part of the period concerned, the effective exchange rate of the guilder appreciated. The direct effect of this appreciation could be a drop of the profits margins. However, in the Netherlands the negative influence of the appreciation of the currency was overcompensated by the real wage moderation, so that on balance the profits could rise. On the other hand the appreciation of the Deutschmark was at the expense of the Germany's competitiveness (see Van Riel and Metten 1996; *European Economy* 1996, 61).

The wage moderation in the Netherlands was supported by the disengagement of the coupling mechanism and tax relief. The latter consisted of a general tax relief policy and selective tax reductions at the lower end of the labour market, in order to promote employment. These measures reduced the wedge end thus enabled the trade unions to support and prolong the moderate-wage policy. The tax relief was made possible by the success of the fiscal consolidation that started in 1982. At that time the Dutch fiscal deficit was at its maximum (6.9% of GDP) (CPB 1994, p. 180) and the debt to GDP ratio was increasing fastly. In the Netherlands the *reform of the social security system*, has laid a solid base for fiscal policy consolidation, as Van de Meerendonk has pointed out in Chapter 4.

The *fiscal consolidation* also created room for additional expenditures in the 1990s, in particular for subsidies to employ people who are unemployed for a long period ('Melkert-jobs'). Finally, the budget came under control, which was a sign for the financial market that the Dutch government was willing and able to take disagreeable measures, if necessary. In this way the budgettary policy supported the central bank's monetary policy.

The central element of the Dutch monetary policy has been to peg the Dutch guilder to the Deutschmark (see Jochimsen, Chapter 6 in this volume). The ultimate aim of this policy is to create a low and stable level of inflation and thus a low level of the long-term interest rate. As will be shown in Section 8.4.3, this low level of the interest rate has been instrumental in increasing consumption in last years.

Finally, *deregulation and privatisation* have been another important element of Dutch policy during the last decade. Gradus (Chapter 7) described the main changes in competition policy in the Federal Republic of Germany and the Netherlands. Both Germany and the Netherlands are changing their legislation to bring it into line with EU law (see OECD 1996a, pp. 61-66; OECD 1996b, p. 137) The results of empirical research on the impact of deregulation of product markets are contradictory. For instance, Nickell 1996 found for a large number of enterprises in the UK a positive relationship between competition and productivity growth. Other research shows that Rhineland enterprises outperform Anglo-Saxon enterprises (De Jong 1996). These contradictory conclusions illustrate the difficulty to estimate the influence of (de)regulation on the economy. Moreover, a number of deregulation measures in the Netherlands, like the Shop Opening Hours Act, the Competition Law and the liberalised Establishment Law are too recent to have any measurable effect. That is why the alleged Dutch employment miracle cannot be explained from more product market functioning, although it may be that on balance the effects are positive for employment.

8.4.3 Favourable External Circumstances

A disadvantage of moderate wage increases is that it reduces domestic demand. This drop in demand did not occur in the Netherlands because of a number of favourable external circumstances (see Delsen and De Jong 1997). In the second half of the 1980s, the Netherlands profited from the synchronous development of the economic situation in the industrial countries. At the beginning of the 1990s, the United States and the United Kingdom ended up in a recession, while in Germany expenditure increased, related to the construction of former East Germany. Within the European Union, the Netherlands, Belgium and Luxembourg benefited most from the *German unification*. Calculations by the European Commission (1992, p. 8) show that both for the Netherlands and the Belgian-Luxembourger Economic Union (BLEU) the German unification resulted in an additional growth of 1.6% over the period mid-1990 to end-1991. For the other EU-Member States (Germany not included) the calculated impulse was 0.6%.

In the following years also continental Europe was hit by a recession, and once again the Netherlands were an exception to the rule. In 1993, the Dutch GDP still increased slightly by 0.3%, while on average for Western European GDP dropped by 0.5% (CPB 1994, pp. 13 and 15). During this recession and in the first part of the recovery (1994 and 1995), the Netherlands benefited from their *specialisation package*. This package is strongly directed at the agricultural sector and related activities (the agro-industrial complex) and at the chemical sector (see CPB 1993). The demand for agricultural products is relatively insensitive to the business cycle. The demand for chemical industry products and other semi-manufactured articles is high at the beginning of the upturn of the business cycle, when stocks have to be replenished. In 1994 and 1995, Dutch industry benefited from this. As the economic situation ripens the Dutch specialisation pattern becomes more unfavourable. The demand becomes more concentrated on investment goods and durable consumption goods, sectors in which the Netherlands are not specialised.

Table 8.1 Average mortgage interest and houses completed/sold in the Netherlands, 1993-1996

Year	Average mortgage interest (percentages)	New mortgages[1] x 1000	Houses completed/sold (a) x 1000	(b) x 1000	(c) x 1000
1993	7,50	339	140	76	84
1994	7,26	431	166	78	87
1995	7,12	406	178	85	94
1996	6,25	563	179	90	89

(a) Total (a) = (b) + (c).
(b) Transactions of all houses sold.
(c) Delivered new estate of houses.
[1] Number of new mortgages on houses (including combinations house/business premises).
Source: Statistics Netherlands (CBS) and Dutch Association of Real Estate Agents (NVM) (transactions of all houses sold).

When in 1996, the Dutch specialisation pattern turned against the Netherlands, it was the low interest rate that came to the rescue. In 1996 the low *interest rate* resulted in a strong increase in consumptive credits and a growth in the number of mortgages. In the second half of 1996, the outstanding amount of consumptive credit increased by 890 million guilders to almost 23.5 billion guilders. Never before in a six months period, the outstanding amount of consumptive credit increased that much (see CBS 1997). Moreover, in the past years the number of contracted mortgage loans increased much more than the number of sales of existent houses and new buildings (see Table 8.1). This suggests that part of the new mortgages has been used to recontract existing mortgages or to finance consumptive expenditures. CPB (1997, p. 67) estimates the real capital gains from the increase of prices of houses at 50 billion guilders. Probably around 10% of this gain will result in higher consumptive spending. The impact of the appreciation of shares is probably much less. Both developments may explain the increased confidence of consumers and the relative high growth of household's consumption, notably of durable goods. In 1996, the volume of the latter increased by 4.25%.

8.4.4 A Dutch Employment Miracle?

The *Dutch job-machine* seems to be working at full speed. The unemployment rate is low, which is a result of the high growth rate of employment. However, the level of the latter still is relatively low. Another positive characteristic of the Dutch labour market is its high level of labour productivity; in 1994 the Dutch level of GDP per hour worked was around 9% above that in Germany, 10% above that in the USA and around 22% above the EU average (see Schmid and Helmer, Table 3.2, Chapter 3 in this volume; OECD 1996a, p. 77).[1] Apart from quantity also quality matters. Between 1987 and 1994 two thirds of Dutch employment growth was in part-time jobs. Between 1994 and 1996 employment growth accelerated. Almost 40% of the recent employment growth was in flexible jobs; 60% of the jobs growth was in small part-time jobs (< 12 hours) and flexible jobs (fixed-term, on-call and agency work).[2] This may explain why in the Netherlands, the proportion of involuntary part-timers is higher than in Germany (see also Schmid and Helmer, Chapter 3 in this volume). However, in the Netherlands the growth of part-time employment and of temporary jobs is mainly, and even more than in other European countries, supply-side driven; relative to other EU countries in the Netherlands a large number of employees prefer a part-time job (see Delsen 1995). Considerable proportions of Dutch working men and women want to reduce working hours at the same hourly wage rate. It is stimulated by change in cultural impediments and reduction in prejudice. There is a growing consensus between the social partners on the value of part-time employment (see Delsen 1997).

The disadvantages of the high share of part-time and flexible contracts can be distinguished into two groups: short-term and structural problems. The *short-term problem* is that the Dutch employment miracle may turn out to be an unstable

---

[1] The growth rate of the Dutch labour productivity is relatively low, so that the level converges towards the lower level of other countries.

[2] These percentages are calculated from Statistics Netherlands (CBS) data. For 1996 only data up to the second quarter are included.

one. These marginal jobs are very sensitive to the business cycle; a turn in this cycle implies that the Netherlands will immediately – and more than other EU-Member States – be confronted with considerable lay-offs and increasing unemployment figures.

Apart from this short-term impact, flexibilisation of the labour market also causes a number of *structural problems*. One may question whether wage moderation and more deregulated labour markets are a solution to the labour market problems at the lower level. The growth of small part-time jobs and flexible jobs may result in poverty when no additional income at the individual or household level is available. Although employment has increased considerably, the volume of work in hours has remained relatively constant. There has been a massive redistribution of work, with a corresponding redistribution of earnings (see Schmid and Helmer, Chapter 3 in this volume). Moreover, there is the real danger of segmentation not only between incumbent workers, the insiders, and the unemployed, but also between the insiders: a segmentation both of the external and internal labour markets (see Delsen and De Jong 1997). Another structural problem occurs because the growth of temporary jobs will affect the *social infrastructure*. The latter may be a threat to durable economic growth (Van Dijk 1997). These flexible jobs may also negatively affect investments in human capital by employers and employees. An active labour market policy can be a solution to at least part of these problems. However, as Schmid and Helmer showed, in the Netherlands and Germany the expenses for active labour market policy are relatively low.

As came forward from previous Chapters 3 and 4, the relatively high labour productivity in the Netherlands is partly due to *exclusion* – more than in any other EU countries and the USA – of those employees with relatively low productivity, for instance disabled persons through disability benefits and older workers through various generous early exit options from the labour market, including early retirement, disability for labour market reasons (see also Delsen and Reday-Mulvey 1996).[3] As a consequence, the number of employed is relatively low. This may cause problems for financing the government budget and the social insurance.

8.4.5 Should Germany Follow the Dutch Example?

Now time has come to investigate whether the Federal Republic of Germany should and can follow the Dutch example. In Section 8.4.3. we argued that part of the Dutch success can be ascribed to good luck. In fact the major part of this

[3] It should be noted, however, that other institutions also matter as came forward from Van de Meerendonk's Chapter 4 in this volume. The social climate in the Netherlands is good relative to Germany and certainly relative to the UK and the USA: stable and peaceful system of industrial relations and relatively few days are lost by strikes, resulting in employees' commitment to the result of a firm and a good basis for business training, contributing to productivity.

luck is that the most important neighbour of the Netherlands, Germany, during some time has followed an expansionary policy, which had its favourable spinoffs for the neighbouring countries. Of course chances are low that Germany will ever have a comparable luck. In discussing the other relevant issues we follow the sequence of the Sections 8.4.2 and 8.4.4.

Wage moderation forms the essential element of the Dutch model. Can Germany generate a wage constraint of a comparable size? With a view toward answering this question, a closer look at the wage bargaining process in both countries is useful. Both the Netherlands and Germany are characterised by sectoral wage negotiations. However, there are considerable differences between these two countries, as Soskice et al. and Van de Meerendonk showed in Chapter 2 and Chapter 4. In the Netherlands more negotiations take place at the central level, and more than in Germany informal coordination takes place of the sectoral level negotiations by trade unions and employers' organisations or by the tripartite Socio-Economic Council. Moreover, in the Netherlands the social partners consult more frequently at the central level in the so-called Foundation of Labour. This limits the influence of the insiders and may explain why wage moderation has a long history in the Netherlands, unlike in Germany. In Germany that coordination is less overt. Moreover, there are cultural differences. The German industrial relation system is characterised by *Tarifautonomie*, while in the Netherlands government involvement in the wage formation process is common. The Netherlands can be characterised, more than Germany, by a *consensus economy*. The latter may be a reason why the January 1996 tripartite 'Bündnis für Arbeit' already is a failure, while the 1982 Central Agreement to reduce unemployment in the Netherlands has been and still is a success. Taking into account these cultural difference it may be questioned whether the overall understanding to negotiate a wage restraint in Germany, recommended by Soskice et al. (Chapter 2) as a cure for the German unemployment problem, may in fact be feasible. The German federal government finds more difficulties in exerting political power than the Dutch, and it may be more difficult for the German government to commit the corporatist parties into a comprehensive policy framework.

Even if the German social partners could agree upon a policy of moderate wage increases during several years, one can argue that the favourable effects are likely to be smaller than in the Dutch case. The arguments for this proposition refer to the differences in size and industrial structure of the two economies. Germany is the dominant economy of the European Union. This implies that chances are high that a policy of wage moderation will be followed by neighbouring countries, so that a *vicious deflationary policy* is set into motion in Europe. Moreover due to the size of the economy, the German export sector makes up a smaller part of GDP and employment than that of the Netherlands. As a result a wage moderation in Germany will almost surely lead to a fall in domestic (and European) demand, so that the favourable effects on employment will be lower than they would have been in the case of the Netherlands. In some sense one can say that the Netherlands have exploited their position of a small open economy. Or in other words, a policy of wage moderation is a beggar-thy-neighbour policy.

As has been put forward by Soskice et al. the share of the services sector in GDP is higher in the Netherlands than in Germany. Services require more low skilled and low paid workers than the industry. Moreover, the German industrial sector follows a *high quality incremental innovation strategy.* The Dutch experience shows that wage moderation has a negative impact on productivity. Wage moderation relieves the pressure on firms to motivate and give workers little incentive to acquire new skills (see for instance Kleinknecht 1996). Productivity growth in the Netherlands is very modest. The latter may be at the expense of future employment growth and competitiveness. According to neoclassical economic thinking low productivity leads to low compensation. However, this causality can also run in the opposite direction: access to labour at low compensation makes the search for productivity increases unnecessary for the employers, and thus undermines the high quality incremental innovation strategy of the German industry.

Hence a policy of wage restraint, if implemented, should be supplemented by other measures in order to be effective for reducing unemployment. Possible candidates are wage differentials, part-time jobs, liberalisation of product markets and fiscal consolidation. Van de Meerendonk pointed out in Chapter 4 that, unlike in the UK and the USA, allowing for more *wage dispersion* may well be an effective solution to the high share of low-skilled unemployed in Germany and the Netherlands, because these countries have well-functioning systems of vocational and company training. Soskice et al. (Chapter 2) are much more sceptical. They think that it "might undercut the attractiveness to young people of investing in lower-level apprenticeships, thus increasing the pool of low-paid unskilled labour" (p. 50). We are of the opinion that these negative effects can be circumvented by including compulsory measures for improving skills in wage agreements and in the conditions for obtaining unemployment benefits. Hence, as Van de Meerendonk, we plea for wage dispersion. Moreover modest wage increases in labour intensive sectors, such as services, can be instrumental in boosting these sectors and thus increasing their share in German GDP and employment. Such a switch may be advantages given the increasing demand for services. The effects of the German reunification also deliver an argument for wage dispersion. As a consequence of the unification there was a massive wave of migration from the East to the West. Unions, employers and government agreed on a national plan for the transition of East German wages to West German wages. In addition a huge fiscal transfer scheme and a special income tax supplement (solidarity contribution of 7.5% in 1995) were put in operation to reduce migration. However, the equalisation of real wages across Germany poses a danger. Such convergence would cause high unemployment, lasting for decades (see Brakman and Garretsen 1997). On the other hand wage discipline needed to reduce the eastern unemployment rate to the western level would require a widening of the wedge between wages in the two regions for an extensive period and either route increases the potential for migration. One possible response would be to seek a compromise between convergence of unemployment and convergence of wages (see Hughes-Hallett et al. 1996).

Although disadvantages are associated with part-time and temporary jobs (see Section 8.4.4), these types of jobs are effective in reducing unemployment and increasing the employment to population ratio. Whether the number of these *atypical jobs* can be increased substantially in Germany, not only depends upon the attitude of German employees but, as the Dutch experience shows, also on a consensus between government and social partners on the advantages of part-time work. Bringing about such a consensus takes time.[4]

Regulation of markets can improve the efficient functioning of the market economy. In fact no market economy can function appropriately without rules. Too much regulation, however, will constrain economic activity. The level of regulation in Germany and the Netherlands are of the same magnitude (see Figure 7.1 in Chapter 7). In Section 8.4.2 we concluded that although it is difficult to measure the effect of deregulation, it might be that in the Netherlands this policy has enhanced employment. Assuming that this conclusion correct, we are of the opinion that a *deliberate deregulation* and privatisation policy can be recommended for Germany as well.

Fiscal consolidation can have various favourable effects. First, if part of it consists of a reduction of taxes and premiums, the willingness of trade unions to accept modest wage increases and the costs of the firms decrease and thus their profits increase. The reduction of taxes is also needed for financing the pensions in the future. In Germany the majority of *pensions* is on a pay-as-you-go system. Given this system, the ageing of the population implies a sharp increase in expenditures, which have to be paid by a steadily decreasing number of people of working age. A restructuring is needed of the German pension system towards the Dutch system, where a large part of the pensions are financed by funds.

In conclusion, the German problems cannot be solved by simply following the Dutch example. The structure of the German industry and the dominant role of Germany in Europe make that a policy of moderate wage increases is expected to be less effective than it has been in the Netherlands. Other measures taken by the Dutch authorities maybe more worthwhile. Examples are: wage dispersion, part-time contracts, a modest liberalisation and fiscal consolidation. On the other hand, in our view the German system of vocational training serves as an example for the Netherlands. Implementing a similar system in the Netherlands can improve the employability of the Dutch employees. Maybe we have left the era of leaders and followers behind us and time has come for walking hand by hand. As argued by Jochimsen in Chapter 6, the creation of the Economic and Monetary Union urges for a cooperative behaviour.

---

[4] The first initiatives of the Dutch government to actively promote part-time work date from the end of the 1970s. This illustrates the path dependency and the importance of governments in changing attitudes and culture as well as policies.

8.5 Lessons for the European Union

Within the European Union there are considerable differences in institutional structures between countries. In fact the economies of members of the EU can be categorised in at least three models: the Anglo-Saxon model, the Rhineland model and the Latin model. This large variance is also found in studies on *cultural values* in different countries. It appears that the differences between the European countries are almost as great as those between countries all over the world (see Hofstede 1993). Previous chapters clearly showed that due to the internationalisation and the common market policy, over the past decades the *institutional structure* of the labour markets, the markets for goods and services as well as the financial markets in Europe has shifted towards the Anglo-Saxon model, i.e. a shift from non-market coordination towards market coordination. This raises the question: will the increased internationalisation and the strife for integration in Europe result in a uniform structure of the economy, i.e. in one European model? Since the previous chapters did not analyse the Latin model we restrict the present discussion to the Rhineland and Anglo-Saxon model.

This change to incorporate more Anglo-Saxon features in the economic system showed itself in a policy of flexibilisation, deregulation, decentralisation and privatisation and was mainly motivated by cost containment and desired flexibility to cope with the internationalisation of the economies and the accompanied increased competition from foreign countries. The increased importance of Anglo-Saxon features also implies a shift from long-term aims towards aiming at short-term results. Increased wage flexibility and improvement of the workings of labour markets by means of institutional changes are indeed advantageous in the short-run, however, they are detrimental to commitment, to the willingness of workers to adapt to technological change and discourage innovation, as has been argued by Soskice et al. in Chapter 2 (see also Kleinknecht 1996). Limitations on flexibility offer the needed stability; they not only involve costs, as supposed by neoclassical economics, but also increase productivity and adaptability. Since a high level of commitment is typical for the Rhineland model and flexibility for the Anglo-Saxon model, we are of the opinion that a particular system of capitalism does not dominate the other systems every time and everywhere.

Not every time, because the preference for an economic system depends upon the *specific economic environment*. In general, due the relatively high level of committment, the Rhineland model works well in a stable economic environment. Consultation leads to an improvement of the quality of the products and processes. The fact that consultation takes time is then relatively unimportant. During periods of structural change, consultation can pospone necessary adjustments. Then, the flexibility of the Anglo-Saxon model is needed.

A particular economic system will not dominate the others *everywhere*, because the characteristics of a country's economic institutions incorporate the *values* of that society. For example, a study of cultural values reveals that

German people put more weight to uncertainty avoidance and collectivism than the inhabitants in the Anglo-Saxon countries do. On both items the score for the Netherlands is in the middle (see Hofstede 1982, pp. 122 and 158). Another more recent study of the managers' aims in these three countries concludes that in the USA the managers are – more than their counterparts in the Netherlands and Germany – forced to deliver short-term growth of earnings per share (Weimer 1995, p. 339). These values are the results of historical processes which last for centuries instead of decades or years.[5] It is unlikely that such long-lasting processes will change dramatically in a few years. The challenge of each society is to adapt its economic system to the needs of the present economic environment. Elements of another system might be useful, however, "societies should be fully aware of the positive and negative aspects of implementation of such alien elements" (Groenewegen 1997, p. 343).

From the previous paragraphs we conclude that, although the structural changes force adaptations of each system, basically the present variety of economic systems will remain in Europe. Since each model has its own merits, this diversity can be regarded an asset for Europe, in the sense that for every economic circumstance there is always a national model that is fit for handling the corresponding challenges. This raises the question whether within Europe these models should compete with each other or that there is a need for co-ordination at the European level. We plead for a "coordinated" competition, i.e. competition forms the basis but is supplemented by European agreements which restrict it. Competition is good since it forces each society to adjust its institutions to changing circumstances. However, since no form of capitalism dominates the others in all circumstances, coordination is needed in order to assure that this competition is not too aggressive. Aggressive competition (subsidies, tax credits etc.) might give rise to retaliation or might destroy the institutional structure of another country. Both results destroy the advantages of Europe's cultural diversity.

---

[5] Pott-Buter, for example, concludes from a comparative study of female labour participation rates in seven countries, that the relative low participation rates of Dutch females during the last century can be explained by the view on the family household as this came into existence in the Dutch Golden Age. At that time the family relationships of the rich bourgeois middle income classes became the dominant form of household behaviour. Underlying this model was that "the well-being of all the members of a household was improved if men provided the financial resources and companionship and women were responsible for raising or maintaining the quality of life of the household This quality-oriented family model gave women working in their own households a higher status..." (Pott-Buter 1993, p. 48), and resulted in a low female participation in the labour market.

8.6 Institutions and Culture Matter

Social capital is like a ratchet that is more easily turned in one direction than another; it can be dissipated by the actions of governments much more readily than those governments can build it up again (Fukuyama 1996, p. 362). Trust or social capital determines the performance of a society's institutions. Trust my not be truly exogenous; it may increase with good past performance of a society's institutions (see La Porta et al. 1997). The stable or self-enforcing systems of norms are a starting point for the explanation of institutional differences between countries. Deregulation may be at the expense of trust and commitment, or in general the social climate (trust, values and norms), the latter being a major source for good economic performance. It is the latter that has often been excluded from economic analyses and overlooked by policy makers in reshaping welfare states (Nyfer 1996). There is a strong cultural element in the way market institutions operate. Economic institutions are for their effectiveness and legitimacy dependent on other institutions and cultural values present in societies (Van Waarden 1997, p. 13). Once the regime is changed because it temporary cannot be sustained, the assumption on which it is based will be eroded, and it will be very difficult to re-establish the regime again (see Layard 1997). Thus in case an economy is performing badly, it may be wise to look at a country with a similar instead of a very different institutional structure and cultural background for obtaining ideas for improving the economy.

Since the German and Dutch economy are both variants of the Rhineland model, this book concentrated on a comparison between the institutional and economic structure of these two countries in order to investigate whether their institutions can be improved. Changes in institutional structure may be necessary given the challenges implied by internationalisation, new technologies, EMU, and demographic aging. In order to put this comparison into a broader perspective, the United Kingdom and the United States of America, representatives of the Anglo-Saxon model, have been used as benchmarks. It appeared that the Rhineland and Anglo-Saxon countries systematically differ from each other with respect to the income distribution and the size of the government sector; in the Anglo-Saxon countries income is always more unevenly distributed and government expenditures are always smaller than in the Rhineland countries. These differences correspond with the prominent place of the individual in the Anglo-Saxon societies (see e.g. Hofstede, 1982, Figure 5.2, p. 158). In the Rhineland countries, especially in Germany, the collectivity is more important.

Since the beginning of the 1990s the Dutch economy is outperforming the economies of other European countries. These results are obtained by a particular mixture of individualistic and collective features of the Dutch society. On the one hand measures have been taken which have increased the responsibility of the individuals and firms for their actions. Examples are the reform of the laws on sickness and disability benefits. Of even more importance (at least for reducing the unemployment) is maybe that many have accepted temporary and part-time labour contracts. On the other hand the core of the Dutch success, wage moderation, is the result of the consensus society. Soskice et al. argue that the structure of the industry and of the wage bargaining process in Germany differ so much from those in the Netherlands that copying the successful Dutch policies would be impossible. Although the two economies belong both to the Rhineland model, the cultural differences are in their view too large. If this is true than the same argument could be applied even more forcefully to other countries in Europe (such as France and Italy). In our opinion it is correct that culture and differences in institutional arrangements matter for economic policy. The differences between countries in this respect along with other factors, such as size and specialisation, imply that policies which are successful in one country need not be the appropriate policies for other countries, even if from a broader perspective these belong to the same model of the market system. Institutions have both advantages and disadvantages. This urges caution in relation to liberalisation initiatives in Europe. However, although cultural differences are important they should never be used as an excuse for delaying necessary adjustments.

References

Baily, M., G. Burtless and R. Litan (1993), *Growth with Equity. Economic Policymaking for the Next Century*, Washington: Brookings.

Brakman, S. and H. Garretsen (1997), Het gat na de val van de muur, *Economisch Statistische Berichten*, 22 January, 64-68.

CPB (1991), Werkgelegenheid in de jaren tachtig, *Werkdocument nr. 41*, CPB Netherlands Bureau for Economic Policy Analysis, The Hague (in Dutch).

CPB (1993), De Nederlandse uitvoerprestatie sinds 1980, *Werkdocument nr. 54*, CPB Netherlands Bureau for Economic Policy Analysis, The Hague (in Dutch).

CPB (1994), *Macro Economische Verkenningen 1995*, CPB Netherlands Bureau for Economic Policy Analysis, The Hague (in Dutch).

CBS (1997), Forse groei consumptief krediet in 1996, *Persbericht*, 26 February, Statistics Netherlands, Voorburg/Heerlen (in Dutch).

Delsen, L. (1995), *Atypical Employment: An International Perspective. Causes, Consequences and Policy*, Wolters-Noordhoff, Groningen.

Delsen, L. (1997), When do men work part-time? in: J. O'Reilly and C. Fagan (eds.) *Prospects and Paradoxes of Part-time Work*, Routledge, London, forthcoming.

Delsen, L. and E. de Jong (1997), Het wankele mirakel, *Economisch Statistische Berichten*, 23 April, pp. 324-327 (in Dutch).

Delsen, L. and G. Reday-Mulvey (eds.) (1996), *Gradual Retirement in the OECD Countries. Macro and Micro Issues and Policies*, Dartmouth Publishing Company, Aldershot.

Dijk, F. van (1997), *Social Ties, Economic Performance and Public Intervention*, Kluwer Academic Publishers, Dordrecht.

European Commission (1992), *Annual Report 1991-2*, Brussels.

Fukuyama, F. (1996), *Trust. The Social Virtues and the Creation of Prosperity*, Simon & Schuster, New York.

Groenewegen, J. (1997), Institutions of capitalism: American, European, and Japanese systems compared, *Journal of Economic Issues*, 31 (2), pp. 333-347.

Hofstede, G. (1982), *Culture's Consequences. International Differences in Work-Related Values*, abridged edition, Sage Publications, California.
Hofstede, G. (1993), *Images of Europe*, valedictory address delivered on the occasion of his retirement as a Professor of Organizational Anthropology and International Management, University of Limburg, Maastricht.
Hughes-Hallett, A., Y. Ma and J. Mélitz (1996), Unification and the policy predicament in Germany, *Economic Modelling*, Vol. 13, No. 4, pp. 519-544.
Jong, de, H.W. (1996), Rijnlandse ondernemingen presteren beter, *Economisch Statistische Berichten*, 13 March, pp. 228-232 (in Dutch).
Kleinknecht, A.H. (1996), Potverteren met loonmatiging en flexibilisering, *Economisch Statistische Berichten*, 11 July, pp. 622-625 (in Dutch).
La Porta, R., F. Lopez-de-Silanes, A. Shleifer and R.W. Vishny (1997), Trust in large organizations, *The American Economic Review*, Vol. 87, No. 2, Papers and Proceedings, May, pp. 333-338.
Layard, R. (1997), Sweden's road back to full employment, *Economic and Industrial Democracy*, Vol. 18, No. 1, pp. 99-118.
Nickell, S.J. (1996), Competition and corporate performance, *Journal of Political Economy*, pp. 724-746.
Nyfer (1996), *Kwartaal Bericht 1996-3*, Nyfer Forum for Economic Research, Sdu Uitgevers, The Hague.
OECD (1990), *Labour Market Policies for the 1990s*, Organisation for Economic Co-operation and Development, Paris.
OECD (1996a), *OECD Economic Surveys. Netherlands 1996*, Organisation for Economic Co-operation and Development, Paris.
OECD (1996b), *OECD Economic Surveys. Germany 1996*, Organisation for Economic Co-operation and Development, Paris.
OECD (1997), *OECD Employment Outlook 1997*, Organisation for Economic Co-operation and Development, Paris.
Okun, A.M. (1975), *Equality and Efficiency: The Big Trade Off*, The Brookings Institution, Washington, D.C.
Porter, M.E. (1990), *The Competitive Advantage of Nations*, Macmillan, London.
Pott-Buter, H.A. (1993), *Facts and Fairy Tales about Female Labor, Family and Fertility: A Seven-Country Comparison*, Ph.D. dissertation, University of Amsterdam, Amsterdam.
Riel, van B. and A. Metten (1996), Reële loonmatiging en de harde gulden, *Tijdschrift voor Politieke Ekonomie*, nr. 2, pp. 114-126 (in Dutch).
Teulings, C.N. (1997), A new theory of corporatism and wage setting, *European Economic Review*, 41, pp. 659-669.
Waarden, F. van (1997), *Institutions of Socio-Economic Coordination: A European Style?*, Ministry of Social Affairs and Employment, The Hague.
Weimer, J. (1995), *Corporate Financial Goals: A Multiple Constituency Approach to a Comparative Study of Dutch, US and German Firms*, Ph.D. dissertation, Technical University, Twente, Enschede.

List of Figures

List of Tables

Author Index

Subject Index

Centre for German Studies

The Centre for German Studies (CDS) is an interfaculty institute of the University of Nijmegen, the Netherlands, in which the Faculties of Policy Sciences, Arts, Law and Social Sciences work together in education, research and services relating to Germany and other German-speaking countries.

Education
CDS was officially opened on 30th October, 1991, although German Studies had already started as an interdisciplinary course in 1989. The four-year programme has both a socio-cultural and a socio-economic variant, and aims to provide students with the general and specialist knowledge and skills that will enable them to hold management and executive positions for which familiarity with Dutch-German relations is necessary. From the commencement of academic year 1997-1998 the programmes of German Studies at the University of Nijmegen and Dutch Studies at the University of Münster (Germany) will be merged to form a bi-national degree programme. Graduates will receive a degree from both universities.

CDS also offers and co-ordinates a post-doctoral professional programme for managers of profit and non-profit organisations. The programme focuses on specific aspects of German trade and industry as well as on Dutch-German economic relations, and was set up in close co-operation with the Nijmegen Institute for Academic Studies (NIVAS) and the Tilburg University Institute for Academic Studies (TIAS).

Research
CDS has developed an interdisciplinary research programme called "Kultur- und Kulturraumforschung". The objective of this research is to identify similarities and differences between the Netherlands and Germany in both the present and in the past. The results of the research are intended to contribute to European policy on integration. The focus is on the image both countries have of each other.

Information and Documentation
Library and information services provided by CDS will be greatly extended for education and research. The emphasis will be on literature concerning culture, economics, history, politics and social geography. Another core activity will be the provision of an easily accessible virtual library.

The Dutch Ministry of Education has supported the activities of CDS since 1996 within the framework of its German Programme for Higher Education.

Address
Centre for German Studies
University of Nijmegen
P.O. Box 9103
6500 HD Nijmegen
The Netherlands
tel. ++24 - 3612958
fax. ++24 - 3615939
internet: http://www.kun.nl/cds/

GPSR Compliance

The European Union's (EU) General Product Safety Regulation (GPSR) is a set of rules that requires consumer products to be safe and our obligations to ensure this.

If you have any concerns about our products, you can contact us on ProductSafety@springernature.com

In case Publisher is established outside the EU, the EU authorized representative is:

Springer Nature Customer Service Center GmbH
Europaplatz 3
69115 Heidelberg, Germany

Batch number: 10725973

Printed by Printforce, the Netherlands